Teach Me Your Paths

Studies in Old Testament
Literature and Theology

Edited by John Kessler and Jeffrey P. Greenman

Dedicated to Donald A. Leggett
with gratitude and esteem

Professor Emeritus of Old Testament
Tyndale Seminary, Toronto, Ontario

Teach Me Your Paths:
Studies in Old Testament Literature and Theology
Copyright © 2001 Tyndale College & Seminary

First edition

Published 2001 by Clements Publishing
6021 Yonge Street, Box 213
Toronto, Ontario M2M 3W2 Canada
www.clementspublishing.com

Typesetting by Steve Masson

All rights reserved.
No part of this publication may be reproduced, stored in a
retrieval system, or transmitted, in any form or by any means,
electronic, mechanical, photocopying, recording or otherwise,
without the prior written permission of the publisher, except in the
case of brief quotations embodied in critical articles and reviews.

Printed in the United States of America

Canadian Cataloguing in Publication Data

Main entry under title:

Teach me your paths : studies in Old Testament literature and theology

Festschrift for Donald A. Leggett.
Includes bibliographical references.
ISBN 1-894667-05-0

1. Bible. O.T. – Criticism, interpretation, etc. 2. Bible. O.T. – Theology.
I. Kessler, John, 1951-   II. Greenman, Jeffrey P., 1959-
III. Leggett, Donald A.

BS1171.2.T42 2001   221.6   C00-932805-X

Contents

Acknowledgments

Our colleagues at Tyndale Seminary contributed enormously to the development and production of this book. We are grateful to Mark Husbands for assisting us with the initial conceptualization of the volume, and for providing both sound advice and constant encouragement as the project advanced. In addition, we owe a large debt of gratitude to Marilyn Chan for handling the administrative details related to the book, and to Ruthi Mathewson for her painstaking thoroughness as a copy editor. We also are deeply indebted to Steve Masson, who designed the book and prepared the manuscript for publication.

We acknowledge with appreciation the contribution made by John Campbell, who assisted us by identifying individuals whose donations helped to finance the publication of this volume.

Finally, special thanks are due to the authors whose work appears here. Their enthusiasm for the project is an indication of their esteem for Donald A. Leggett, whom we honour with this *Festschrift*.

John Kessler & Jeffrey P. Greenman
October, 2000

Contributors

Nancy Calvert-Koyzis (PhD, University of Sheffield) has been Professor of New Testament at Tyndale Seminary since 1996. Her areas of research and writing include early Judaism, Pauline studies, women in early Christianity, and sociological approaches to New Testament studies.

Jeffrey P. Greenman (PhD, University of Virginia) has been Vice-President and Academic Dean of Tyndale Seminary since 1998. He also serves as Professor of Christian Ethics. His areas of research and writing include virtue ethics, friendship, Anglican theology, issues of work and vocation, biomedical ethics, and the relationship between spirituality and ethics.

Mark Husbands (PhD cand., University of St. Michael's College) is Director of Spring/Summer School and Extension Education at Tyndale College & Seminary. He also serves as Professor of Theology at the Seminary. While his primary research interest pertains to the work of Karl Barth, his research extends to cover the range of systematic theology, the thought of Calvin and Luther, theological hermeneutics and moral theology.

John Kessler (Docteur de l'Université, Sorbonne-Paris IV) is professor of Old Testament and Chair of Biblical Studies at Tyndale Seminary. His areas of specialization include the Book of Haggai, the historical and cultural context of Judah in the early Persian Period, and Old Testament theology.

Barbara M. Leung Lai (PhD, University of Sheffield) is Professor of Old Testament and Director of the Chinese Ministry Program at Tyndale Seminary. Her research and writing are in the areas of Wisdom literature, biblical interpretation and postmodernism, social sciences and the interpretation of the Hebrew Bible, and gender-culture studies.

Roy R. Matheson (ThD, Dallas Theological Seminary) has been Professor of New Testament at Tyndale Seminary since its inception in 1976. For the past 20 years he also has been teaching pastor at Chartwell Baptist Church in Oakville, Ontario. His teaching interests include how one moves from exegesis to exposition, particularly how preachers use the Greek text as a tool to give substance to their public communication.

Dennis K.P. Ngien (PhD, University of St. Michael's College), formerly a Senior Fellow at the Centre for Reformation and Renaissance Studies in the University of Toronto, has served as an associate faculty member in Systematic Theology at Tyndale Seminary since 1998. He is the author of *The Suffering of God according to Martin Luther's 'Theologia Crucis'* (Bern: Lang, 1995). His areas of research and writing include Luther, German theology, Trinity, Christology, issues in Calvinism and Arminianism, and eschatology.

Ian S. Rennie (PhD, University of Toronto) is Professor Emeritus of Church History at Tyndale Seminary, where he served as Vice-President and Academic Dean between 1981-1995. Recognized as a leading authority on Canadian church history, he served on the faculty of Regent College and has pastored several churches of the Presbyterian Church of Canada.

Victor A. Shepherd (ThD, Victoria University, University of Toronto) is Chair of Wesley Studies and Professor of Historical Theology at Tyndale Seminary. He is the author of 5 books, including *The Nature and Function of Faith in the Theology of John Calvin* (Macon, GA: Mercer University Press, 1983), as well as scholarly essays on Wesley and the Methodist traditions. Between 1978 -1999, he served as Senior Minister of Streetsville United Church in Streetsville, Ontario.

Terrance Tiessen (PhD, Loyola School of Theology, Ateneo de Manila University) is Professor of Systematic Theology at Providence Theological Seminary, Manitoba. He is author of *Irenaeus on the Salvation of the Unevangelized* (ATLA Monograph Series, No. 31; Metuchen, N. J: Scarecrow Press, 1993), and *Providence and Prayer: How Does God Work in the World?* (Downers Grove, IL.: InterVarsity Press, 2000).

John A. Vissers (ThD, University of Toronto) has been Principal of The Presbyterian College, Montreal and Faculty Lecturer in Theology at McGill University since 1999. Previously he served as Professor of Systematic Theology at Tyndale Seminary and as Senior Minister of Knox Presbyterian Church, Toronto. His areas of teaching, research and writing include Reformed theology, especially Calvin and Barth, North American neo-orthodoxy, the doctrines of revelation, church and atonement, and Canadian Presbyterianism.

Abbreviations

AB   Anchor Bible

ABD   *Anchor Bible Dictionary*, 6 vols. ed. D.N. Freed-
            man, New York: Doubleday, 1992

ATR   *Anglican Theological Review*

Bib   *Biblica*

CBQ   *Catholic Biblical Quarterly*

CBQMS   CBQ, Monograph Series

CRINT   Compendia rerum Iudaicarum ad Novum Tes-
            tamentum

CSCO   Corpus scriptorum christianorum Orientalium

CSR   *Christian Scholar's Review*

FP   *Faith and Philosophy*

HSM   Harvard Semitic Monographs

IDBSup	*The Interpreter's Dictionary of the Bible,* Supplementary Volume, ed. K. Crim, Nashville: Abingdon, 1976
JBL	*Journal of Biblical Literature*
JSOT	*Journal for the Study of the Old Testament*
JSOTSup	JSOT, Supplement Series
JSPSup	Journal for the Study of the Pseudepigrapha, Supplement Series
NIB	*New Interpreter's Bible,* Nashville: Abingdon, 1998
NICOT	New International Commentary on the Old Testament
NovTSup	Novum Testamentum, Supplements
OBT	Overtures to Biblical Theology
RB	*Revue Biblique*
RelS	*Religious Studies*
SBLSP	*Society of Biblical Literature Seminar Papers*
SJT	*Scottish Journal of Theology*
TDNT	*Theological Dictionary of the New Testament,* 10 vols. ed. G. Kittel and G. Freidrich, Grand Rapids: Eerdmans, 1964-76
TOTC	Tyndale Old Testament Commentaries
T(P)APA	*Transactions (and Proceedings) of the American Philological Association*
VT	*Vetus Testamentum*
WBC	Word Biblical Commentary

Chapter 1

Introduction

John Kessler & Jeffrey P. Greenman

*T*eaching and learning are among the most ancient as well as the most foundational experiences of human existence. As long as society has existed, teachers have occupied a critically important position. Furthermore, viewed from an historical and global perspective, teaching consists of far more than the mere transmission of cold data. In addition to the communication of the factual aspects of any discipline, truly great teachers form their students in many other ways. They stimulate them to reflection and careful thought. They fill them with interest and enthusiasm for the subject. They inspire their students to believe that, contrary to the doubts and hesitations they may feel, that they are capable of great things. They impart to their students vital skills and abilities which enable the student to move into new and uncharted areas of study, investigation and growth. They shape the student's character so that knowledge gained is used well, and thus enriches not only the student but the community as a whole. This broader understanding of teaching and learning reflects the biblical vision of the teacher as one who is wise, and who imparts that wisdom to others.

Donald A. Leggett is one who well understands and embodies what it truly means to teach and to learn, and most especially to be "taught of God." We feel that the volume's title reflects that which is at the very centre of Don's life and ministry. This *Festschrift* consists of

1

a series of essays by several of Don's friends and colleagues. The articles deal with a variety of biblical and theological issues, and their outworking in life experience. They are a good reflection of Don's wide-ranging interests.

Ian Rennie provides a warmhearted personal appreciation of Don's life and ministry. In the area of biblical studies, Victor Shepherd insightfully explores Luther and Calvin's understanding of Genesis 22, with its deeply challenging account of the divine command for the sacrifice of Isaac. John A. Vissers integrates Reformed theology (Don's own theological rooting) and exegesis in a study of Psalm 19 as it relates to knowledge of ourselves and knowledge of God. Barbara Leung Lai engages the question of the contemporary reading of the "Virtuous Woman" of Proverbs 31. This reflects Don's deep interest in wisdom literature, and its application to the practicalities of daily life. Nancy Calvert-Koyzis examines the interesting subject of Paul's usage of the Abraham materials in Genesis in comparison to the portrayals of Abraham by the Jewish historian Josephus.

In a more theological vein, Terrance Tiessen provides a defense of the Reformed position regarding divine foreknowledge in the light of recent critiques of that view. Dennis Ngien, who presents a theological counterpoint to the volume's more Reformed contributors, emphasizes the importance of the biblical concept of the God who is emotionally engaged in the experiences of his covenant people, and the practical and pastoral relevance of the passionate nature of God. Mark Husbands develops the question of the role of the Holy Spirit giving access to the understanding and application of Scripture, a topic which is especially important to Don. Jeffrey Greenman explores the relevance of the disciplines of *lectio continua* and *lectio divina* in order to highlight the richness of the classical Christian tradition for spiritual formation. In an essay underlining the use of the Old Testament in the church, Roy Matheson provides insight into how the discipline of narrative criticism can be of great help to those who preach from the Hebrew Bible, looking particularly at the Book of Ruth.

Don will be remembered not only for his abilities in the classroom, but also as an author. In addition to a series of articles at the popular level and contributions to study Bibles, he produced two fine monographs, both of which have made significant contributions to the study and appreciation of the Old Testament. In a more scholarly vein, his *The Levirate and Goel Institutions in the Old Testament: with special attention to the Book of Ruth* (Cherry Hill, NJ: Mack, 1974), provides an in-depth study of the legal and sociological issues related to the interpretation of the Book of Ruth, as well as a detailed analysis of various aspects of that book. Addressing a broader readership, his more recent *Loving God and Disturbing Men : Preaching from the Prophets* (Burlington, ON: Welch, 1990) gives an introduction to the prophets and their importance to the Christian faith, as well as practical guidelines for preaching from the prophets. This is followed by a discussion of the meaning and message of the books of Habakkuk, Haggai, and Malachi, which illustrates how these books may be communicated in a meaningful way to contemporary hearers.

As editors we have sought to honour Donald A. Leggett by presenting a volume which would be of interest and use to former students, pastors, and teachers. As a result the essays are intended to be easily accessible to non-specialists in the various disciplines represented, yet of significant depth and thoughtfulness. It is our hope that this book will be both a source of enrichment and insight to its readers, as well a heartfelt tribute to a great teacher, pastor, scholar, colleague and friend.

Chapter 2

Donald A. Leggett:
An Appreciation

Ian S. Rennie

*H*aving had the opportunity to work with Don Leggett day in and day out for fourteen years, it is a privilege to be able to write a personal and collegial appreciation of him.

When God created Don he made him to be a great character, larger than life. Don is full of humour which is often expressed in tumultuous laughter. He delights in sports, enjoys good food and exhibits in full measure the enthusiasm and exuberance for which Americans are justly famous. Don is a "people person" - strongly relational. On occasion he will share his deepest self with fellow faculty members, or join some of his students for a game of basketball after class with shirt-tail flying. He is visited regularly by a steady stream of graduates. Since Don does nothing by halves, both his disinterest in organizational process and his absentmindedness are monumental. This aspect of his character can also result in lecture tangents, misplaced papers and keys, and enough books left on the Toronto subway system between Union Station and Finch to provide the core of a good theological library.

In addition to being an engaging and very human person, Don is an utterly genuine and wholehearted Christian. He underwent a deep and transforming conversion in 1953 when he was eighteen years of age. This experience has given motivation and direction as well as a spirit of consecration and servanthood to his life. Don has given an account of this life-changing event:

> I was raised in a liberal Methodist Church in the States, and was very involved in church work as a young person. Upon graduation from high school I attended Lehigh University, Bethlehem, PA, for one year. Near the end of the year, I went with a number of dorm friends to see the movie, 'The Titanic'. This turned out to be an event which profoundly changed my life. I left the movie faced with the reality of death and consequently the meaning of life. Under some anguish of soul, I went to talk with my minister who advised me to go into the ministry. I transferred schools to begin preministerial study, winding up at Dickenson College in PA - mainly because of the basketball court, since I had played freshman basketball at Lehigh. Early in the first semester I went to a meeting of Inter-Varsity Christian Fellowship. After the meeting I heard talk of an itinerant preacher at a local church. That Sunday I went to hear him and for the first time, I heard a forceful Christ-centred message. I attended the services all week and that Friday I accepted Christ.

The reality and wonder of this momentous experience has remained with Don throughout his life and ministry.

In the Independent Baptist congregation of strong Calvinistic persuasion which he attended, Don received an extensive grounding in biblical and theological studies. Both doctrine and implications for life were stressed.

Not only was Don spiritually transformed and well-taught, but he also gave evidence that he had received the gift of teaching whereby he would instruct and edify Christians. As a result he was able to discern what was positive and constructive about his undergraduate education, and then proceed from 1956 to 1959 to be engaged in theological study for his M.Div. at the Reformed Episcopal Theological Seminary in Philadelphia. After his basic academic theological preparation, he went across the city for his M.Th. to Westminster Seminary, which was in its most distinguished period. Faculty members included Ned Stonehouse in New Testament, John Murray in Theology, Cornelius Van Til in Apologetics, and, in Don's special field of Old Testament, E. J. Young. Young was arguably the leading evangelical American Old Testament scholar of his day, along with his junior colleague, the stimulating Meredith Kline. Don partook liberally of the riches offered at Westminster. Then, wisely, he was off to Europe, with its exhilarating intellectual and cultural life, to secure his Th.D. under the eminent Reformed Old Testament professor, N. H. Ridderbos, of the Free University, Amsterdam. Don's spiritual and theological foundations remained strong, and were stretched and expanded, as expressed in his published doctoral thesis, *The Levirate and Kinsman Redeemer Institution in the Old Testament*, which has been appreciatively recognized by various Old Testament scholars. This academic formation was an indispensable element in preparing Don to be a teacher in Christ's Church.

Don's first appointment was at Ontario Bible College, where he served from 1964-76. In 1976, he became a founding faculty member of Tyndale Seminary, where he has remained for twenty-four years. Students have consistently found his teaching to be highly stimulating. His love for Christ, his confidence in the Bible as the Word of God, his sense of God's call upon his life and his academic background meant that the serious Christian student preparing for ministry was never disappointed. Student evaluations indicated overwhelmingly that the lectures and discussions in Don's classes had resonated with his love of Scripture and of the Lord Jesus Christ.

Don's teaching also was enriched in many ways. Throughout all his professional life he was an active family man, with the strong, intelligent, energetic and creative Linda as a constant source of support and wisdom. God certainly provided the ideal wife for Don, in Linda. Then there were their five children who drew out his great heart of love even more, preparing him uniquely to relate to students. Don's relational abilities have been evident at Village Green Baptist Church in London, Ontario, where he has been the preaching pastor for some twenty years. In addition, in this setting he learned the value of loyalty to his own Fellowship Baptist denomination, of fellowship with other clergy in the community and of involvement with such parachurch ministries as Inter-Varsity Christian Fellowship - all these components were invaluable assets in a transdenominational training institution such as Tyndale. Don's more recent experience teaching in Third World theological seminaries, particularly at the South Asia Institute of Advanced Christian Studies in Bangalore, India, has also increased his desire and ability to train students for Christian ministry. His books, articles, translations and annotations have also served to enrich and extend his ministry as a teacher.

Throughout his career at Tyndale Seminary Don has been an indispensable agent of institutional health. His spirituality, his theology, his ecclesiology, his personality, all bound together, have done much to positively influence the direction of Tyndale Seminary. So we thank God for him, and trust that many faculty and students may find in Don a model of all-round ministry.

Chapter 3

Abraham and Isaac in Genesis 22:
Hope as the Reconciliation of Command and Promise

Victor Shepherd

Concerning the account of the *akedah* ("binding")[1] Gordon Wenham comments, "No other story in Genesis, indeed in the whole OT, can match the sacrifice of Isaac for its haunting beauty or its theological depth."[2] No doubt its literary beauty[3] helped keep the story in the forefront of the people's consciousness even as its theology informed and formed Israel for centuries throughout the people's anguished engagement with God, their relations with the surrounding nations, and contemporary Jewry's self-understanding in the wake of 20th century depradations.

Notwithstanding the story's formative role in Israel's self-understanding, it has exercised Christian exegetes and philosophers[4] in every era. Two exegetical giants, Martin Luther and John Calvin, both architects of the Protestant Reformation, wrestled with this narrative inasmuch as it had first gripped them, not allowing them to rest until they, like Jacob of old, had found their grappling with it yielding its God-appointed blessing.

This essay, then, probes the account of Abraham and Isaac and their joint sacrifice, together with the anguished contortions of two thinkers who persisted in wrestling with the text despite the profound torment it occasioned for them.

The Story

Abraham's test[5], of course, is not "temptation" in the sense of seduction into sin. It is *Anfechtung* (Luther), trial, that occasion of torment which discloses the nature, depth and scope of one's faith; in a word, what is undeniably the state of one's heart. In many respects the command is stupefying. Isaac, after all, was granted to Abraham and Sarah when realistically no child could have been expected. More to the point, Isaac's survival is essential to the fulfillment of God's promises to Abraham. Having cut himself off from his entire past — "Go from your country and your kindred and your father's house to the land that I will show you" (12:1) — Abraham must now renounce his future, and with it the future of his people, including not only the future of his descendants but also that of innumerable nations who were to be blessed through his descendants.[6]

The crux of the story is this. Abraham, the prototype of the person of faith, has been promised spiritual descendants as numerous as the sand on the seashore. If the promise is to be fulfilled, two conditions must be met: Abraham must *persevere in faith* (or else he cannot be the foreparent of descendants-in-*faith*), and Isaac must *survive* (or else there will no *descendants*-in-faith.) The dilemma is plain: If Abraham obeys God and offers up his son, then God's promise is null and void, since Isaac has not survived; if Abraham second-guesses (i.e., disobeys) God and preserves Isaac, then God's promise is null and void, since Abraham's disobedience exemplifies unfaith.

Abraham's obedience threatens to nullify the promise as surely as his disobedience would nullify it. Abraham decides to stake everything on trusting God to fulfil his promises in ways that Abraham cannot imagine at this point. He will obey God even though such obedience, from a human perspective, ensures the non-fulfillment of the promise.

God tests Abraham[7], the sole, true and living God, the Holy One whose address is as undeniable as it is unmistakable. It is little wonder that the text obviates all sought-after speculations concerning all reductionist psycho-religious "explanations": the story has point and force only if *God* has spoken unambiguously and Abraham has heard unambivalently.[8]

Testing as such is nothing new for Abraham.[9] The nature of this test, however, is highlighted by the fact that here, for the first time in the Abraham narratives, testing appears in the opening words of the narrative; and here too there appears a test so severe as to appear wantonly destructive.[10] The earlier nexus of command and test included the promise of a rich future, new land, numerous descendants, and blessing for all nations. The present command includes no such promise. In fact obedience to it precludes future, land, descendants and blessing — for all of these presuppose Isaac's survival. Yet the severity of the testing does not imply insensitivity on God's part. "*Take* (your son)" has the force of "Please take."[11]

God's sensitivity notwithstanding, the request is outrageous. The terrible tension it precipitates is heightened yet again as Abraham is told to take "your *only* son, Isaac, whom you *love*." By now the narrative has slowed to a crawl as the reader is forced to linger over the perseverated detail, Isaac who is loved unspeakably, and therein forced to reflect on a command whose ever-narrowing specificity fosters ever-increasing anguish. "Whom you love", exquisitely protracted, precludes any "easy out" that Abraham's love for his son was deficient in any case.[12]

The content of the test pertains, as already noted, to the promise and its (apparent) nullification. The context of the test is Abraham's unsurpassable love for Isaac. Both are needed. Just as it is nowhere suggested that Abraham's love for Isaac is deficient, nowhere is it implied that Abraham's love for Isaac is inordinate. God approves its intensity. Apart from a love as intense as it is proper, the dilemma concerning the promise would be but a cold abstraction devoid of human significance. Apart from the dilemma concerning the promise, the story would not be trivialized (the loss of a child can never be trivial), but it would none the less lack the creation-wide significance it is meant to have.

Abraham is to give up Isaac as a "burnt offering." Later Levitical ritual will designate this particular offering as the only one to be completely consumed. While the reader's awareness of the conclusion[13] of the story (e.g., the provision of the ram) mitigates the story's horror and incomprehensibility, for Abraham himself there was no such relief. The test remains consummate *test* only if horror and incomprehensibility perdure.

The drama takes a remarkable turn when Abraham, intending nothing but that resolute obedience which undeniably includes the death of Isaac, departs for the site with Isaac alone and, upon leaving the servants behind, adds, "[we]...will come again to you." (22:5) On the one hand Abraham releases the servants in that he cannot endure seeing anyone else behold the ghastly event. On the other hand he indicates that he *expects* to return with Isaac, however illogical or inchoate his expectation here. Thus now Abraham is trusting God to fulfil the promise in a manner wholly unforeseeable yet not to be doubted. Paradoxically, the narrator speaks in such a way as to leave the reader the understanding that on the one hand Abraham intends nothing but the slaughter of Isaac, and yet is relying on the promise *fulfilled*, an event that presupposes Isaac's being spared.[14]

Isaac, meanwhile, is aware that he and his father are on their way to worship, and aware, of course, that worship entails sacrifice. Unsuspecting, he calls out, "My father." Abraham replies, "Here am I, *my son*." Abraham's heart remains knit to Isaac's as strongly as it was the day he received the baby from Sarah. The iron-fast bond of affection only magnifies the tension as Isaac, not suspicious but certainly bewildered, notes that all is on hand for the sacrifice except the victim. "Where is the lamb for a burnt offering?" Isaac's trust in his father is one with his father's trust in God.

While much religious art depicts Isaac as a child, if not still an infant, the story makes plain that Isaac is strong enough to carry wood sufficient for that conflagration required to consume his remains. He is also sophisticated enough to apprehend the accoutrements of sacrifice. Not surprisingly, then, Jewish tradition deems Isaac to be 37 years old.[15] Isaac thus willingly accepts his role as sacrificial victim. A vigorous young adult could readily overpower a very aged father. The test for Abraham is therefore a test for Isaac as well. Isaac, after all, could not be bound unless he complied.

Since Isaac submits to being bound he is not *mere* piacular victim. He is as much an agent in the event as his father. To the extent that Abraham is ready to obey God at all cost, Isaac is ready to obey his father — and therefore obey God through his father — at all cost. Lest the subtlety of all such considerations distract the reader from the shock-aspect of the deed, the narrator comments, "Abraham ...bound Isaac *his son.*" (22:9) The event at Moriah remains grisly. Nothing can reduce the bizarreness, horror and enormity of what is about to happen.

Precisely at the moment of the knife's descent God (I am reading "angel of the Lord" as God himself in his immediacy, intimacy and intensity apperceived in *this instance*) calls, "Abraham, Abraham." The name repeated is a Hebrew way of denoting urgency, typically a way of stopping an action that someone is on the point perpetrating.[16] God's forbidding the dreaded act is now as pressing as his earlier command to sacrifice Isaac. God has "seen enough." Abraham's willingness to sacrifice is sufficient proof of his undeflectable obedience and trust in God. God's unaffected awareness and candid acknowledgement, "*Now* I know that you fear God" (22:12), dovetails exactly with Abraham's utter surprise at the provision of the ram.[17] Earlier (22:8) Abraham had attempted to remedy Isaac's bewilderment with "God will provide a lamb", and then had moved ahead in obedience to God on the assumption that there were no *this-worldly* grounds for such intervention (the proof of Abraham's mind and heart being his raising the knife over Isaac.) Then the ram is brought forth. Abraham's surprise is no more feigned than his intent to obey God at any cost. Both dimensions must be underscored: it is true simultaneously that Abraham never doubts that "God will provide" (or else he has abandoned faith's trust in the promise-fulfilling God) *and* that he is genuinely astounded at the appearance of the ram (or else he has abandoned faith's obedience to the uncompromising claim of God.) Abraham is genuinely surprised, profoundly surprised, that the promise has been fulfilled in this manner.

Abraham names the place "The Lord will provide." In naming the place he does not mention himself. He does not seek to exalt himself, never mind memorialize himself. He wants only to magnify the act of God wherein *God's* mercy and wisdom are enlarged. Nothing in the story suggests that Abraham understands himself to be anything more than an "unprofitable servant."

The second address of the "angel of the Lord" to Abraham (22:15-18) is by no means an "add-on", let alone embellishment, but is rather an integral aspect of the story itself. Indeed the angel's words "are the last and most emphatic statement of the promises given to Abraham."[18] For nowhere else does a divine oath, "By myself I have sworn" (22:15), occur in the patriarchal stories. Again, the singularity of the divine oath (emphasized by "by myself") is matched by the divine acknowledgement of Abraham's singular obedience: "Because you have done this"; "[because you] have not withheld your son, your only son"; "because you have obeyed my voice." *On account of Abraham's obedience* blessing will abound. "I will indeed bless you, really bless you" (22:17), the infinite absolute of "bless", used here alone in Genesis, underlines the truth that *this* promise surpasses all others.[19]

As enormous as the ordeal has been, the blessing is "super-enormous." Abraham himself will be blessed, as will his descendants, as will (by his descendants) *all* the nations of the earth. The content of the blessing is specified in the case of his descendants. They will be uncountable ("as the stars of heaven and as the sand which is on the seashore"), victorious ("shall possess the gates of their enemies"), and used of God in his prospering others ("shall all the nations of the earth bless themselves.") Abraham's faithfulness is the occasion, under God, of a divinely ordained beneficence whose scope and profundity are inestimable.

In all of this one must be careful not to undervalue the unsubstitutably *human*. Abraham's faithfulness and obedience and unwavering trust are a human event/act/affirmation upon which the blessing of the whole world hangs. The thrice-uttered "because *you*..." can only mean that the human "dialogical partner"[20] of God conditions God's response. What *God* will do (can do?) for all the nations turns on the integrity of a *human* agent. Heretofore the promise of God has been grounded in the will of God; now it is grounded in both the will of God and the will of Abraham. Not only has the test found Abraham unbroken, the test has been the occasion of the crown and climax of his walk with God.[21] And the test has permitted God to bless both Israel and the entire Gentile world.

It is little wonder, then, that the oath God has sworn to Abraham will be recalled repeatedly throughout scripture (e.g., Luke 1:55), for this oath gathers up and guarantees all God's promises to the patriarch.

Luther

Luther knows what is at stake in the *akedah*: Isaac "had the promise of God concerning the future blessing of the entire world."[22] Yet the command of God, in light of the promise of God, has issued in a "contradiction with which God contradicts himself."[23] For Luther it is humanly impossible to understand this, for we should "inevitably conclude that God is lying — and this is blasphemy — or that God hates me — and this leads to despair."[24] Whereas God formerly seemed to be Abraham's friend, God now appears to have become "an enemy and a tyrant."[25] Confronted by the God who is enemy and tyrant, Abraham is unable to believe that he is *merely* being tested, since he would know that in the face of *Anfechtung* he must recall, cling to and declare the promise of God — and this Abraham appears unable to do, no longer having "remained sure of the promise."[26] As profoundly discomfited as Abraham is by the ordeal, the episode is recorded for *our* comfort "in order that we may learn to rely on the promises we have."[27]

The dialectic Luther suggests here seems bizarre. Since the promise is now the occasion of logical contradiction, Abraham cannot be sure of the promise. Yet the purpose of the story of Abraham is to teach us that *we* must ever rely on the promise. Notwithstanding the oddity, Luther knows that *Anfechtung* does not arise ultimately in the face of "woman, gold, silver, life or death"; it arises, rather, when God "shows himself differently from the way the promise speaks."[28] *Anfechtung* overtakes us when God's self-disclosure contradicts God's self-utterance, not merely now in one situation and now in another, but rather *simultaneously*. When faced with contradiction (apparent or real) between God's *self*-disclosure and the promise, what are we to do? Luther's answer is unambiguous: we are to cling to the promise. And yet Luther appears to contradict himself immediately as he declares that "Abraham's faith shines forth with special clarity in this passage, inasmuch as he obeys God with such a ready heart when He gives him the command."[29] Here Luther identifies faith as obedience to command rather than as trust in promise. At once, however, Luther adds, "And although Isaac has to be sacrificed, he nevertheless has no doubt whatever that the *promise* will be fulfilled even if he does not know the manner of its fulfillment."[30] "No doubt" can only mean "faith." Here, then, faith is confidence in the promise fulfilled.

Nowhere in his commentary on Genesis concerning the matter under discussion does Luther speak of the command of God in terms of the law of God, and then contrast it sharply (as is his custom) with the gospel (promise). Were he to do this, of course, he would have to relegate the significance of the command to fostering in the hearer that despair which drives one to the gospel (promise). Were command to be understood as law, however, the tension in the incident would disappear and the "trial" would evaporate. Throughout his exposition of Genesis 22 Luther presupposes promise and command as the one gospel of God seen from two different angles. While the law/gospel distinction is crucial in Luther's thought as a whole and therefore characteristic of him, it is plain that so far as Abraham is concerned the command is not to be understood in terms of law but in terms of gospel. When Luther probes the three-day journey to Moriah he notes that Abraham's reliance on the *command* "strengthened and preserved him."[31] Everywhere in Luther the law, so far from strengthening and preserving, breaks people down for the sake of that which does: the gospel. Plainly Luther relates obedience to command even as he implies promise (rather than law). The obedience he has in mind, of course, is that obedience which pertains to (promise-quickened) faith. Obedience "does not exist where there is no divine promise."[32] Clearly there is a subtle mutuality between promise and command. While from a human perspective promise and command may appear to contradict each other, ultimately the promise is the meaning of the command.

Obedience to the command is no small matter. For when Abraham heard the command of God "he hastened without hesitation to carry it out. This is an extraordinary example of a description of perfect obedience."[33] Unlike Adam, Luther notes, Abraham does not ask why.[34] Adam's *Anfechtung*, whatever else it may have involved, did not involve contradiction. Then how did Abraham manage to meet it? He met it only "through the power of the command of God."[35] Although, from a human perspective, Abraham "did not have a heart of iron but was of a very tender nature...emotions undoubtedly were accompanied by inexpressible groans, sighs, sobs, and fatherly tears", his obedience "extended to his innermost being"[36], there being no room in him for doubt, let alone defiance. The resilience of his obedience, insists Luther, was attributable to the fact that the *command* "rules and lives in him."[37]

Immediately the reader recalls the New Testament insistence that Jesus Christ (i.e., the gospel) alone rules and lives in believers. Once more, then, Luther is relating obedience (to the command) to gospel- (promise-) quickened faith. In this context it should be noted that Luther maintains faith to arise as we open our ears and shut our eyes. Ears (metaphorically) receive the Word of God; eyes behold what is everywhere a contradiction of the Word of God. Abraham "hears" the (promise-grounded) command, and "sees", as it were, Isaac slain — and then proceeds to slay Isaac, trusting God to fulfil the promise.

Reason, Luther rightly sees here, is helpless before the conundrum: "If Isaac must be killed, the promise is void; but if the promise is sure, it is impossible that this is a command of God."[38] Reason aside, Abraham cannot doubt that God has announced both promise and command.

At this point Luther brings forward a theme that will recur throughout his discussion of the episode; *viz.*, the sacrifice of Isaac, and Isaac's subsequent restoration (necessary if Isaac is to have descendants), is an anticipation of the resurrection of the dead.[39] Within a few lines, however, Luther recognizes that to rely on Isaac's being resurrected *after* he has been slain is to denature the event as *incomparable* trial. If Isaac is to be resurrected and thereby rendered the progenitor of a people, then strictly speaking there is no trial. There remains psychological tumult for Abraham (he must still *slay* his son), but no theological/spiritual conundrum, no trial with respect to faith in the promise of God and the future blessing of the world. Admittedly, God can continue to "try" Abraham's trust in and love for One who visits assorted afflictions on Abraham, but appealing to the resurrection of the dead undercuts the nature of that trial which tries faith in the promise of the God whose promise has become an impossibility; i.e., tries faith in the God *who has himself become an "impossibility."* Luther maintains that the Word of God is "equal to God", as is God's "spoken word"[40] (i.e., God's self-utterance.) The contradiction between the spoken utterance (command) and the Word (promise) renders God *self*-contradictory.[41] God has thus, in Luther's eyes, become an impossibility for Abraham.

In reflecting on the *akedah* Luther reminds us that the Word of God and faith in that Word are correlative, and wherever "these two are, there follows the third, namely, the cross and mortification. These three make up the Christian life."[42] And what is the extent of mortification? Mortification entails self-denial, to be sure, yet a self-denial so far-reaching as to involve the cancellation of everything and everyone whose significance is connected to the "self" undergoing trial. Mortification, self-denial, is nothing less than utmost deprivation. In this regard Luther comments, "Abraham has now [i.e., upon hearing the command] nothing more, so far as the promise is concerned, than he had before Isaac was born; and yet, because of God, he is ready to give up not only his son, Sarah, an inheritance, his house and his church, but even his own life. Isaac's death included all of this inasmuch as the promise was attached to Isaac."[43] Isaac's death entails an obliteration that is nothing less than total. And since, as was noted earlier, a *self*-contradiction in God renders God an impossibility, obedience to the command of God will not only cancel the promise of God *but thereby effect the ultimate* nihil. Abraham, faced with an obedience to God that effects the ultimate *nihil*, finds a sympathizer in Luther who suggests this is to be the reason why Abraham told no one of his trial: no one would have understood it (the same conclusion Kierkegaard was to announce, exemplify and suffer for centuries later.)[44]

As Isaac's initial bewilderment ("Where is the lamb for the burnt offering?") gives way to his awareness that he is to be the offering, Luther highlights the obedience of father *and* son. On the one hand Luther maintains that so profound, so moving, is this development that nothing is said about it in that "the subject matter is greater than can be expressed by any eloquence."[45] On the other hand, he does manage to say something: "With the exception of Christ, we have no similar example of obedience."[46] With his subtle grasp of so very many ramifications Luther points out that Abraham's sacrifice of Isaac is not only Isaac's *self*-sacrifice but also Abraham's as well. For "death has a soul and a body", and to die "in the truest sense of the word" is not to undergo biological cessation but rather "to feel the violence of real death."[47] In this sense "*both* are killed, since they see and feel *nothing but death*."[48] And while Abraham is everywhere commended for his faith in the promise, Isaac's faith is no less remarkable. For at the moment that the knife is held to Isaac's throat, *Isaac* insists, "I am the son of promise. Therefore I must beget children even if heaven collapses."[49] God's promise is so very sure, and so very sure is Isaac's faith in the promise, that heaven will "collapse", the cosmos will de-create, before the promise fails — even as obedience to the command precipitates the ultimate *nihil.*

Plainly Luther views the Abraham-Isaac story as having cosmic significance. It is no surprise, then, that he ruminates, concerning the appearance of the ram that dies in place of Isaac, on two possibilities: the animal could have been brought to the site or been brought *into existence* at the site. He prefers the latter.[50] For Luther God's provision is not a providential rearranging of what already exists; God's provision is nothing less than *creatio ex nihilo.*[51] The Abraham/Isaac promise/command matrix, together with the blessing soon to be pronounced, means that the *world's* life can begin again.

The resolution of the trial finds God swearing by himself. Such singular swearing has the force, says Luther, of God's saying, "I desire so greatly to be believed and long so intensely to have my words trusted that I am not only making a promise but am offering myself as a pledge....If I do not keep my promises, I shall no longer be who I am."[52] The promise made to Abraham must be fulfilled or God has annihilated himself. That God does not (cannot) annihilate himself is God's pledge that this promise is not merely something that God has said and now makes good; i.e., as related to the faithfulness of God *this* promise is integrally related to the *being* of God. This promise, then, is like no other. For this reason Luther rhapsodizes that by this God "enlarges His promise to such an outstanding extent that it surpasses all thinking and faith."[53] In other words, this promise transcends thought so as to leave us unable to comprehend it, even as the enlarged promise dwarfs our faith. Yet since promise and faith are internally related, an enlarged promise *must* issue in enlarged faith. For precisely this reason Luther adds, "What could be said or thought that is surer and more powerful for increasing faith?"[54]

With respect to the scope of the blessing spreading out from Abraham, Luther speaks first of David. David apprehends (Pss 89:35; 132:11) that by God's oath the promise "has come into my [i.e., David's] tribe, into my line, person and body....I am he to whom the promise is attached, just as it was attached to the person of Abraham."[55] In short, David is now the embodiment of the original promise. But then David's enemies must have been anticipated in Abraham's enemies and those of Abraham's immediate descendants. Not unexpectedly, then, Luther comments that regardless of however "powerful and violent" the enemies of Abraham's descendants might be, victory "will be with the sand and the stars, but especially with the Son."[56] With *the Son*? Luther's final word concerning the scope of the ever-expanding boon could not be stronger: "The blessing promised Abraham is eternal."[57]

Calvin

In his *Institutes* Calvin admits that Abraham's trial concerning Isaac is quantitatively different from all tests and afflictions (the greatest of which was childlessness) visited upon Abraham earlier, since "for a son to be slaughtered by his father's hand surpasses every form of calamity."[58] All such tests, however, have merely facilitated Abraham's mortification. Now, however, Abraham is pierced by a wound that is qualitatively different, "a wound far more grievous than death itself."[59] Here Abraham is tormented not merely at the prospect of bereavement, but rather at a faith-obedience wherein "the whole salvation of the world seemed to be extinguished and to perish." The exercise of faith issues in "the destruction of faith." It is little wonder that Abraham finds his "piety" a consuming "distraction."[60]

Calvin's reference to "piety" is significant. For him *pietas* is a noble word and carries none of modernity's pejorative freight; *viz.*, a saccharine, cloying, ethereal, self-indulgent and meritorious religiosity. *Pietas*, rather, is "that reverence joined with love of God which the knowledge of his benefits induces."[61] In his earlier catechism, written more expansively than the compressed *Institutes*, Calvin had said, "True piety consists rather in a sincere feeling which loves God as Father as much as it fears and reverences Him as Lord, embraces His righteousness, and dreads offending Him worse than death."[62] Paradoxically it is Abraham's piety that is now the ultimate spiritual threat. To adore God is now one with abhorring him. Previous tests presupposed the veridicality of the promise; this test ensures its cancellation, and with it even the possibility of humankind's salvation. The cancellation here, moreover, entails an inconsistency *in God* that renders God thoroughly opaque and therefore utterly untrustworthy. If trusting a treachery "proves" faith, what is the nature of such faith? If to exercise faith is to be left with none, and not to exercise faith is to be left with none, then what is meant by "faith?" Lest the reader think that Abraham might be "hearing things" in all of this, Calvin, reading the text with exquisite attentiveness, insists Abraham cannot doubt that God has spoken.[63]

In view of the fact that Calvin is notorious for insisting that word and faith cannot be separated, he displays his own "distress" when, in the context of proving faith, he speaks uncharacteristically of the "disappearance of the word."[64] While Calvin everywhere else maintains that the word can no more disappear than God vanish, here he magnifies the uniqueness of Abraham's test by insisting that God tries Abraham's faith by drawing Abraham into a contest with God's own word.[65] Amplifying this, Calvin avers (again uncharacteristically) that "God would shake the faith that Abraham had placed in His *word*, by a counter-assault of the word itself."[66] In short, God would test Abraham by juxtaposing word as promise (previously vouchsafed to Abraham) and word as living voice of the One whom Abraham knew with undeniable immediacy, "since all occasion of doubt is removed."[67]

It is impossible to exaggerate the manner in which Calvin has heightened, in expounding this narrative, the tensions in his own theology. Calvin rigorously maintains that the word alone is the author and object of faith. "Word" and "faith" always imply each other. For Calvin any deviation here is seen as the "fanaticism" of the 16th Century radicals.[68] Since the word is now *self*-contradicted, no human reasoning can reconcile the immolation of Isaac (word) and the promise concerning his descendants and the salvation of the world. This singular simultaneity of self-contradiction has the force of making "full trial" of Abraham's faith.[69] Such a trial is "full" not in the sense of "not partial" but rather in the sense of a *novum*, unprecedented, categorically different from the trials that have tested Abraham and all believers. Whereas temptation to disobey God is normally "shaken off"[70] by recalling and clinging to the promise, such recourse now appears impossible, since "God, in a certain sense, assumes a double character."[71] While word-quickened faith is kept constant as we "apply all our senses to the word of God"[72], such application is now useless since the *word itself* (God himself) has become the problem, God now being two-faced. God's "forked tongue" can only bespeak a Jekyll-and-Hyde monstrosity. Calvin reminds the reader that when believers are assaulted they are always to arm themselves with the word, "the sword of the Spirit." Now, however, he asks rhetorically what the predicament of believers must be if God at this moment attacks believers with that weapon wherewith he had previously protected them.[73] While the predicament cannot be untangled at the level of thought, the predicament can still be lived. Abraham, forswearing the futility of immobilizing himself before it or speculating beyond the concrete occurrence of the unmistakable summons, wrestles with the test *by faith*.[74] In it all he remains the paradigm of the person whose faith keeps him fixed on the immediacy of the *command* of God. Faith, in moments of dreadful testing, fixes itself to the immediacy of the command, obeying the command while trusting the promise. Calvin exalts the obedience of Abraham by pointing out that while believers of less rigorous faith are prone to be carried off "in whatever direction the breath of a doubtful vision may blow"[75], Abraham resolutely obeys God when, from a human perspective, he is faced not by a doubtful vision but by undeniable nightmare; and when from a believer's perspective, he is faced with a command incomprehensible in itself, ruinous for his family, and catastrophic for the wellbeing of the world. As if the "double character" of God were not enough, horrible on account of the confusion it engenders, God appears to gloat in his torturing Abraham by mocking him: God's requiring Abraham to exercise faith by obeying the command to wield the knife becomes itself the knife that dismembers the promise. As a result Abraham is commanded, as an act of faith, to "cut in pieces the charter of his salvation"[76] — and that of the whole world's.

Then is Abraham's faith anything more than irrationality or impulsiveness? Is he merely a self-negating inverted romantic? Little if anything could be said to spare Abraham (and therefore Calvin) this accusation were Genesis 22 the whole history of Abraham's engagement with God. While the test with Isaac is certainly unparalleled, it is not the only test or the first. In light of Abraham's decades-long, rich acquaintance with God and his understanding of God arising from this intimacy, Abraham, Calvin insists, concludes, *notwithstanding the present crisis,* that God "could not be his adversary."[77] Abraham's having concluded this much, however, still does not permit him to see *"how* the contradiction might be removed."[78] All of this is to say that Abraham, not yet permitted to walk by sight, must continue to walk by faith; he can reconcile promise and command only "by hope."[79] Again, however, such hope is never wishful thinking; Abraham's history of "walking" with God saves hope from the charge of irrationality, impulsiveness or romanticism even as it allows Abraham to affirm the fact of such reconciliation, content to leave the manner of it with God.

At this point in his analysis of the narrative Calvin appears to have said as much as he wants or needs to say. Apparently mesmerized by the story, however, and unable to let it go, he circles back relentlessly upon the contradiction between command and promise and all its consequences for a world unaware. Having already told his readers that God has contradicted himself *by reason of his word* (something Calvin will admit here in light of the intractable text of Genesis 22 yet something he will deny as absurd everywhere else in his theology), Calvin now directs our attention to a similar problem: Isaac is the *only* pledge of grace.[80] This sole pledge is now to be taken away, leaving — leaving a graceless God? (Again, such an implication occurs nowhere in Calvin outside the Abraham/Isaac story.) Admittedly, in view of the age of Abraham and Sarah, the occasion of the conception of Isaac was one of *human* impossibility. The destruction of the only pledge of God's grace, however, is the occasion of a *divine* impossibility, for the pledge and he of whom it is pledge cannot be separated: destruction of the pledge is the self-willed destruction of God. Whereas the promised conception of Isaac had required Abraham to trust God in a way that redounded to Abraham's praise as well as God's, now Abraham is to trust God in a situation that renders God, promise, faith and blessing a farrago of inconsistency and incomprehensibility. Still, says Calvin, in all of this there remains the fact of a promise whose meaning is affirmed in the face of what appears to void the promise of meaning. Abraham's test, Calvin adds laconically, is the prototype of test for every believer: God "reduces all their senses to nothing, that he may lead them to a complete renunciation of themselves."[81] With self renounced and understanding immobilized, Abraham suspends trying to "measure, by his own understanding, the method of fulfilling the promise."[82] Instead Abraham relies on the "incomprehensible power of God."[83] He will cling to the promise *of God* not only in the face of human impossibility but even divine.

At this point it is important for the reader to understand, in view of what Calvin has said already, that God's power is "incomprehensible" not in the sense that God is to be counted on for a mighty act whose mightiness is beyond human comprehension; rather, God's power is "incomprehensible" in that God is to be counted on to resolve his "double character." He whose nature is mercy[84] now wills the disappearance of his *only* pledge of mercy (grace.) Since "pledge" and "promise" imply each other, God's power is "incomprehensible" at present in that the promise is to be vindicated (and Abraham's faith with it) precisely where promise (and therefore pledge) wills its self-obliteration.

Still mesmerized, Calvin circles back yet again, examining the story from yet another angle of vision. Isaac is the "mirror of eternal life and the pledge of all good things."[85] "Mirror", one of Calvin's commonest metaphors, is never mirror only. When Jesus Christ, for instance, is said to mirror God, Calvin never means that those beholding the Nazarene are given a substance-less reflection. Similarly, when the sacraments are said to mirror Christ, Calvin never suggests that believers receive elements that somehow deceptively depict Christ but are devoid of him.[86] The purpose of a mirror, for Calvin, is to render substance accessible. Then the death of Isaac as "mirror" can only mean the disappearance of eternal life. And since "eternal life" is uniquely the life of God, the death of Isaac entails the death of God. It is *this* human opacity and divine impossibility, "incomprehensible", according to Calvin, that God's power can remedy.

Unable to let the matter go, Calvin returns to it once more, stating that the death of Isaac does not merely wound Abraham's "paternal heart"; it "tramples upon His [i.e., God's] own benevolence.'[87] Everywhere in Calvin God's "benevolence" is his inmost nature turned outward salvifically upon the world. If God's benevolence has been "trampled" (i.e., pulverized), then God himself has been de-natured.

Still haunted, Calvin comes back to the conundrum, this time stating that Isaac "was not a son of the common order but one in whom the person of the mediator was promised.'[88] Calvin insists in *Institutes* and *Commentaries* alike that there is no knowledge of God (i.e., no participation in God's life) apart from the mediator.[89] Then the death of the person of Isaac plainly implies the non-existence of the mediator. Abraham's obedience incontrovertibly deprives humankind of its sole saviour and thereby dooms it.

Calvin is so very reluctant to move past the perplexity he needs to point out only once in that he is evidently aware of its inherent shock: the person who embraces all of the foregoing embraces it as an act of *faith*. Calvin appreciates the correlation between an affirmation of the "incomprehensible" and a risible instance of the ludicrous, for he maintains that Abraham left the servants behind, on his way to Moriah, lest they find him "a delirious and insane old man.'[90] While Calvin is speculating here, the speculation is none the less profound. Abraham is "insane" in that he is about to do what only psychotics do; "delirious" in that Calvin assumes Abraham to be hysterical. Abraham is understandably hysterical, for Isaac's cry, "My father", is a *"new* instrument of torture.'[91]

Like Luther before him, Calvin maintains that Isaac is no infant but rather is middle-aged. Isaac "voluntarily" surrenders himself, and does so, says Calvin, only because he is "acquainted with the divine oracle.'[92] In view of Isaac's willing collaboration, therein rendering his death *self*-sacrifice, Isaac is bound not lest he change his mind and bolt at the moment of immolation but rather lest anything extraneous impede his act.[93] Again like Luther before him Calvin states that the sight of Isaac slain would be enough to kill Abraham.[94] In other words, Isaac's willing submission renders Abraham's obedience a joint perpetration on the part of father and son, even as it renders father and son joint victims.[95] Abraham's unalloyed obedience in faith destroys faith, son and *Abraham himself.* There is no other conclusion. And in view of Calvin's understanding of the person of God inherent in all the acts of God, the destruction of the promise (act) is also the destruction of the promiser.

As a result of Abraham's unvarying obedience God has come to know that Abraham fears him. Did God not know as much already in light of earlier tests? Yet as Calvin has averred repeatedly, this test is categorically distinct; this text exposed a "double character" in God and summoned Abraham to obey and trust the God self-exposed as such. Isaac's release completes and terminates Abraham's *"true* trial."[96] *Verus,* ("true") has the force of real, actual, genuine. The concrete actuality of the *akedah* has become the reality of Abraham's life, even the reality (albeit hidden) of the world, since the *akedah* lends the world its unacknowledged but no less real truth and substance: a divine blessing whose ramifications are inestimable.

Yet something can be "estimated", even counted on: (i) even though Israel's enemies will overrun her occasionally, Israel's enemies can never defeat her definitively[97] ; (ii) the victory promised to Israel is fulfilled in Jesus Christ and his people "so far as they adhere under one head."[98] Calvin, it should be noted, adduces both without indicating any inconsistency or even tension in the two-fold outcome. Israel will never be exterminated; neither will the church (Christ and his people.) Calvin does not develop at this point in his Genesis commentary anything approaching Paul's treatment of Israel and the church in Romans 9-11, or even his own understanding that Jesus Christ, the one and only mediator, was salvifically present to Israel under the economy of the torah. Yet his affirmation of the certainty that, based on Abraham's obedience, neither Israel nor the church will ever be destroyed is both sobering and pregnant. This point is especially relevant in light of the ongoing contemporary Jewish reflection on the question, "Why did no ram appear at Auschwitz?"

In his examination of Genesis 22 Calvin says nothing about the relation of Isaac and the church. Yet the reader may legitimately ask after and probe this relationship, for in his exposition of Genesis 21:1 Calvin writes, "in his [Isaac's] very birth God has set before us a lively picture of the church."[99] What does Isaac's birth portend for the church, even as the arm of the sacrificer is stayed, but only at the moment of the church's unconditional willingness to give itself up to death in demonstration of its trust in the promise? And how firm is the church's confidence that "God never feeds men with empty promises"?[100]

Comment: Contemporary Illustration and Theological Consideration

Imagine someone announcing in church that she has received a divine summons to slay her offspring. It is inconceivable that fellow-congregants would nod knowingly, all the while telling her they understood why she must proceed and assuring her of their support throughout it. Instead they would insist she undergo psychiatric assessment, thinking her to be psychotic. Now imagine that she submits to such assessment and is shown to be non-psychotic. It is still inconceivable that anyone would agree that, horrific as the deed appears, she must proceed as an act of faith. Most likely assertions would tumble out of many that God does not ask such hideous things of his people. If the woman in question were to reply, "Why not?", then likely it would be said that God would not or cannot, on the grounds of the character of the God we apprehend through his self-disclosure. Willful slaying of one's offspring is not the sort of thing that the God known in the church asks of his people, not the sort of thing that honours him in any way. Then the question cannot be avoided: why would anyone concur that Abraham was divinely summoned to slay Isaac? If God's character forbids such today, why would it not have forbidden it then? Conversely, if God's "voice" rendered sacrifice non-murder then, why would it not do as much today?

In framing a reply to this question we must consider the narrative itself: Yahweh rejects the offering. We must also consider the laws in Exodus and Deuteronomy regarding the redemption of the firstborn; and the abhorrence of child-sacrifice in the prophets.[101] All of these considerations taken together preclude the possibility that God would ever again ask such a thing.

Yet more can be said. Another clue to coming to terms with the question is suggested by Luther and Calvin in their insightful discussion of the *akedah*: in view of Isaac's consensual complicity, the son is as much sacrificer as the father; and in view of the fact that Isaac's death is tantamount to a fatal knife-thrust in the heart of Abraham, the father is as much the sacrificed as the son. Father and son are one in offering up and in being offered up; father and son are one in their obedience, their suffering and their trust.

I am convinced that we must ponder, in light of the critical comments adduced already in this section, the simultaneity of Father and Son with respect to the Atonement, presupposing as it does the *homoousion* as reflected in the apostolic confession of Jesus Christ and articulated in Athansius's assertion at the Council of Nicaea. In the context of the Arian heresy, Athanasius insisted, following the apostles, that the Son was of the *same* nature as the Father, not merely of a *similar* nature. If Father and Son were merely of a similar nature, then the Father's appointing the Son to the cross on behalf of humankind would be no more than the Father's appointing an innocent yet hapless third party to misery in the interests of appeasing a wrath the Son did not share. Yet precisely because Father and Son are of the same substance, same identity and being, the Son's free, self-willed identification with sinners is the Father's; the Son's sinbearing love is the Father's; the Son's cry of dereliction is the Father's heart-cry of self-alienation for the sake of sinners that demonstrates Father and Son to be one in their judgement of humankind, one in their determination to redeem it, one in their self-identification with it, and one in their pain suffered for its restoration.

The Son's God-forsakenness (not merely his feeling that he was) for the sake of humankind, together with the Father's self-same "God-forsakenness"[102] means that no human being is — or can be — God-forsaken. Looked at from a different angle, the cross means that that to which God appointed himself at Calvary *no human being will be appointed to now: namely, the sacrifice of one's offspring.*

Abraham and Isaac are together a prolepsis of God the Father and Son. The prolepsis, however, having been fulfilled in actuality in the event of Good Friday, is thereafter rendered impossible *as prolepsis*; i.e., any slaying of one's offspring could thereafter be regarded as murder only, never as sacrifice. Abraham and Isaac are not an instance, or even *the* instance, of the "teleological suspension of the ethical."[103] They are, rather, an instance of the unity of Father and Son in the event of the cross, no subsequent "anticipation" ever being possible in the light of *this* anticipation's definitive fulfillment. What Father and Son did in the cross is nothing less than that "one oblation…once offered, a full, perfect, and sufficient sacrifice, oblation and satisfaction, for the sins of the whole world."[104] Such an act needs no supplementation *or duplication*, neither does it permit one.

Conclusion

The force of Genesis 22:1-19 is that hope alone reconciles promise and command of God. Such hope, however, must always be distinguished from wishful thinking. Wishful thinking is but "dead" hope; "living" hope, on the other hand, is rooted in the event of the resurrection of Jesus Christ from the dead. (1 Pet 1:3) From a biblical perspective, *hope* is always a future *certainty* grounded in a present reality. Any lessening of hope as *certainty* merely denatures "hope" and moves it in the direction of wishful thinking. The resurrection of Jesus Christ is that reality which is ultimately the fulfillment of the promise of Exodus 3:14: "I

shall be who I shall be."[105] In the resurrection of his Son, God definitively resolves any suggestion or imputation of a "double character"
(Calvin) in his kingdom-establishing event. The resurrection is that act of
God whereby promise and command are reconciled; hope is the human
counterpart that finds promise and command reconciled in the believer.
Accordingly, the resurrection of Jesus Christ is ultimately the truth and
reality that gave Isaac *back*; hope, that which gave him back to *Abraham*,
the resurrection being the guarantee of all the promises of God to all
believers. Because Jesus Christ has been raised from the dead; because his
resurrection and all it implies is the truth of the world (albeit hidden and
therefore unacknowledged), as well as the truth of the church (an "open
secret" and therefore acknowledged in faith), hope can never finally dis-
appoint God's people. The future certainty of what is hoped for pertains to all the promises of God, whether now only partially fulfilled or
not yet fulfilled at all. They *will* be fulfilled, and will be seen to be such.

Instances without end can be given with respect to promises that
appear to remain unfulfilled, as well as of commands that seem to per-
petuate the non-fulfillment. One such promise/command appears to be
the promise that the powers of death will not prevail against the church
(Matt. 10:18), even as the church, defined by the gospel and charged to
live by the gospel, must announce Jesus Christ with no little urgency in
season and out of season. (2 Tim 4:2). Related to the command to announce the gospel is the promise that God's word does not return to
him fruitlessly (Isa 55:11), as well as (among others) the promise that
whoever hears the herald of the Lord hears that selfsame Lord himself
(Luke 10:16).

Yet the command appears to vitiate the promise, as the church
dwindles numerically (at least in the west) week by week. The gospel has
been promised to be fruitful beyond our imagining, while the command
to declare it appears to ensure the church's fruitlessness. After all, the
gospel appears too narrow in an age of inclusiveness, too sharply-de-
fined amidst the blurred vaguenesses of pluralism, too confident of its
effectiveness in a time of polite opinions, too real for an era that prefers
romanticism, too specific for those who like generalities, too precisely

parameterized to suit the taste of those who want no boundaries. It appears that insofar as the church attempts to live by the gospel it will die by the gospel. Then what is the church to do?

Like Abraham of old it can trust God to fulfil promises in ways that the church cannot see at present. It can obey the command of God even though its obedience must render all such fulfillment *hope*. Or it can second-guess God and attempt to ensure the fulfillment of the promise by "improving" on the command as it resorts to gimmicks, entertainment, sure-fire techniques, agendas that "work" with other institutions and whose "success" the sociologist can explain.

For those who have agonized with Abraham there is only thing to be done: live in hope, confident that hope will see, in God's own way and in God's own time, the reconciliation of promise and command.

Notes

[1] With respect to the Hebrew word itself H. C. Brichto (*The Names of God* [London: Oxford University Press, 1998] 286) comments, "…only the Hebraist will know that the verb for *bind* here never occurs again, so that rabbinic tradition can refer to this entire chapter as the *Akedah*, the (one and only) Binding."

[2] Gordon J.Wenham, *Genesis 16-50* (WBC; Waco: Word, 1994) 112.

[3] Von Rad maintains that "the narrative [is]…the most perfectly formed and polished of the patriarchal stories", and cites this as evidence that the story existed independently long before it was gathered up into the redacted work. Gerhard von Rad, *Genesis: A Commentary* (OTL; Philadelphia: Westminster, 1972) 238.

[4] Kierkegaard was plainly overwhelmed by the narrative. It precipitated *Fear and Trembling*, one of his most powerful works.

[5] The entire event will turn out to be as much a test for Isaac as it is for his father.

[6] While Brichto (*The Names of God*, 288) is undoubtedly correct in denying that a protest against the pagan practice of child sacrifice is *the* point of the story, his insistence that such a point is not to be found in the story at all seems one-sided. He writes, "How can one read such a repudiation of child sacrifice into a story in which the central theme throughout is Abraham's readiness to make the sacrifice, and in the denouement of which that readiness of Abraham's is explicitly hailed as meritorious and certain to elicit reward?" It can be argued readily that Abraham's readiness to make the sacrifice, only to have God stay his

hand, tellingly bespeaks Israel's awareness that child sacrifice henceforth has no place in its worship or ethos. The incident is an instance of pierastic irony: the speaker wants the opposite of what is called for.

[7] With Wenham, Genesis, 104, I am interpreting the definite article here (lit. "the God") as forbidding the reader from finding relief in such vagaries as "Perhaps Abraham merely *thought* he heard God speak, merely projected an intra-psychic oddity." While "God" (without the article) is used in the story wherever the narrator refers to the deity, the article is added whenever God himself addresses Abraham. Not to be overlooked is the use of *Elohim* rather than *Yahweh*: is there a hint here of what the outcome of the story is to be?

[8] Martin Buber's question to anyone who claims to have heard such a summons today, "Are you really addressed by the Absolute or by one of his apes?" (Martin Buber, *Eclipse of God* [New York: Harper and Row, 1952] 119), is a question asked and answered in the text.

[9] Abraham had been tested already with respect to famine (12:10ff — at which he behaved ingloriously) and again with respect to the three visitors (18:1ff).

[10] von Rad, *Genesis*, 239.

[11] Notwithstanding the debate about the precise force of the enclitic ("please"), rare in a divine command, I am reading it here as lending the force of entreaty to the command. God manifests his awareness of the outrageous nature of his request. See Wenham, *Genesis*, 113; Hamilton, *The Book of Genesis: Chapters 18-50* (TOTC; Grand Rapids, Eerdmans, 1995) 101.

[12] This point has to be made lest it be thought that Abraham is unconcerned about Isaac. After all, Abraham "did not hesitate to haggle on behalf of a tiny percentage of possible innocents in Sodom's moral sinkhole." (Brichto, *The Names of God*, 280).

[13] The reader is told at the start that this is a test. This information makes the narrative bearable.

[14] I am puzzled at Wenham's suggestion that Abraham's "we will come again to you" can mean any or all of the following: a lie to spare Isaac anxiety, Abraham's decision not to sacrifice Isaac after all, or an affirmation of faith. I find nothing in the text to support the first two suggestions. Everything in the story supports only the third. Wenham, *Genesis*, 107.

[15] Gen. Rabbah 56:8, quoted in Hamilton, Genesis, 100.

[16] For scriptural illustrations of this point see Hamilton, *The Book of Genesis: Chapters 1-17* (TOTC; Grand Rapids: Eermans, 1994) 111.

[17] A full-grown ram rather than a lamb is a fitting substitute for a full-grown Isaac.

[18] Wenham, *Genesis*, 111.

[19] Wenham, *Genesis*, 111.

[20] The expression is Martin Buber's.

[21]For an amplification of this point see Derek Kidner, *Genesis: An Introduction and Commentary* (Downers Grove, IL: InterVarsity, 1967) 142-43.

[22]Martin Luther, *Luther's Works: Volume IV* (Saint Louis: Concordia, 1964) 92.

[23]Ibid., 93.

[24]Ibid., 93.

[25]Ibid., 94.

[26]Ibid., 94.

[27]Ibid., 94.

[28]Ibid., 94.

[29]Ibid., 94.

[30]Ibid., 95 (emphasis added).

[31]Ibid., 110.

[32]Ibid., 124.

[33]Ibid., 102.

[34]Ibid., 103.

[35]Ibid., 103.

[36]Ibid., 103, 109.

[37]Ibid., 109. In his customary law/gospel scheme Luther, insisting that the law is death-dealing, would never say that the law "lives and rules" in any *believer*.

[38]Ibid., 95.

[39]Ibid., 96.

[40]Ibid., 106.

[41]Ibid., 131, Luther will say, when God commands Abraham not to slay Isaac after commanding him first to sacrifice his son, "It is God's nature to do contradictory things when things are contradictory." The contradiction is between God's "strange work" and God's "own work." The "strange work" is the trial, and is undertaken for the sake of God's "own work." Despite Luther's repeated use of "contradiction", however, it must be understood that it is the situation befalling Abraham that is contradictory. The situational contradiction of "slay...do not slay", however, is entirely different from the inherent contradiction in God himself. It is the latter that torments Abraham and is the crux of the story.

[42]Ibid., 101.

[43]Ibid., 98.

[44]Abraham's inability to communicate is a major element in his trial. For an exposition of this point, together with a discussion of the literary context pertaining to it, see Jean Louis Ska, "Gn 22,1-19. Essai sur les niveaux de lecture," *Bib* 69 (1988) 324-39.

[45]Luther, *Works*, 112.

[46]Ibid., 114.

[47]Ibid., 115.

[48]Ibid., 115, emphasis added.

[49]Ibid., 119.

[50]Luther, 137.

[51]Luther does not use the expression *creatio ex nihilo*, but incontrovertibly it is what he intends.

[52]Luther, *Works*, 143.

[53]Ibid., 143.

[54]Ibid., 144.

[55]Ibid., 150,151.

[56]Ibid., 175.

[57]Ibid., 151.

[58]John Calvin, *Institutes of the Christian Religion* (Philadelphia: Westminster, 1960) 2.10.11.

[59]Calvin, *A Commentary on Genesis* (London, The Banner of Truth Trust, 1965) 560.

[60]Ibid., 560.

[61]Calvin, *Inst.*, 1.2.1. (1559).

[62]Calvin, *Catechism* (1538); quoted in F. L. Battles, *Interpreting John Calvin* (Grand Rapids: Baker, 1996) 289.

[63]Calvin, *Genesis*, 561.

[64]Ibid., 562.

[65]Ibid., 562.

[66]Ibid., 562. (Emphasis his).

[67]Ibid., 561.

[68]See Calvin, *Institutes*, 1.9.1-3.

[69]Calvin, *Genesis*, 561.

[70]Ibid., 561.

[71]Calvin, 561. For massive documentation from his *Commentaries* that a "double character" in God is impossible, see Victor Shepherd, *The Nature and Function of Faith in the Theology of John Calvin* (Macon: Mercer University Press, 1983) 72ff.

[72]Calvin, *Genesis*, 561.

[73]Ibid., 562.

[74]Ibid., 562.

[75]Ibid., 562.

[76]Ibid., 563.

[77]Ibid., 563.

[78]Ibid., 563. (Emphasis added.)

[79]Ibid., 563.

[80]Ibid., 564.

[81]Ibid., 568.

[82]Ibid., 564.

[83]Ibid., 564.

[84]For Calvin's insistence that mercy is not merely an aspect of God but rather characterizes God, see Shepherd, *The Nature and Function of Faith in the theology of John Calvin*, 12ff.

[85]Calvin, *Genesis*, 565.

[86]Any such suggestion would deny them to be *sacraments*.

[87]Calvin, *Genesis*, 565.

[88]Ibid., 565.

[89]See, for instance, *Inst.* Book Two, *passim*.

[90]Calvin, *Genesis*, 567.

[91]Ibid., 568. (Emphasis added.)

[92]Ibid., 569.

[93]Ibid., 569.

[94]In comparing Luther and Calvin here I am in no way suggesting that Calvin borrowed from Luther.

[95]"Our narrator's intent cannot be mooted: In this text Isaac is Abraham and Abraham is Isaac." (Brichto, *The Names of God*, 287.)

[96]Calvin, *Genesis*, 570. (Emphasis added.)

[97]Ibid., 572.

[98]Ibid., 572.

[99]Ibid., 537.

[100]Ibid., 538.

[101]E.g., Leviticus 20:1-5; Deuteronomy 21:15ff; 2 Kings 16:3; 21:6; Jeremiah 7:31; 19:5.

[102]There is a point, of course, at which comprehension falls short and gives way to sheer adoration.

[103]Kierkegaard's affirmation of "the teleological suspension of the ethical" has rendered him notorious. He insists that as long as one is aware merely of ethical obligation, one does not stand *in relation to* God. The ethical "hero" lives in a penultimate reality; the real is known only by those who, like Abraham in Genesis 22, exist in an absolute relation (higher than the category of the ethical) to the absolute (God), "or else Abraham is lost." Soren Kierkegaard, *Fear and Trembling* (Princeton: Princeton University Press, 1983) 55.

[104]*The Book of Common Prayer, Canada, 1962,* (Toronto: Anglican Book Centre, 1962) 82.

[105]For the future translation of the Hebrew verb here see Brevard S. Childs, *Exodus,* (OTL; Philadelphia: Westminster, 1974) 76.

Chapter 4

The Knowledge of God and of Ourselves in Psalm 19

John A. Vissers

An Introductory Tribute

Nearly all the wisdom we possess, that is to say, true and sound wisdom, consists of two parts: the knowledge of God and of ourselves."[1] These well-known and often quoted words of John Calvin from the *Institutes of the Christian Religion* might well be used to summarize the message and ministry of our friend and colleague Donald Leggett as a teacher of the Old Testament. For Don, Christian faith is rooted in the texts of the Bible through which we are invited into a personal and practical knowledge of God. Passionate about what may be known about God through the Scriptures, Don believes this knowledge causes us to look at our own lives in a new light.

As a teacher of the Old Testament, Leggett constantly reminds his students that the knowledge of God which issues from faith is more than mere assent to rational truths revealed once for all time. As the practical discipline of godly wisdom, theology has to do with an experiential knowledge of God. This practical knowledge of God, however, is not the result of human reasoning about human experience. It is, rather, a knowledge of God which emerges from a sustained engagement with the texts of the Old and New Testaments. As a result, Don Leggett has never tired of urging his students to read the Hebrew Scriptures from a Christian perspective. In the tradition of the biblical prophets, he has warned the evangelical church that it must not neglect the Old Testament and, turning to the Reformed tradition, especially the Puritans, Don has been nourished and nurtured in this approach to biblical hermeneutics.

At the same time, Don has also made it clear that the knowledge *of* God and *of* ourselves revealed through the pages of the Old Testament is not simply a knowledge *for* ourselves but for the church as a whole. It is a privilege, then, to offer this theological and homiletical reflection on Psalm 19, written largely within the framework of Calvin's Reformed exegesis, as part of this tribute to his work as a preacher, teacher, and Old Testament exegete and theologian. It is intended to reflect Donald Leggett's emphasis on the theological exegesis of the Old Testament in the service of preaching, only one of the many contributions for which we honour him.

The Wisdom of Psalm 19

Psalm 19, in all its parts, provides both an exegetical basis and biblical illustration of Calvin's dictum regarding the knowledge of God and of ourselves. Calvin writes:

> David, with the view of encouraging the faithful to contemplate the glory of God, sets before them, in the first place, a mirror of it in the fabric of the heavens, and in exquisite order of their workmanship which we behold; and, in the second place, he recalls our thoughts to the Law, in which God made himself more familiarly known to his chosen people. Taking occa-

sion from this, he continues to discourse at considerable length on this peculiar gift of Heaven,
commending and exalting the use of the Law. Finally,
he concludes the psalm with a prayer.[2]

For Calvin, the significance of Psalm 19 is that it introduces us
to the knowledge of God and a right understanding of ourselves before God. Psalm 19, to be sure, has played an important role for others besides Calvin. C.S. Lewis described Psalm 19 in this way: "I take
this to be the greatest poem in the Psalter and one of the greatest
lyrics in the world."[3] Indeed, as Craigie reminds us, there is little doubt
that this psalm "combines the most beautiful poetry with some of the
most profound of biblical theology"[4] ever written. And when we remember that Psalm 19, with its powerful poetry and profound theology, was sung by the people of ancient Israel as a doxology of praise,
we enter into the radically God-centred worship of the Old Testament. It is within the context of this God-centredness an appropriate
self-understanding and human response emerges.

Indeed, this knowledge of God and of ourselves, and the appropriate human response, may be seen in the psalm's structure. Psalm
19 may be divided into two main parts and a conclusion: (vv.1-6) the
revelation of the glory of God in creation, particularly the heavens;
and (vv.7-11) the revelation of the law of God. In a third concluding
section (vv.12-14) the psalmist, now standing before a vision of the
glory of God and the law of God, recognizes his condition and need
which leads to the final petition. Since the psalm's structure, however,
so clearly falls into two main parts, and since the movement from the
first part to the second part appears to be so abrupt, some scholars
have questioned the psalm's unity and concluded that Psalm 19 was
originally two separate psalms.[5] There is much to commend this argument. There is a clear difference of substance between the two parts
of this psalm. In the first part we find a hymn to creation, with particular emphasis on the sun, not unlike many of the nature hymns in
the ancient near east. In the second part we find a meditation upon

the *Torah*, the law of God, which has the character of wisdom poetry. Furthermore, the name for God changes and the length of the lines also changes. In the first part, "God" *(El)* is used as the divine name whereas in the second part the psalmist speaks of "Lord" (Yahweh).

While it is likely that the origins of this psalm might be traced to a nature hymn and wisdom poetry, "it is reasonably certain that the psalm in its present form is a unity, either composed as a single piece, or else the author took a fragment of an old hymn and extended it by means of a theological commentary and comparison."[6] Indeed, it is precisely this movement from the first part of the psalm to the second part which forms the heart of its theological epistemology. The knowledge of God which might be available and accessible in the creation has been rendered inadequate for a true knowledge of God and ourselves by our disobedience of God's law. By setting forth the first part of the psalm in a manner similar to the ancient Egyptian and Babylonian hymns, the psalmist emphasizes the need for a turn from general revelation to special revelation while maintaining an integral connection between creation and the law. This makes the second part of the psalm all the more powerful. Without the law of God the witness of creation is used by sinful hearts to sow the seeds of idolatry.

The Knowledge of God the Creator

In the first part of Psalm 19 the psalmist points to the glory of God in what has been made, specifically the heavens and the skies. The heavens by their very existence declare the glory of God, and the skies by their very existence proclaim the work of God's hands (v.1). Older translations render "skies" as either firmament or expanse. The first rendering reflects the Septuagint's language, while the second seeks to locate the meaning of the Hebrew noun *raqia'* in terms of its verbal root *rq'* which signifies "to spread abroad, to stretch forth, to extend, or to expand." Calvin opts for the latter translation because he sees a similarity with other texts which speak of the Creator as "stretching out" the heavens as a curtain, and spreading them out as a tent to dwell in, as in Psalm 104:2 and Isaiah 40:22.[7] The psalmist's point is clear: when we look *up* we are confronted by an array of witnesses to the glory of God. Day and night the sun and the stars and the movement between light and darkness testify to the reality of God's presence and power. It should be noted that the psalmist is not speaking here about nature in general, but rather about a very specific part of God's universe: the heavens or the skies. The psalmist is primarily interested in the glory of God in its grandest expression and expanse rather than in its minutest detail, and his text invites us into an outward and upward-looking theological cosmology. The psalm emphasizes transcendence rather than immanence, and while it will lead us to look inward and examine our own response to the revelation of God, it does so by first introducing the "heavens as witnesses and preachers of the glory of God, attributing to the dumb creature a quality which, strictly speaking, does not belong to it, in order the more severely to upbraid us for our ingratitude, if we should pass over so clear a testimony with unheeding ears."[8]

We are living at a time when we know a great deal more about the universe than did the people of ancient Israel, or so we believe. But given how little we still know by comparison with the vastness of the universe, and how frequently we ignore what for ancient Israel was central, namely that the heavens declare the glory of God, the declaration of the psalmist remains poignant. The psalmist's interest is not primarily scientific, romantic or even mystical, but theological. The vastness of the universe and the beauty of the heavens speak to our author of one thing and one thing only: the glory of God the creator. The language of the heavens has a twofold thrust. It is addressed to God as praise, yet it also is addressed to humankind as a revealer of knowledge. Craigie notes that as "mankind reflects upon the vast expanse of heaven, with its light by day and its intimation of a greater universe by night, that reflection may open up an awareness and knowledge of God the Creator, who by his hands created a glory beyond the comprehension of the human mind."[9] For the psalmist, then, the heavens and the skies invite us to know God and share in the praise of God by all creation. We fulfill our vocation to glorify God and enjoy the reflection of his glory in what has been made. Following the thoughts of this psalm Charles Haddon Spurgeon asked himself these questions. "Does not all nature around me praise God? If I were silent, I should be an exception to the universe. Does not the thunder praise God as it rolls like drums in the march of God's armies? Do not the mountains praise him when the woods upon their summits wave in adoration? Does not the lightning write his name in letters of fire? Has not the whole earth a voice? And shall I, can I, silent be?"[10]

After this opening declaration, the psalmist goes on to describe the character of this testimony in verses 2-4b in three ways. First, this witness to the glory of God is continuous. The knowledge of God in nature is not an intermittent revelation but continues day and night. Secondly, this witness to the glory of God is abundant. "They pour forth speech...and they display knowledge." The image is literally of a gushing spring. However, not everyone perceives and understands this witness, for reasons to which we shall return. But God has willed that he should be seen and known through what has been made. As Paul reminds us in Romans 1, through this abundant witness God has made it plain: "Since the creation of the world God's invisible qualities - his eternal power and divine nature - have been clearly seen, being seen from what has been made" (Rom 1:19-20).

Thirdly, this revelation of the glory of God is universal (v.3). This is a difficult text and something of a paradox when rightly understood. The psalmist seems to be saying that the heavens and the skies constitute a silent but universal witness. The Hebrew text reads literally: Verse 3: "No speech, no words, voice not heard." Verse 4: "Voice all the earth, words to the end of the world." The New Revised Standard Version captures the text in this way: "There is no speech, nor are there words; their voice is not heard; yet their voice goes out through all the earth, and their words to the end of the world. " This is what Craigie describes as "the paradox of 'inaudible noise'." "On the one hand, there is no speech, no noise, from a literal or acoustic perspective (v.4); on the other hand, there is a voice that penetrates to the furthest corners of the earth."[11] The skies and the stars are silent. Nevertheless by their very existence they speak to the ends of the earth in witness to the glory of God. But now the subtlety of the psalmist's theology begins to emerge with even greater force. The power of this silent-speaking witness to the glory of God in the heavens extends to the furthest and remotest ends of the earth. It speaks to all people, cutting across all linguistic difference and variety. And here we bump up against what appears to be another subtle paradox: the preaching of the skies is heard, but it is not heard; the language of the heavens is understood, but it is not understood. Creation may sound forth the praise of God but not all of God's creatures welcome it. This witness goes out the ends of the earth and transcends all linguistic barriers, excluding no one from its power. At the same time, this means that this witness leaves no one in its wake without excuse, because God has made it plain (Rom 1:20).

By putting it this way, the psalmist sets forth the reality of a revelatory purpose for nature but also hints at a limitation in the way that revelation functions for human beings. This is a silent witness: it may leave us without excuse, but it also points to the need for something more. The fullness of the witness is revealed to those who know God. As Craigie puts it: "In this hymn of praise, it is not the primary purpose of the psalmist to draw upon nature as a vehicle of revelation, or as a source of the knowledge of God apart from the revelation in law (or *Torah*); indeed, there is more than a suggestion that the reflection of God's praise in the universe is perceptible only to those already sensitive to God's revelation and purpose."[12]

The praise of God in nature concludes in verses 4c-6 with the glory of the sun as the crowning achievement of God's creation of the heavens. In one sense, as John R.W. Stott has put it, the sun is a particular example of the universal witness to God by the heavens.[13] However the psalmist appears to portray the sun as having a very central position in God's creative purposes. In the heavens God has pitched a tent for the sun. The reference probably refers to the darkness into which the suns appears to retreat each night and from which it appears to emerge each new day. The psalmist uses two similes to describe the dawning of the sun: it is like a bridegroom coming forth from his pavilion and like a champion rejoicing to run his course. The images convey power, strength, and energy as well as splendour and glory. While the psalmist may not have known what we know about the sun - that it stands at the centre of our solar system and that it consists of gases burning itself up - the psalmist also knows something that we seem to have forgotten: God created the sun, and its heat and light radiate and reflect the glory of its creator.

The Nature of General Revelation

As one of the great nature psalms, then, the knowledge of God described in the opening section of Psalm 19 is the knowledge of God the creator. The revelation of God in nature is what theologians refer to as general revelation, the self-disclosure of God to all persons at all times and in all places.[14] Sometimes referred to as "natural revelation" or "external revelation," it is that revelation which is available and accessible universally. Traditionally theologians have identified three main loci of general revelation: the glory of God in nature, the providence of God in history, and the image of God in human beings. Psalm 19 refers only to the first of these, general revelation in nature, and not all of nature, but to the heavens and the skies and the stars and the sun.

But in what sense does this revelation cultivate within us a knowledge of God? On this point, Christians have not always agreed. In the first instance, and again popular today, are those who argue that the revelation of God in nature is sufficient in and of itself to cultivate within us a right knowledge of God and a right knowledge of ourselves. This view may be described as an example of *creation spirituality*. Many contemporary theologians, including certain feminist theologians seeking an environmentally responsible theology, have turned away from an emphasis on transcendence to immanence, from rationality to spirituality, and from the outward and exterior life, to the inward and interior life of the self. By doing so, they claim to be recovering a lost dimension of the Christian tradition whose neglect has led to what they consider a truncated and damaging form of Christian faith and life.

Creation spirituality is associated with the names of Thomas Berry, Matthew Fox, Brian Swimme, and their followers. Feminist theologian Sallie McFague, who expresses appreciation for their insights while also levelling some serious criticisms, describes creation spirituality as

> a critique of a sin-centred, redemption-oriented interpretation of Christianity that focuses on guilt, sacrificial atonement, and other-worldly salvation. Positively, it is a celebration of cosmic evolution and splendour that we learn about in the common creation story and that provides us a sense of personal grandeur and responsibility as the only creatures who consciously know this story. Creation spirituality redresses centuries of an increasingly narrow focus of divine concern on human beings, especially Christian human beings, with the virtual elimination, at least in Protestant circles, of creation, which, at most, becomes the backdrop for redemption.[15]

By allowing the revelation of God in creation to be eclipsed by special revelation, it is argued, the Christian tradition has contributed to such things as the environmental crisis and the exploitation of women. True knowledge of God and self, it is concluded, is accessible by getting in touch with the revelation of God which we experience as creatures of God in the midst of God's rich and diverse creation. Special revelation may prove useful by providing symbols to interpret such experience but the knowledge of God is already universally available and accessible.

As one of the so-called nature psalms, does Psalm 19 provide a theological basis for creation spirituality? If verses 1-6 stood alone, apart from what follows concerning the law of God, a case might be made for such a reading of the psalm. But even then, one would also have read the psalm apart from its canonical context. Furthermore, the orientation of the psalm is outward and upward, towards transcendence, outlining a cosmology, rather than inward and downward, pointing towards immanence and a narrower psychological viewpoint.

Secondly, there are those who argue that general revelation cultivates within us a general knowledge of God upon which a more particular knowledge of God may be developed. The revelation of God in the universe cultivates belief in the existence of God and perhaps even the power of God. This may be described as an example of *natural theology*. "Natural theology is traditionally that knowledge of God and the divine order which reason can acquire without the aid of revelation."[16] Saving faith, in this sense, is not created out of nothing. It is based upon a knowledge of God gained through the revelation of God in nature. This general revelation, in and of itself, is never enough to cultivate a knowledge of God's love and mercy, God's triune nature, or God's redemptive purposes. However, it is sufficient to establish a foundation for faith. In this sense, it is argued, Psalm 19:1-6 can stand on its own while at the same time providing a platform for what follows. The challenge for Christian theology today, then, is to coordinate the cosmology of verses 1-6 with the picture of reality coming to us in contemporary science on the one hand, and with the knowledge of God in special revelation, on the other.

In the third instance, there are those who vehemently deny that any form of general revelation cultivates a knowledge of God within us. This may be described as an example of a radically *christocentric* or *particularist theology*. The revelation of God in nature (and for adherents of this position, it is doubtful whether it should be described this way) does not cultivate within us a knowledge of God upon which Christian faith may be established. Any such possibility was eradicated in the Fall. The substance of revelation, and therefore of our knowledge of God, is found in Jesus Christ, and in him alone. Karl Barth believed the silent witness of Psalm 19 really is silent. He sounded this note most loudly in his notorious polemic against Brunner during the German Church struggle of the 1930s. Brunner sought to affirm a distinction between natural and special revelation and argued that Scripture testifies not only to the revelation given in Jesus Christ, but also to the revelation given in creation. Brunner believed that the Bible "assumes that God's action always leaves an imprint of the divine nature upon creation and history and it repeatedly asserts or implies that genuine knowledge of God is attainable through knowledge of the law."[17] Barth stood strongly against this position. He maintained that one can only speak about the reality of revelation in the person of Jesus Christ testified to in the Scriptures of the Old and New Testaments. The only knowledge of God is the knowledge of God the redeemer through which we come to a knowledge of God the creator. In this sense, Psalm 19:1-6 reflects the perspective of someone who has a knowledge of God the redeemer. These verses could never stand on their own, nor do they provide a platform for what follows. Rather, they represent a theological worldview already shaped not only by what follows, but by the whole history of redemption.

Finally, in a fourth approach, we find those who affirm the reality of revelation in nature as described in vv.1-6 but who conclude that human beings in their sinful state inevitably use this revelation to cultivate a distorted knowledge of God. In short, humanity uses the reality of divine revelation in nature as the basis for idolatry. This position may be described as an example of *Reformed epistemology,* and it owes its origins to John Calvin who saw Psalm 19 this way. Calvin believed that "the knowledge of God shines forth in the fashioning of the universe and the continuing government of it."[18] The clarity of God's self-disclosure strips us of every excuse because the divine wisdom is displayed for all to see.[19] But we turn ungratefully against God and confuse the creature with the creator.[20] Calvin makes it clear: "We ought not to rack our brains about God; but rather, we should contemplate him in his works." We are called to a knowledge of God:

"not that knowledge which, content with empty speculation, merely flits in the brain. But that which will be sound and fruitful if we duly perceive it, and if it takes root in the heart."[21] "Knowledge of this sort," Calvin believed, "ought not only to arouse us to the worship of God, but also to awaken and encourage us to the hope of future life."[22] Calvin concludes that we fail to know God and worship God, we fall into superstition and confusion, and the evidence of God in creation does not profit us.[23] In short, "the manifestation of God in nature speaks to us in vain."[24] Therefore, "Scripture is needed as a guide and teacher for anyone who would come to God the creator."[25] God bestows the actual knowledge of himself upon us only in the Scriptures: "Just as old or bleary-eyed men and those with weak vision, if you thrust before them a most beautiful volume, even if they recognize it to be some sort of writing, yet can scarcely construe two words, but with the aid of spectacles will begin to read distinctly; so Scripture, gathering up the otherwise confused knowledge of God in our minds, having dispersed our dullness, clearly shows us the true God."[26]

This need for Scripture as a guide and teacher is reflected in Calvin's understanding of the second part of Psalm 19. After having shown that the heavens teach all human beings so clearly that there is a God, as to render them inexcusable, the psalmist now turns to the law as expressed in the covenant made by the Lord with the people of ancient Israel, to whom God had communicated a fuller knowledge of himself by means of his word.

> Thus, God vouchsafes to those whom he has determined to call to salvation special grace, just as in ancient times, while he gave to all men without exception evidences of his existence in his works, he communicated to the children of Abraham alone his Law, thereby to furnish them with a more certain and intimate knowledge of his majesty.[27]

Calvin believes, then, that Scripture can communicate to us what the revelation in the creation cannot.[28] Scripture functions in a particular way as a form of the special revelation for those who would come to a knowledge of God the creator. In Psalm 19 the form of this special revelation is law *(Torah)*. The second part of Psalm 19, then, is a description of the knowledge of God the redeemer as the giver of the law, without which we would never come to a knowledge of God the creator, and through which we come to recognize our desperate need of salvation. The law of God opens up for us what remains cut off in the contemplation of nature: the will of God the creator for our lives, and the knowledge of ourselves as fallen creatures in need of God's grace. Or, as Calvin describes the role of the law of God in Psalm 19: "since God in vain calls all peoples to himself by the contemplation of heaven and earth, this is the very school of God's children."[29] *Torah* thus cultivates the right knowledge of God the creator and the right knowledge of ourselves before God. To this school of God's children in the second part of Psalm 19 we now turn.

The Knowledge of the Lord as Law-Giver

The psalmist shifts from creation to *Torah* in what appears to be a rather abrupt manner. This shift in the psalm makes it clear that the psalmist believes it would be a very great mistake to stop after verse 6. The purpose of the psalmist is not to draw upon the heavens as a sole source of the knowledge of God. There is more to knowing God than this and it is to be found in the law of the Lord. Rhetorically and theologically, there is a link in the text which points to the fact that the hymn of praise to God the creator in verses 1-6 does not and cannot stand alone. In fact, the last line of verse 6 marks the transition: "nothing is hidden from its heat." C.S. Lewis has pointed out that this is the key clause which marks "the transition between the two parts of the psalm and at the same time links them intimately together."[30] Like the sun, Torah dominates our lives day by day, penetrates, warms, and gives us life. Just as nothing is hidden from the heat of the sun, so too is nothing hidden from the searching, testing, and purifying reaches of

Torah. Both are essential. Both the sun and the revealed word of God are essential for authentic human life. Within this basic framework the psalmist sets forth six characteristic features of the law of God and its benefit to the believer. Verses 7-9 contain a superb example of Hebrew poetic parallelism in which there are six couplets or parallel statements which use six terms for the law of God, six adjectives to describe it, and six statements of the effect of the Torah.

Six words are used to define the law of God. First, the psalmist uses the word *law* or *Torah* as the most embracing term. In the life of Israel Torah referred to the Ten Commandments where the law of God found its supreme expression. But it was also used in a more general sense to refer to the first five books of the Old Testament. In its most basic sense Torah is not limited to law per se but refers to all divine instruction. As Calvin notes, law comprehends the covenant by which God had distinguished the people of Israel from the rest of the world.[31]

The other five terms used in verses 7-9 for divine instruction are to be understood within this same context. Craigie has noted that "from a poetic perspective, these terms may be seen as synonymous, though from a theological perspective, they may be seen as all-embracing."[32] Each of the terms sets forth a slightly different aspect of the law of God. Statutes (v.7) refer to the testimony of the Lord in which the truth of these words is attested by God himself. Precepts (v.8) are the precise instructions by which God addresses his people. Commands (v.8) are authoritative words calling for obedience. Ordinances (v.9) are authoritative directions or decrees enacted by those who have authority to render judgments or verdicts. The only word which is not strictly synonymous with law is the word "fear" (v.9). As an aspect of Torah, fear refers to the effect God's law produces in those who are addressed by the revelation.

Secondly, the psalmist uses six different adjectives to describe the attributes of the Torah in verses 7-9. The sense here seems to be that in every way the law of God is good. In v.7a the revelation of the will of God in the law is perfect in the sense that it is complete and all-sufficient. Nothing is to be added or subtracted from that which God has spoken. In v. 7c the statutes of the Lord, to which the Lord himself bears testimony, are trustworthy. The law of the Lord is worthy of our trust because the Lord himself stands behind this word. He is the reality to which it corresponds. The statutes of the Lord, in this sense, are self-authenticating. The precepts of the Lord are right (v.8a). The word "right" is not to be understood as the opposite of "wrong" in this verse. The term refers to that which is straight as opposed to that which is crooked and it is linked to the idea of righteousness. The Lord provides precise instructions through which his people may find the fullness and freedom of righteous living rather than being caught up in crooked and perverse ways. In v.8c the commands of the Lord are said to be radiant, that is they give illumination. As noted above, here the psalmist draws upon the reference to the sun in verses 4-6. Just as nothing is hidden from the radiance of the sun, the commands of the Lord call forth obedience by piercing the darkness of our lives and illuminating the path on which we are called to travel. In v.9a the fear of the Lord is pure. The basic sense is that of being uncorrupted. It is a divine law revealed by God which, when rightly heard and understood, creates a thorough-going response of pure reverence and awe as the basis for obedience. And finally, in v. 9c the ordinances of the Lord are sure and altogether righteous. The last of these six adjectives does not follow the precise parallelism of the other five because it adds the phrase "and altogether righteous." The phrase is added as a transition to verse 10 in which the psalmist introduces a rich description of the law of God which appeals to sense and desire: the law of God is more precious than pure gold and sweeter than honey from the comb. Verse 11 re-introduces the parallelism which has been only slightly delayed by verse 10. The description of the law of God in verse 9 is clear: as authoritative decrees enacted by the One whose right it is to judge, the ordinances of the Lord are sure and certain and altogether righteous. They are true, never false, ever faithful, and always right. When rightly understood, Torah instills confidence and faith in the One whose word the law of God is. This law may be trusted since the Lord who gives it is faithful and righteous.

Thirdly, throughout these verses the psalmist depicts the effect of the Torah on the lives of those who receive it. The Torah has a purpose for the people of God. In the New Testament this understanding of the nature and function of Scripture is found in 2 Timothy 3:16-17: "All Scripture is God-breathed and is useful for teaching, rebuking, correcting and training in righteousness, so that everyone who belongs to God may be proficient, equipped for every good work."

In Psalm 19 the law of God does six things. The law of God revives the soul. Since the law of God is an all-sufficient revelation, it is able to convert, restore, and revive our souls. Soul (*nephesh*) is meant to refer to the fullness of human life as living beings animated by the word and Spirit of God. The law of God energizes, feeds and nourishes us as living beings created in the image of God and animated by the Spirit of God. Life lived by the fruit of obedience to the expressed will of God is life lived in the way God intended it to be lived in all its fullness and freedom in fellowship with God. Jesus testified to this reality when he quoted Deuteronomy 8:3 during his temptations in the wilderness: "Man does not live by bread alone, but on every word that comes from the mouth of God" (Matt 4:4).

The law of God makes the simple wise. As a wisdom psalm, v.7 reminds us that the law of God is to be understood as instruction in wisdom. Those who walk outside the revealed will of God walk in folly. Those who think themselves too wise to attend to the wisdom of God show themselves to be fools. In the New Testament Paul picks up this theme with reference to the gospel and shows that God has turned the wisdom of the world on its head (1 Cor 1:19-21). In 1 Corinthians 3:18-19 he urges us not to deceive ourselves : "If you think that you are wise in this age, you should become fools so that you may become wise. For the wisdom of this world is foolishness with God."

The law of God makes the heart rejoice. Spurgeon saw a progression in the first three statements about the law of God that sets forth a movement in the Christian life: having revived (converted, restored) the soul, instructed (taught) us in wisdom, the law of God now gives joy to the heart.[33] In a similar manner, Calvin saw this joy as rooted in a right understanding of ourselves before God:

> This implies that there is no other joy true and solid
> but that which proceeds from a good conscience; and
> of this we become partakers when we are certainly
> persuaded that our life is pleasing and acceptable to
> God. No doubt, the source from which true peace of
> conscience proceeds is faith, which freely reconciles
> us to God. But to the saints who serve God with true
> affection of heart there arises unspeakable joy also,
> from the knowledge that they do not labour in his
> service in vain, or without hope of recompense, since
> they have God as the judge and approver of their life.
> In short, this joy is put in opposition to all the corrupt
> enticements and pleasures of the world, which are a
> deadly bait, luring wretched souls to their everlasting
> destruction."[34]

The heart rejoices, says Calvin, when we know ourselves as approved by God.

The law of God gives light to the eyes. In Psalm 119:5 the psalmist declares that the word of the Lord "is a lamp to my feet and a light for my path." The law of God enables the believer to see things clearly as they are, not as they might be imagined. The Bible reminds us that we in our sin are always being given over to self-deception. The law of God, on the other hand, beckons us into the real world of God. The law of God is not a set of rules to be mastered. The law of God invites us into a way of life which conforms to God's intentions for life in his world. As Calvin reminds us, that way of life may not be readily apparent to us by looking at the world itself. But when we look through the lens of God's law, the law of God pierces our darkness and gives light to the eyes.

In v. 9 the effect of the law of God is substituted for the cause: "The fear of the Lord is pure, enduring forever." Craigie suggests that the nuance shifts here and that we should understand the proper fear or reverence for the Lord, instilled by the law of God, as that which is pure and endures forever. Boice, on the other hand, argues that most commentators maintain the poetic parallelism and conclude that the law of God is pure and enduring.[35] If, however, the purpose of these verses is to set forth the attributes of the law of the Lord and their effect on those whose lives are shaped by that law, this difference is of no practical significance for the overall meaning of the psalm.

Verse 11 concludes this section of the psalm by stating that there are two benefits to keeping the law of God. First, the one who knows the law is warned by the law. The law of God warns us against the clever deceptions of a world in rebellion against its creator. Secondly, the one who keeps the law is rewarded. This does not necessarily mean that those who obey God's commands should expect to receive a great reward, although that is not discounted. It means, rather, that the keeping of the law is its own reward. Augustine once said that sin is its own punishment. In the same way, virtue is its own reward. Obedience to the law of God does not lead to joyful living in the presence of God, rather, it *is* joyful living in the presence of God. When rightly understood, a joyful faith is an obedient faith and a joyful obedience is a faithful obedience.[36]

In sum, then, the second part of Psalm 19 is a hymn of praise to the Lord who has revealed his will in the law. But why does the psalmist focus on this particular form of general revelation and this particular form of special revelation? And how, if at all, are these two particular forms of general and special revelation related to each other? And what, if any, is the significance of these related forms of revelation for our knowledge of God?

Law and Creation

The answer to these questions is found, it seems to me, in a persuasive argument made by Clines in an article called "The Tree of Knowledge and the Law of Yahweh (Psalm XIX)."[37] Clines argues "that each of the characteristics of the *Torah* listed above contains an allusion to the tree of knowledge (Gen 2-3), and that by means of these allusions the psalmist is expressing the superiority of the *Torah* to the tree of knowledge."[38] In Genesis 2:16 the Lord God gives the man a command: "You are free to eat from any tree in the garden; but you must not eat from the tree of the knowledge of good and evil, for when you eat of it you will surely die." As Genesis 2-3 describes it, our first parents were faced with a fundamental decision: would they eat from the tree of the knowledge of good and evil or would they obey the command of God their creator? By choosing to listen to the lie of the serpent they turned away from the very thing that could give them the life for which they longed: the will of God as expressed in the command of God, i.e. the law. They thought they could live in God's world, knowing the glory of God in the heavens, without obedience to the revealed will of God.

Psalm 19, then, describes the superiority of the will of God as expressed in the law of God over that which they chose, the tree of the knowledge of good and evil, and the psalm does this by using precisely the language of Genesis 2-3. Whose word is perfect, trustworthy, right, radiant, pure, certain, and righteous? Is it the word of the Lord or the lie of the evil one? What is it that can truly revive the soul, make wise the simple, give joy to the heart, give light to the eyes, and endure forever? Is it the law of the Lord or the tree of the knowledge of good and evil? What is to be desired more than pure and precious gold? What is sweeter than honey from the comb? Where is the real reward? Is it to be found in eating from the tree of the knowledge of good and evil or in keeping the law of the Lord? Psalm 19 makes it clear that our first parents did not choose well. Although they lived in God's world, they doubted God's word and they disobeyed

God's law. They were banished from the garden and forfeited the joy of God's immediate presence. Now, more than ever, they, and all humanity with them, need the law of God to help them understand the depth of the crisis into which they have been plunged by their willful disobedience. They need the law of the Lord to bring light, life, and rejoicing. The law of God reveals the life they, and all humanity with them, left behind in the garden. *Torah* is the means through which the word of God and the will of God heard by our first parents may be heard again. While our first parents disobeyed, *Torah* issues an invitation to obedience. *Torah,* as the revelation of God, the will of God, and the law of God, is not simply the way to life *with* God, although it is that; it *is* the good life with God which God reveals, wills, and commands for his people.

But Psalm 19 is more than a subtle exposition of Genesis 2-3. There are also striking and obvious parallels between the first part of the psalm (verses 1-6) and Genesis 1:1-2:3. The heavens and the skies declare the glory of God (Gen 1:1; Ps 19:1). Through the day and the night the heavens and skies pour forth speech and display knowledge (Gen 1:3; Ps 19:2). The voice of God goes out into all the earth and to the ends of the world (Gen 1:3,6,9,14,20,24,26,29; Ps 19:3,4). The imagery of the tent and the bridegroom mirror the Genesis description of the sun's creation (Gen 1:14-19; Ps 19:5-6).

In short, the psalm begins with the glory of God in creation and moves to *Torah,* the revealed will of God for his people in the world which God has created. This mirrors the movement in Genesis 1-3 which begins with the glory of God in creation and ends with the failure of the Lord's people to obey the revealed command of God. As Craigie notes, "...when this internal progression within the psalm is perceived, then a further progression may be noted - a progression in revelation."[39] While the glories of the heavens reveal God (Hebrew *El*) in Psalm 1:1-6 (compare Gen 1:1-2:3 where the related divine name *Elohim* is used), the glories of the *Torah* reveal the *Lord* (*Yahweh*) in Psalm 19:7-11 (compare Gen 2:4-3:24 where the compound name *Yahweh-Elohim* is used). The *Torah* is given by the Lord who has revealed himself to a people by entering into covenant with them and redeeming them. God gives them, through this covenant, a knowledge of himself as redeemer and as creator. The knowledge of God the creator in creation does not stand alone as a solitary witness. If it did, then we, as children of Adam and Eve, would be condemned to life with no memory, or at best a distorted memory, of the God who created us and revealed his will to us. Rather, we come to a right knowledge of God the creator through a right knowledge of *Torah*, for a right knowledge of God the creator is not to be confused with a general knowledge of some divine reality. The right knowledge of God the creator is a knowledge of the will of God the creator as the basis of a life lived in response to God. The knowledge of the Lord as lawgiver leads us therefore to this right knowledge of God the creator. Psalm 19 bears witness to the covenantal unity of this revelation already found in Genesis 1-3.

Law and Gospel

The dialectical nature of this covenantal unity helps to make some sense out of the relationship between law and gospel. If the law points back to God's will in creation it also points forward to God's saving purpose in Jesus Christ, gathering up the knowledge of God in both creation and gospel. This is, for example, to be seen in Paul's use of Psalm 19:4 in Romans 10:18. In Romans 10 Paul has been arguing that God has opened a new way of justification and salvation through the gospel of Jesus Christ, open to all, and foreshadowed in the prophets of old. The opportunity to believe in Christ has been offered to all, but especially to Israel, and therefore Israel cannot claim that it did not hear this gospel. How then does one explain the unbelief of Israel? Paul asks rhetorically, "Did they not hear?," and answers his own question, "Of course they did." And then he cites the Septuagint version of Psalm 19:4: "Their voice has gone out into all the earth, their words to the ends of the world."

For Paul, it is simply not possible to conclude that Israel has not heard the gospel. He believes that his Jewish brothers and sisters have heard the message about Christ. He believes there has been a real opportunity for them to hear the gospel. It is simply incomprehensible, in Paul's mind, that the apostolic messengers described in verses 14-15 have been ineffective. And by way of proof Paul applies the words of Psalm 19:4 to the preaching of the gospel. Just as the heavens declare the glory of God to the ends of the earth, so too has the gospel been preached to the ends of the earth. The gospel witness, like the revelation of the knowledge of God in creation, has a universal character. Israel, therefore, like the rest of the world, has heard the gospel.[40] In short, the gospel has been preached, the message has been heard because the voice of the heralds has gone to the ends of the earth, and all are without excuse.

For our purposes, it is important to note that most commentators conclude that Paul's appeal to Psalm 19:4 is based on an analogy between the universal revelation of God in creation and the universal witness of the gospel. But most assume that Paul does this for purely rhetorical reasons. Stott, for example, argues that Paul's choice of Psalm 19:4 is surprising, since what it celebrates "is not the worldwide spread of the gospel, but the universal witness of the heavens to their Creator."[41] Stott continues by noting that Paul knew perfectly well what he was doing and "it is entirely gratuitous to conclude that he misremembered, misunderstood or misrepresented his text."[42] Stott argues, therefore, that Paul transferred the eloquent language of Psalm 19:4 about the universal revelation of the knowledge of God in creation to the particular revelation of the knowledge of God in the gospel of Jesus Christ, taking the former as symbolic of the latter. For modern commentators the choice seems clear: either Paul misremembered, misunderstood, or misrepresented Psalm 19:4 and therefore made a mistake in its application to his argument in Romans 10, or he remembered and understood Psalm 19:4 perfectly well but chose to set aside its meaning and use it as an analogy in the rhetorical argumentation of Romans 10.

At times, pre-modern commentators have a sense of the theological meaning of texts which has been lost in post-Enlightenment
critical scholarship. Calvin's interpretation of Paul's use of Psalm 19:4
in Romans 10 is a good example. In his commentary on Romans,
Calvin notes the difficulty in Paul's use of Psalm 19:4 in this context.
On the one hand, he points to ancient interpreters, followed by later
writers, who "have been led by this passage to explain the whole of
the Psalm in allegorical terms. Thus the sun going forth as a bridegroom from his chamber without question was Christ, while the apostles were the heavens."[43] Calvin is not persuaded by this reading and
cannot find in Romans 10:18 the basis for an allegorical and
christological interpretation of Psalm 19. On the other hand, Calvin is
not persuaded that Paul has misconstrued the passage by transferring
to the apostles what the psalmist had properly said of the architecture
of heaven.[44]

Instead, Calvin explains Paul's use of Psalm 19:4 by pointing to
the relationship between the knowledge of God available to the Gentiles and the Jews. He writes:

> From the very beginning of the world, God has dis-
> played His divinity to the Gentiles by the testimony
> of His creation, if not by the preaching of men. Al-
> though the gospel was not heard at that time among
> the Gentiles, yet the whole workmanship of heaven
> and earth spoke and proclaimed its Author by its
> preaching. It is, therefore, clear that, even during the
> time in which the Lord confined the favour of His
> covenant to Israel, He did not withdraw the knowl-
> edge of himself from the Gentiles, without continu-
> ally inflaming some spark of it among them. He did
> indeed manifest himself more closely at that time to
> His chosen people, so that the Jews might justifiably
> have been compared to domestic hearers, who were
> taught intimately by His holy mouth. Since, however,

He also spoke to the Gentiles at a distance by the
voice of the heavens, this prelude revealed His desire
to make Himself known at length to them also.[45]

For Calvin, Paul's argument is clear: neither Gentile nor Jew is
without excuse because both Gentile and Jew have had access to the
revelation of God. Thus, both Gentile and Jew have had access to the
voice of God in the heavens. Furthermore, the Jews have had a privi-
leged relationship with God through the favour of the covenant. The
covenant with Israel, however, did not nullify the knowledge of God
in the testimony of the heavens for the Gentiles, i.e., God did not
withdraw the knowledge of himself from the Gentiles, and therefore
the Gentiles are still accountable for this revelation even after the revelation of Torah to Israel. Likewise, the covenant with Israel did not
nullify the knowledge of God in the testimony of the heavens for the
Jews either. Rather, God has spoken to them in creation and the law,
and through the law in a manner which makes them doubly accountable for the knowledge of God in the heavens. What is more, both
Gentile and Jew have been recipients of the knowledge of God through
the preaching of the gospel. So when Paul appeals to Psalm 19:4 in
Romans 10:18, he is declaring that the truth of the gospel has been
proclaimed to the Jews, and that this proclamation had already begun
in the revelation of God in the heavens, and that the revelation of the
Lord their God in the *Torah* provided for them the knowledge of the
will of God their creator and the meaning of a life lived in response to
God. The Jews are accountable, Paul says, not simply because the
word of Christ has gone out into all the earth, and the preaching of
the gospel to the ends of the world, in the same way that the heavens
declare the glory of God, but because the Jews themselves have also
been the recipients of the revelation of the knowledge of God in
creation and law. To be sure, they are accountable for the proclamation of the gospel gone out into all the earth. But that gospel did not
appear out of nowhere. The knowledge of God in the gospel of Jesus
Christ stands in continuity with the knowledge of God in creation and
law. The analogy which Paul draws, then, finds its force in a theologi-

cal reality. It is not just that there is an outward similarity between the universal witness of the heavens and the universal proclamation of the gospel, and that Paul extends the one to the other. The rhetorical value of the analogy is grounded in something far more significant than a formal similarity. Paul's appeal is based on a theological reality and a covenantal unity.

At this point, however, we are confronted by one final and highly significant issue: it has been assumed by most Protestant interpreters in the past that Paul sets aside the psalmist's affirmation of the positive characteristics of the law of God. How do we make sense of this? If Paul affirms the kind of covenantal unity described above, why does he sometimes describe the law of God in such negative terms? How can the law of God revive the soul if it is a dead and deadly letter? How can the law of God give joy to heart if it brings a spirit of bondage and strikes the heart with terror? How can the law of God give light to the eyes if it casts a veil before our minds and excludes the light which ought to penetrate within?[46] Most commentators in the past, Calvin included, explained this difference by arguing that Paul was dealing with persons who perverted and abused the law, and separated it from the grace and the Spirit of Christ.[47] Recent biblical scholarship, however, has placed the relation between law and gospel in an entirely new context, namely that of first-century Palestinian Judaism. The result has been that *Torah* is now to be seen not only in terms of Paul's polemic against the failure of the law but also in terms of an appreciation for the righteousness of the law rightly understood in the first century.[48] A great deal of Lutheran biblical scholarship and theology has been revised in light of these arguments, and Reformed theology done in the light of Calvin's exegesis has also had to revisit earlier conclusions. At the same time, some of Calvin's insights, including his appeal to the so-called "third use of the law," point to the righteousness of the law which recent interpreters of Paul wish to emphasize. More importantly, Calvin sees this emphasis in a covenantal unity between law and gospel centred in Jesus Christ. When the psalmist speaks of the law, as we noted above, Calvin believes he comprehends the whole covenant by which the descendants of Abraham have become the people of God. The will of God for his people, as set forth in the law, also includes the promise of salvation, namely the gospel promise in Jesus Christ. For Calvin, Christ does not abolish the law but fulfills it (Matt 5:17). Christ is the sum and substance of the covenant through which the knowledge of God in creation and the knowledge of God in the law find their fulfilment. In short, there is a covenantal unity between creation, law and gospel centred in Christ in whom, through whom, and upon whom this covenant is founded. By grace, through faith, Christ is known as creator, redeemer, and law-giver, regaining for us the life with God, in God's world, and according to God's will, which was forfeited by our first parents. The law of the Lord remains as the expression of God's will for his people. Psalm 19, in all its glory, points backwards and forwards to this reality.

The Knowledge of Ourselves Coram Deo

In his devotional commentary on the Psalms, W. Graham Scroggie describes verses 12-14 as the revelation of God in experience. "The skies tell us much," he writes, "the Scriptures tell more, but the soul tells most of all, for it is only for the sake of the soul that God has revealed himself to us at all."[49] This is, in my judgment, an unfortunate way of describing Psalm 19 because it leaves us with the impression that the revelation of God in human experience supersedes the revelation of God in creation and in the Bible. Furthermore, it narrows the cosmic and universal scope of God's revelatory purposes to the individual human soul alone. Contemporary Christian faith and life, driven as it is by human experience, and plagued as it is by a self-absorbed consumer culture of individualism, hardly needs to be encouraged in this direction by providing for it biblical warrant. To be fair, Scroggie was writing for an earlier generation of Christians who were concerned that the realities of God's saving grace be a reality for those to whom God reveals them. And despite the unfortunate way in which his description of these verses reads in the context of our contemporary culture, he does in fact point to a significant theological turn taken in these concluding verses in relation to the earlier sections of the psalm.

When confronted by the glory of God in creation, and when confronted by the will of God in the law, and when confronted by the law of God as the will of God the creator, the psalmist becomes aware of his own need to be drawn back into God's will and way in the world. A profound knowledge of self emerges when confronted by the revelation of God. The knowledge of God has led him to a truly theological knowledge of self. The psalmist knows that his fellowship with God in the world needs to be restored. The law has made him conscious of his alienation from God and of the fact that the cause of this alienation originates within himself. In short, he knows himself to be a sinner in need of forgiveness and cleansing. He knows that fellowship with God rests upon the grace of God. Theologians throughout the history of the church as diverse as Calvin and Schleiermacher have emphasized that consciousness of sin comes into existence only through consciousness of God. Human beings come into an awareness of their sin only after they have been awakened by the knowledge of God. Sin is a profoundly theological category, then, and we know ourselves as sinners when we know ourselves *coram Deo* (before God).

All this is signalled by the change of tone in the concluding portion of the psalm. These songs of praise - the praise of God in creation and the praise of God in the law - these songs evoke in the psalmist a deep awareness of his situation in life before God and of his unworthiness. The transition is sharp but it is entirely natural. Craigie puts it this way:

> The psalmist began by looking at the heavens and reflecting on the divine law, and such reflection naturally evoked praise; but, as his eyes turn back from this double and glorious vision to gaze upon himself, the shock is almost too much.[50]

Aware now of his own insignificance and unworthiness in so glorious a context he can do nothing but pray. He turns inward, to introspection, but he does not wallow in his own despair. And he doesn't stay there. Having looked within, he turns to God. The prayer of response to God's self-revelation is twofold.

First, the psalmist prays that God will forgive his sin and deliver him from additional transgressions. He seeks to be acquitted and set free from all that has alienated him from God so that once again he might be a complete person in a right relationship with God. His prayer emerges from a conscience quickened by the truth of divine self-revelation. The law of God revealed not only the holiness of God's character, but also the depravity of the psalmist's own heart. Boice has noted that the psalmist treats his sin seriously, aware of its subtle nature and complexity, dividing it into three categories. First, the psalmist asks, "Who can discern his errors?" acknowledging that wrongs innocently committed cannot be excused when exposed by the law of God. Forgiveness is required for sins of omission as well as sins of commission, for sins without malevolent intent as well as sins of willful disobedience. Secondly, he asks God to forgive his hidden faults. These are the sins unknown to himself because they are so deeply ingrained in his personality. These are the attitudes and actions so deeply imbedded in his psyche that the psalmist does not know, indeed cannot know, just how destructive these sins can be. Out of sight and out of mind, these hidden faults work as demons of destruction in the life of the psalmist. And wherever and whenever they may make an appearance in the light of day, these sins are often rationalized and justified, transformed from vices into virtues. But they are not hidden to God, and the psalmist now knows this. Standing before the law of God as before a mirror, he seeks forgiveness for what could never have been known about his life apart from the law. Thirdly, he prays to be kept from willful sins. He does not want to be governed by the sins of deliberate presumption. He wants to be out from under the law of sin, set free, blameless, and innocent of great transgression. The great transgression might refer to the original sin of our first parents. If so, the psalmist is praying for deliverance from the curse of sin inflicted upon the human race by the Fall. The great transgression might also refer to the psalmist's own particular gross sin. In the ancient world adultery was commonly identified as the great sin, in which case, the psalm might refer to David's sin with Bathsheba. Whatever the case, the psalmist seeks deliverance from sin and wants to live his life in obedience to the law of God, experiencing the fullness of life and liberty in God's world that comes with joyful obedience to the will of God.

Secondly, in verse 14 the psalmist appeals to the Lord as his Rock and Redeemer. The psalm ends where it begins: with the Lord his God. We are not only led to see ourselves as we really are in this psalm, as sinners exposed by the law of God, but we are also led to the One who delivers us from ourselves and from our sin. And who is this One named Rock and Redeemer by the psalmist? This is the same One who has revealed himself gloriously in the heavens.[51] The psalmist began by describing the speech of the heavens, extolling God's glory; he concludes by praying that his own mouth, in its speech, may be acceptable to God. Having found his rightful place once again in God's world, the psalmist wishes to join the heavens to declare the glory of God and the skies to proclaim the work of his hands. He longs to be part of the chorus which sounds forth the continuous, abundant and universal praise of God, proclaiming worthiness to God, who is his "Rock" and "Redeemer." He has rediscovered his true vocation and found his voice: participation in the praise of God by all creation. In sum, "the final words, describing the psalmist's relationship to God, transform God's universal and cosmic glory, with which the psalm began, into the glory of an intimate relationship between a human being and God, who offers solidarity and redemption."[52]

In three brief movements through fourteen verses the psalmist has invited us into the world of God. Beginning with the *reality* of revelation in creation, the psalmist moved us along by pointing to the *superiority* of the will of God in the law, and concluded by confronting us with the *necessity* of God's redeeming grace. In short, Psalm 19 is a grand and glorious vision of all the wisdom we can possibly possess: the knowledge of God and of ourselves, in creation, law and gospel, for the purpose of our full redemption and true vocation.

Notes

[1] John Calvin, *Institutes of the Christian Religion* (Library of Christian Classics 20; ed. John T. McNeill; Philadelphia: Westminster, 1960) 35.

[2] John Calvin, *Commentary on the Book of Psalms* (trans. James Anderson; Grand Rapids: Eerdmans, 1949) 307.

[3] C.S. Lewis, *Reflections on the Psalms,* p. 56, cited by Peter C. Craigie, *Psalms 1-50* (WBC; Waco: Word, 1983) 183.

[4] Craigie, *Psalms,* 183.

[5] James Montgomery Boice, *Psalms,* vol. 1 (Grand Rapids: Baker, 1994) 169; Craigie, *Psalms,* 179.

[6] Craigie, *Psalms,* 179.

[7] Calvin, *Psalms,* 308.

[8] Ibid., 309.

[9] Craigie, *Psalms,* 180.

[10] Charles Haddon Spurgeon, cited in A.W. Tozer, *The Pursuit of God* (Camp Hill, PA: Christian Publications, 1995) 118.

[11] Craigie, *Psalms,* 181.

[12] Ibid., 181.

[13] John R. W. Stott, *Favourite Psalms, Selected and Expounded* (Chicago: Moody, 1988) 21, cited in Boice, *Psalms,* 165.

[14] Millard Erickson, *Christian Theology* (Grand Rapids: Baker, 1983) 153.

[15] Sallie McFague, *The Body of God: An Ecological Theology* (Philadephia: Fortress, 1993) 70.

[16] Alan Richardson and John Bowden, *The Westminster Dictionary of Christian Theology* (Philadelphia: Westminster, 1983). See Sallie McFague, *The Body of God,* 73.

[17] Gary Dorrien, *Theology Without Weapons: The Barthian Revolt in Modern Theology.* (Louisville, KY: Westminster John Knox, 2000) 118.

[18] Calvin, *Institutes,* 51.

[19] Ibid., 51-53.

[20]Ibid., 55,56.

[21]Ibid., 61-62.

[22]Ibid., 62.

[23]Ibid., 63.

[24]Ibid., 68.

[25]Ibid., 69.

[26]Ibid., 70.

[27]Calvin, *Psalms,* 317.

[28]Calvin, *Institutes,* 73.

[29]Ibid., 73.

[30]Craigie, *Psalms,* 183.

[31]Calvin, *Psalms,* 318.

[32]Craigie, *Psalms,* 181.

[33]Spurgeon, *Psalms,* vol. 1 (The Crossway Classic Commentary Series; ed. Alister McGrath and J. I. Packer; Wheaton: Crossway, 1993) 68.

[34]Calvin, *Psalms,* 321.

[35]Boice, *Psalms,* 173.

[36]Ibid., 174.

[37]D. J. A. Clines, "The Tree of Knowledge and the Law of Yahweh," *VT*, 24 (1974) 8-14.

[38]Craigie, *Psalms,* 182.

[39]Ibid., 182.

[40]Joseph A. Fitzmyer, *Romans: A New Translation With Introduction and Commentary* (AB. New York: Doubleday, 1993) 595, 599.

[41]John R. W. Stott, *Romans: God's Good News For the World* (Leicester: InterVarsity 1994) 287.

[42]Ibid., 287.

[43]John Calvin, *The Epistle of Paul to the Romans and the Thessalonians* (trans. R. Mackenzie; ed. David W. Torrance and Thomas F. Torrance., Edinburgh: Oliver and Boyd, 1960) 234.

[44]Ibid., 234.

[45]Ibid., 234.

[46]Calvin, *Psalms,* 321.

[47]Ibid., 321-22.

[48]See E.P. Sanders, *Paul and Palestinian Judaism* (Philadelphia: Fortress, 1977) and Stephen Westerholm, *Israel's Law and the Church's Faith* (Grand Rapids: Eerdmans, 1988). It is beyond the scope of this article to rehearse the arguments in detail.

[49]W. Graham Scroggie, *The Psalms*. (Old Tappan, NJ: Revell, 1965) 127.

[50]Craigie, *Psalms*, 182.

[51]Boice, *Psalms*, 175.

[52]Craigie, *Psalms*, 183.

Chapter 5

Making Sense of the Biblical Portrait:
Toward an Interpretive Strategy for the "Virtuous Wife" in Proverbs 31:10-31

Barbara M. Leung Lai

The portrait of the wife par excellence in Proverbs 31:10-31 appeals to generations of readers, across time, cultures and contexts. As a young girl, I was greatly intrigued by the 'fairy tale-like' feel to this portrait. The woman seemed just too ideal to be real! As an adult, I am still amazed by the high standard set by the sages. The fact that the portrait begins with a rhetorical question, "A virtuous wife who can find?" emphasizes the difficulty of such a search. As contemporary Christian women face the constant struggle between family and career, role-expectation and personal aspiration, my peers often find that this portrait exasperates and frustrates them. This resentment creates an obstacle in hearing the text and its intended message. Now as I gain more experience in the interpretation of the Hebrew Bible, the impetus of coming to terms with this 'virtuous wife' is still high on the agenda of my interpretive interest. To read this old wisdom classic afresh is both a challenging and inspiring endeavour.

Interpretive Strategy and Objective

In a discussion of interpretive interests, Mark Brett has pointed out the interrelatedness of 'strategy' and 'goal.'[1] Shaped by my own cumulative interests, the ultimate goal of this essay is to move from 'what it meant' to 'what it means' (to the Christian church at large). From the perspective of doing Old Testament theology today, Robert L. Hubbard describes this goal as the examination of both the 'descriptive' and 'normative' aspects of the text.[2] This 'both-and' operation entails paying due attention to the intrinsic textual elements as well as their normative values in the context of the collective lived experience of the faith community. I seek to describe 'what the text meant' in its original historical context[3] and strive to understand 'what the text means to us today' through a two-centre approach: text-centred and reader-oriented.[4] My reading of the text is therefore a 'both-and' operation, seeking both 'descriptive' and 'normative' aspects of the passage.

My own context as a woman, wife, mother, shepherd-teacher (Eph 4:11) and scholar-saint inevitably shapes the way I hear, interact with and interpret the Proverbs 31:10-31 text. It also contributes to my understanding of how the text relates to the church today. Being a partner in leadership with my husband sharpens my reading of the text in areas that have long been neglected.[5] Bruce K. Waltke's recent essay, "The Role of the 'Valiant Wife' in the Marketplace"[6] is a significant contribution in this respect in its affirmation of women's role in business as entrepreneurs. It is my intention here to build on and interact with Waltke's analytical results and seek to carry his interpretation further with additional observations.

In hammering out an interpretive strategy for Proverbs 31:10-31, I have found five promising points of entry. They serve as windows as we strive to make sense out of this biblical portrait. It is my hope that the results which emerge from each point of entry can cumulatively provide valuable direction toward an interpretation that is more than simply 'suggestive.'[7]

The Figure: A Real Wife or Wisdom's Ideals Personified?

The crux of the interpretation of this poem lies in the ways that the "virtuous wife" (אשת־חיל, v. 10) is understood. In the current interpretive scene, she is taken by some as a real figure without ruling out her significance in representing wisdom's ideals.[8] Others follow the symbolic interpretation and recognize her as Wisdom personified.[9] There are still others who hold that the portrait is not that of a real woman, but both a representation of the ideal wife and the epitome of wisdom.[10] This line of interpretation has profound implications on the intended message for the first recipients as well as the strategic place of this poem in the book.[11] In essence, 'the virtuous wife' serves as a role model for both women and men, an ideal for which all humankind should strive.[12]

As Claudia Camp observes, this conclusion of the book (Prov 31:10-31) corresponds to the prominent role of the feminine figure in the prologue (chs. 1-9). The prologue and epilogue together form the intentional 'inclusio' which frames the collection.[13] Waltke rightly points out that the similarities between the symbolic Woman Wisdom in 9:1-6 (and other feminine portrayals) and 31:10-31 do not necessarily rule out the understanding of a 'human figure' in 31:10-31. "Similarity does not establish identity."[14] While Woman Wisdom in 9:1-6 is purely symbolic, the real foolish woman in 9:13-16 incarnates folly.[15]

Among the feminine figures in the book, the only other occurrence of the phrase "virtuous wife" (אשת חיל) is in 12:4. There it undoubtedly refers to a real woman in the immediate context. On the one hand, by means of an antithetical parallelism, 12:4 balances the sage's teaching towards men (12:3). On the other hand, it reflects the social and cultural contexts of that time where 'honour' and 'shame' are an integral part of a woman's concerns. Syntactically, the other occurrences of (אשה) also support the real woman/wife designation.[16] This then positions the wife in the historical realm. As Waltke observes, the term is never used as personified Wisdom in 1:20-33; 8:1-36; and 9:1-6.[17]

Reading 31:10-11 straightforwardly and contextually, v. 10 does denote the praise of the 'virtuous wife' and her worth to her husband. In a didactic context of the royal mother's teaching to her son Lemuel (31:1-9), no one has challenged the 'women' referred to in verse 3 as real life figures. The queen's warning is set in the life setting of the ancient society of Israel. Given that Proverbs is a collection of collections of wisdom materials, it is still a legitimate strategy to read chapter 31 as a cohesive whole. This entails a reading perspective that takes seriously the dominant role of the woman figure (i.e., the king's mother, the 'women' in v. 3 and the 'virtuous wife' in v. 10) in the socio-cultural-historical setting as reflected in the text. Coming to terms with the extraordinary ideals that this 'virtuous wife' embodies seems to be at the heart of this 'real wife or wisdom personified' inquiry. Our preunderstanding often shapes our reading perspective which in turn, shapes our interpretation. In searching for the keys to unlock the message here, it is necessary to move on to the other points of entry.

Form, Structure, Poetics and Function: What is behind the Deliberate, Artful Design?

The analysis of Hebrew poetry has experienced a much welcome revival in recent years. This observation is also reflected in the recent interest in the structural analysis of Proverbs 31:10-31.[18] Prov 31:10-31 is one of the most complete acrostic poems (i.e., the first consonant of its 22 verses follows the same sequence as the 22 Hebrew letters) in the Hebrew Bible. As an acrostic, it has its distinct functions and also carries with it inevitable limitations. One way of looking at the limitations of an acrostic is the observation that it contains intentional ambiguities. As Waltke points out, the epigrammatic nature of proverbial literature entails presenting a truth in a most concentrated way and not representing the whole truth.[19] Within the confines of the 22 Hebrew letters in their exact sequence, the purpose of the acrostic may well be to present a succinct piece that aids memory. The compact nature of the acrostic will naturally leave room for ambiguities. In this sense, even the artful 'ambiguities' are deliberate.

If meaning is genre dependent, then what is intended behind the deliberate, artful design? Recent structural-analytical studies point to the fact that there are logical, thematic and structural arrangements beyond the alphabetical sequence.[20] Approaching the poem form-critically, Wolters concludes that the 'valiant woman' is deliberately described in terms borrowed from a tradition of heroic poetry.[21] Waltke carries this observation further and has come up with the most far-reaching results through his analysis of the three-fold dimension: form, structure and poetics.[22] Focusing solely on the literary aspects, I shall underscore the key elements that are crucial to answering the question posed previously: What is behind the deliberate, artful design?

First, replete with military imagery, the 'virtuous wife' is presented as a heroic figure, one who is full of strength and power.[23] The wife in this poem is described primarily through a portrait in verbs. She is depicted as a woman always in action. Her activities are itemized in vv. 13-27, the main body of the poem.[24] It is remarkable to observe that all her activities are placed in the domestic (her entire household and the needy in the community) and economic (her cottage industry) realms. Yet, the depiction of her activities and the praise of her values are so significant that they demand a 'heroicizing' in the portrayal. In essence, to 'heroicize' this wife is to give diction to the idea of (חיל), that she is truly a wife par excellence.

Second, to read the poem as a 'eulogy' to the excellent wife,[25] three broad-stroke thematic divisions are obvious: (1) an introduction of the virtuous wife and her worth (vv. 10-12); (2) an elaboration of her values by itemizing her activities (vv. 13-27); and (3) a conclusion calling for her praise (vv. 28-31). This reading strategy provides an interpretive key in that her itemized activities are not necessarily set within the 24-hour day time frame. Rather, they could be taken as pointing to different areas of her contribution/accomplishment through her whole lifetime.[26]

Third, a study of the syntax and poetics of this acrostic further reinforces its thematic unity. Syntactically, an initial verb form (i.e. "she does X") begins each verse in the first half (vv. 13-18) and an initial non-verbal form is used in the second half (vv. 19-27).[27] Poetically, the first half is structured after the alternating pattern and the second half is developed according to the chiastic pattern.[28] As K. C. Hanson observes, Proverbs 31:10-31, as well as the other acrostics in the Hebrew Bible, employ a "variety of interactive structures."[29]

These three literary observations collectively point to the fact that a thematic development, a distinct structure and some remarkable poetic techniques can be detected from a detailed analysis of this acrostic which is in the pattern of a heroic hymn. Further, they support the assertion that Prov 31:10-31 goes beyond merely following the sequence of the complete Hebrew alphabet. It is a deliberate, artful piece of literature.

The above conclusion leads to another crucial question: What is then the function of this artful design with such vigorous structure? While the classical theory views poetry as an imitation of reality, the emotional theory "construes it as the spontaneous outpouring of powerful feelings."[30] In terms of the audience's response, Waltke suggests that the sage and his first audience would have felt "all has been said, from A to Z" and that the poet has fully expressed himself.[31] If the function of a poem is to engage the feeling and emotion of its readers, then as a reader, I strongly feel that my response goes beyond this sentiment of "something has been expressed fully." The fact that even the artful 'ambiguities' are intentional, leaves more room for its audience/readers to appropriate its message to their own context. As I read on from א to ת (i.e., from A to Z), my interaction with the text escalates and my emotive response abounds.

With regards to the function of this 'heroic' acrostic, three modes of emotive escalation could be at work. First, it ascends from the appraisal of her values in the prologue (vv. 10-12) to the inviting call for her praise and reward in the epilogue (vv. 28-31). Second, in the depiction of her accomplishments, the emotive impact upon the audience/readers moves from her contribution to the poor (v. 20) to the household (v. 21), to her own well being (v. 22), to her husband (v. 23), and to the merchants in the broader community (v. 24). The third area of audience response arises from the description of her strength. It escalates from a depiction of her as energetic (the verbs of actions in vv. 13-18), diligent ("works with diligent hands," v. 13; vv. 15a, 18b; 27), skillful (v. 19), and physically strong (v. 17) to a depiction of her inner strength (v. 25) and wisdom (v. 26). In essence, I think the vigorous and interactive structures of this poem enhance the emotive response of the reader/audience. I would, furthermore, suggest that is the intended function of this poetic artistry.[32]

The Hebrew Concept of Time: A 24-hour Day Description?

As previously mentioned, this 'virtuous wife' is depicted as a woman of action. Coming to grips with the boundless activities (basically covering every sphere in life) that her hands perform within the span of a 24-hour day creates significant tension. On this ground, contemporary readers would see her as wisdom's ideals personified. It appears too unreal if "she gets up while there is still dark" (v. 15a) and "her lamp does not go out at night" (v. 18b).

A crucial step in making sense of this biblical portrait is to understand that the Hebrew concept of time differs fundamentally from contemporary usage. In classical Hebrew mentality, "there is no conceptual separation between an event and the time in which it occurs. Time, like the event or series of occurrences defining it, is a dynamic, phasic phenomenon."[33] Since there is no abstract concept of time in the Hebrew thought, recognition of time is determined by the events that take place in it. In essence, time is content-determined, highly subjectively perceived, and phasic in nature.

This unique Hebrew conception of time serves as an interpretive key for the sequential listing of the 'virtuous wife's' endless activities. Daily life in the Old Testament tradition is not reckoned on the basis of a 24-hour time period. As Simon DeVries observes, this distinctive time-concept gives definition and quality to one's existence. Time is perceived as an experience-filled, meaningful continuum.[34] Thus it follows that a 'life-time' or 'life-span' would refer to the streams of events/occurrences, which collectively give meaning and relevance to the individual, and which together make up a biography.[35] Reading Prov. 30:10-31 as a 'eulogy' of the 'virtuous wife's' lifetime accomplishments, covering the different spheres/aspects of her life is therefore, a proper reading strategy.

Textual evidence also supports this reading perspective. "All the days of her life" (כל ימי חייה, v.12) in the Introduction frames the portrait as one that depicts her experience-filled life span. It makes more sense once we recognize that the whole portrayal is cast within the framework of an acrostic poem, which denotes the distinctive concept of whole-ness, completeness, content-filled phasic development (through the se-quence of the entire alphabet).

The Uniqueness of this Acrostic Poem among Others in the Hebrew Bible

Fourteen acrostic texts are commonly identified in the Hebrew Bible (Psalms 1, 9/10[36], 25, 34, 37, 112, 119, 145; Lam 1, 2, 3, 4; Nah 1:2-8; and Prov 31:10-31).[37] Within the constraint of the demanding acrostic form, the authors all seek to embellish their work with fine literary devices and employ interactive structures. Beside these gen-eral characteristics, Prov 31:10-31 is unique on two grounds. First, as discussed in the previous section, it fits into the category of "heroic Hymn."[38] While others in the praise-hymn category (e.g. Ps 9/10, 34, 37, 119, 145) are all directed to God as the object of praise, Prov 31:10-31 and Ps 112 are the only occurrences where an acrostic hymn is devoted to a human object. Psalm 112 praises a man, whereas Prov 31 praises a 'virtuous wife.' Second, in the context of praise-hymn, Prov 31:10-31 concludes with a double emphatic, the most emphatic ending: an im-perative (נתן, "give")[39] and a Piel jussive (ויהללוה, "and let …praise her") calling for her praise and recognition.

Given the fact that (הלל, "praise") occurs also in vv. 28 and 30, and the fact that vv. 28-31 constitute the conclusion of this episode as well as the Book of Proverbs, this observation is quite remarkable. On the one hand, it relates and underscores the first unique feature - that is that a human object (a 'virtuous wife') deserves a 'heroic' commendation and honour. On the other hand, at the high point of her appraisal, the sage calls for giving this 'virtuous wife' her proper recog-nition and rewards. He exhorts, "Give her of the fruit of her hands and let her works praise her in the [city] gates" (v. 31).

The Place of Proverbs 31:10-31 in this Collection of Collected Wisdom Materials

The book of Proverbs is a collection of collections of Wisdom materials.[40] The question being considered here is this: Is Prov 31:10-31 a fitting conclusion to the whole book, or it is an appendage to the book? Camp affirms that, by virtue of their shared female imagery, the pro-logue of the book (chs. 1-9) and conclusion (31:10-31) function as an inclusio.[41] If this is deliberate, then what is the intention behind this fram-ing?

Based on the nature of the book, I shall present a number of points with regard to its editorial intentions. (1) As an intentional compi-lation, guided by divine inspiration, the sages/editors of the work would not have chosen Prov 31:10-31 randomly. The fact that they saw fit to conclude the whole collection with Prov 31:10-31 must be intentional. What is then the divinely driven agenda? We can carry Camp's observa-tion further by proposing that, since Prov 1-9 (the prologue) predomi-nantly presents womanhood as the source of temptation and evil (e.g., chs. 5, 6, 7), the final editor(s) intended to balance the portrayal of wom-anhood in the conclusion. The call for the praise and reward to the 'vir-tuous wife' in the literary form of an acrostic heroic poem is most fitting if such a balance is to be sought. (2) Since Prov 31:10-31 concludes the whole collection by employing the acrostic technique, it brings forth the **idea of 'totality' and 'completeness.' Further, it highlights the fact that the book of Proverbs is meant for complete, holistic didactic purposes,** echoing the purpose of the book as spelled out in 1:1-7. (3) There is little dispute about the first target audience/recipients of the book. It was intended for eligible young men, future leaders in the ancient society of Israel. This emphasis has a sudden twist as the book approaches its conclusion, that is the portrayal of the praise and value of the 'virtuous wife.' It gives a double message to its first audience in that the qualities of the woman par excellence invite all women of special status to aspire to the same excellence. Furthermore, the poem also encourages all young men to seek after women of such quality. Proverbs thus appeals to its first audience/recipients as a wisdom book for men and women. The contents of chapters 10-30 also place the relevance of the book in the general socio-cultural setting of the ancient society of Israel, and reflect the compiler's concern for community maintenance. (4) Following the thematic and structural movements of the poem, vv. 28-31 concludes the acrostic. As the depiction of the wife's values and qualities ascends to the conclusion of the poem (vv. 28-31), she receives praises from members of her immediate family (children, v. 28, and husband, v. 30). Emphatically, the sage calls the whole community to give her the praise and reward she deserves.[42] Moreover, this recognition has to be carried out in public and in a very prominent place ("let her works praise her in *the [city] gates*").[43] To affirm the strategic place of Prov 31:10-31 in the book is significant, yet to grasp the impact of v. 31 against the original *Sitz im Leben* is even more inspiring.

From What It Meant to What It Means

The cumulative results drawn from the preceding discussion of the five entry points support the following points of departure as we move from 'what it meant' to 'what it means' to the Christian church at large. It is my intention here to integrate the textual observations and the contextual meaning-making; to move beyond the literary/descriptive elements to normative claims.

What It Meant

To read the 'virtuous wife' as a real wife determines the target first audience/recipients. Because of her exceptional qualities and value (vv. 10b-12), young men are encouraged to seek after her and young women are commended to aspire to her as a role model. The fact that this poem begins with a rhetorical question (v. 10a) underscores the difficulty of the search.

The introductory statement in the appraisal (vv. 10b-12) together with the conclusion of the episode (vv. 28-31) place the high point of the portrayal in the familial relationships - her worth to husband and children and the praise she receives from them. The first audience would have known the literary characteristics of a heroic poem, especially if they were (as seems most likely) members of the aristocratic class. They would readily be able to identify this poem as acrostic and would have known the function and deliberate ambiguities of such a genre. Hearing and reading the poem as an informed audience, they would expect a highly articulated portrayal in its totality and completeness. Among other aspects in this heroic-hymn, what would be most striking to them would be her capabilities (in both domestic and economic realms) and strength (both physical and inner strength).[44]

"All the days of her life" (v. 12) sets the stage for the long list of the wife's activities. Reading this depiction from the perspective of a eulogy, the first readers would have perceived her as a relatively older woman. Through the various accomplishments (in different spheres: domestic, business, community, and her well being) in the different stages of her life, she advances from being an able and strong woman, to one that is full of wisdom, with inner strength and dignity (vv. 25-26).

To the first audience, the surprising notion in this poem would be its ending (vv. 28-31). On the one hand, this conclusion re-sharpens the focus on the praises to the 'virtuous wife.' They are from her own children and husband, as a blessed woman (v. 28) and a woman par excellence (vv. 28b-29). On the other, the audience is reminded of the two fleeting physical qualities, charm and beauty, in sharp contrast to the fear of the Lord ("a woman who fears the Lord is to be praised" [v. 30b]). In **a way, it echoes and restates the motto of the book in 1:7.**

Furthermore, the first audience would have been personally implicated as this poem emphatically calls for their proper response in public, "Give her of the fruit of her hands and let her works praise her in the [city] gates" (v. 31).

What It Means to the Christian Church at Large

The context of readers shapes the way they hear the text. Since Prov 31:10-31 is a heroic hymn in praise of a woman, there is no doubt that this poem appeals to generations of woman readers. Some aspire to her qualities and capabilities; others see the portrayal as far too idealistic. Yet there are others who are upset by the role-expectations as reflected here (unless we confine the text's application to the context of the patriarchal society of ancient Israel). For this group, there is still a big gap between the 'then' and 'now,' and thus a huge step is necessary to appropriate its intended message to 21st century Christian readers. If the thrust of completeness and totality is behind this acrostic, our challenge is to present its whole truth and not just pieces of the truth as contained in the text. The intended first audience were eligible young men and women of the ancient society of Israel. However, the concluding imperative ("Give her…," v. 31) is not directed to the young eligible adults only, but to husbands, children and the wider community "at the [city] gates." It is then a legitimate interpretive strategy to appropriate its message to the whole faith community, women and men, single and married, young and old.[45] As a woman reader, I am proposing here first, a gender-'specific' meaning. This is followed by a faith-seeking-understanding attempt to come up with a more holistic appropriation to the contemporary situatedness of the Christian community.

(1) Christian women should strive for excellence in every sphere of life: domestic responsibilities, career, community engagement, personal well being (vv. 22, 25) and spirituality. The wife so depicted is a woman par excellence in all these aspects. As Waltke sums up, all the superb qualities are in her: "energetic, strong, charitable, competent and skilled entrepreneur and manager."[46] Reading the portrait as an 'eulogy' is inspiring and also comforting. All Christian women have their whole lifetime to develop and advance in these areas of excellence, in accordance with their God-given potentials and opportunities.

(2) The depiction of her inner strength and spiritual qualities are remarkable. These are the virtues that all Christian women from all walks of life should strive for. She is clothed with 'strength' and 'dignity' (v. 25a) that correspond to her outstanding appearance — dressed in fine linen and purple (v. 22b). "She can laugh at the days to come" (v. 25b). I am amazed at her inner strength and dignity, qualities which enable her to embrace the future with all its uncertainties with a smile. Yet among all these glamorous descriptions, one summary appraisal stands out: "Charm is deceptive, and beauty is fleeting; but a woman who fears the Lord is to be praised" (v. 30).

(3) The goodness or benefit she brings to her husband is empowerment (vv. 11, 23). Her husband is respected at the city gate, serving in a position of leadership among the elders (cf. Exod 3:16, 4:29). If v. 31 ("and let her works praise her in the [city] gates") and v. 23 correspond to each other, and if leadership is defined as 'empowerment,' then we have here a portrayal of husband and wife's partnership in leadership. As the 'woman in ministry/leadership' issue and the 'mutual submission between husband and wife' controversy (Eph 5:21-33) are still unsettled among denominations today, Prov 31:10-31 provides an affirmative answer for both.

(4) A harmonious family relationship is presented here. Children as well as the household are well cared for (vv. 15, 21). Her children call her blessed (v. 28a); her husband has full confidence in her (v. 11) and praises her as the woman par excellence (v. 30). There is absolutely no conflict between family responsibilities and personal aspirations as both husband and wife, each in their own right, contribute to the community in positions of leadership. The demand for appreciation is called for here - for children to bless their mother, and for husbands to appreciate their spouses. As today's Christian family still struggles in these areas, Proverbs 31:10-31 serves as a timeless biblical model that calls for our own adaptation in various contexts.

(5) The concluding verse is inspiring (v. 31). If that is the intentional climax of the whole collection as well as the book, please join me in affirming all women in the God-given roles of empowerment. Acknowledge women's contributions as missionaries, homemakers, mothers, wives, pastors and Christian workers. Give them the reward they deserve. Moreover, this recognition has to be proper and in public: "and let her works praise her in the [city] gates."

My Tribute to Dr. Donald Leggett and Mrs. Linda Leggett -- Shepherd-Teachers

On the occasion of writing this essay in honour of Dr. Donald Leggett, I have a deep sense of appreciation for him, both as a friend and a colleague. My acquaintance with Linda and Don can be traced back to the year at Tyndale House, Cambridge, as we were both working on research projects in Isaiah, and occasionally fighting for books in that area. As I sat down to work on this essay, what was prominent in my mind was the beautiful portrait of a harmonious family, a mutually empowering and appreciative couple. These impressions have made a lasting impact on me in fulfilling my God-given roles as a woman in ministry, wife, mother, shepherd-teacher, and scholar-saint.

Notes

[1] As a methodological procedure, "any talk about method should be preceded by an analysis of interpretative interests; a 'method' will only be coherent if it is guided by a clearly articulated question or goal." Mark G. Brett, "Four or Five Things to Do with Texts: A Taxonomy of Interpretative Interests," in *The Bible in Three Dimensions: Essays in Celebration of Forty Years of Biblical Studies in the University of Sheffield*, ed. David J. A. Clines et al. (JSOT Sup 87; Sheffield: JSOT, 1990) 357-77; quotation from 357.

[2] "Doing Old Testament Theology Today," in *Studies in Old Testament Theology*, (ed. Robert L. Hubbard Jr., Robert K. Johnston, and Robert P. Meye; Dallas: Word, 1992) 35.

[3] Or 'what the text meant' to its first recipients/audience.

4 Grant R. Osborne's 'hermeneutical spiral' best explicates the dynamics of this interpretive process. See *The Hermeneutical Spiral: A Comprehensive Introduction to Biblical Interpretation* (Downers Grove, IL: InterVarsity, 1991) 5 - 7. My three criteria for the reader's perspective are Bible believing (2 Tim 3:16); God-fearing (2 Tim 2:15); and faith-seeking-understanding (Rom 1:17).

5 For example, the possible relationship between v. 23 and the concluding appeal in v. 31.

6 Bruce K. Waltke, "The Role of the 'Valiant Wife' in the Marketplace," *Crux* 35 (3, 1999) 23-34.

7 Scholarly research in the past has been largely focused on the form and structural dimension of this acrostic poem. In my opinion, most studies fail to carry the analytical results to the fullest and to come up with a more holistic interpretation. In this respect, Waltke's "Valiant Wife," (23-34) is a significant step towards this goal. In response to the postmodern ethos, it is also my intention here to arrive at an interpretation that is not merely "suggestive" but "affirmative." Cf. David J. A. Clines, *The Theme of the Pentateuch*, (2d ed.; Sheffield: Sheffield Academic Press, 1997) 130 where he draws the distinction between "suggestive" and "normative."

8 See Waltke, "Valiant Wife," esp. 30-31; Al Wolters, "Proverbs XXXI 10-31 as Heroic Hymn: A Form-Critical Analysis," *VT* 38 (1988) 446-57, esp. 455-57.

9 See Thomas P. McCreesh, "Widsom as Wife: Proverbs 31:10-31," *RB* 92 (1985) 25-46; repr. in *Learning from the Sages: Selected Studies on the Book of Proverbs*, ed. Roy B. Zuck (Grand Rapids: Baker, 1995) 391-410. Ignatius G. P. Gous, "Proverbs 31:10-31 – the A to Z of Women Wisdom," *Old Testament Essays* 9 (1996) 35-51. Note that while Claudia V. Camp opts for the wisdom-personified interpretation, she maintains that the portrait cannot be totally removed from a historical context. A full interpretation of the female wisdom figure should be tied to a certain socio-historical locus where such figure could give and receive meaning. See C. V. Camp, *Wisdom and Feminine in the Book of Proverbs* (BLS 11; Sheffield: Almond, 1985) 12; and the assessment of this view in Madipoane Masenya, "Proverbs 31:10-31 in a South African Context: A Reading for the Liberation of African (Northern Sotho) Woman," *Semeia* 78 (1997) 55- 68, esp. 61. This approach minimizes the gap between the real woman and personified female wisdom interpretations.

10 Cf. Tom Roger Hawkins, "The Meaning and Function of Proverbs 31:10-31 in the Book of Proverbs," (Unpublished Ph.D. Thesis, Dallas Theological Seminary, 1995); Madipoane Masenya, "Proverbs 31:10-31 in a South African Context,"61-62; K. T. Aitken, *Proverbs* (Philadelphia: Fortress, 1986) 158.

11 I shall return to this issue below in the section on "The Place of Proverbs 31:10-31 in this Collection of Collected Wisdom Materials."

12 See Hawkins, *The Meaning and Functions*, passim; Masenya, "Proverbs 31: 10-31 in a South African Context," 62.

13 Camp, *Wisdom and the Feminine*, 183-91.

14 Waltke, "Valiant Wife," 30.

[15]Ibid.

[16]See for example, 9:13; 11:16, 22; 14:1; 18:22; 19:13, 14; 21:9, 19; 25:24; 27:15; 30:20; 31:3.

[17]Waltke, "Valiant Wife," 30.

[18]As observed by J. Kenneth Kuntz, "Biblical Hebrew Poetry in Recent Research, Part I," *Currents in Research: Biblical Studies* 6 (1998) 31. This is also evident in the 1999 Society of Biblical Literature Annual Meeting in Boston. Two papers were devoted to the textual analysis of Proverbs 31:10-31 (Robert E. Longacre, "Proverbs 31:10-31 as a Biblical Hebrew Lyric Poem," and Bruce Waltke, "The Structure of the Valiant Wife [Proverbs 31:10-31]"). See *AARSBL Abstracts* (1999).

[19]See Waltke, "Valiant Wife," 30.

[20]See Waltke's comprehensive assessment of the structural-analytical results conducted by scholars on this pericope (Waltke, "Valiant Wife," 57).

[21]The 7 characteristics that can be found in Prov 30:10-31 are: (1) the description of the woman as manifesting חיל; (2) the recurrence of חיל in v. 29 creating an inclusio; (3) the frequent mention of her "strength" (vv. 17, 25); (4) a number of terms that have military connotation ("plunder" [v. 11], "prey" [v. 15], and the military expressions in vv. 19, 29); (5) the use of the verb תנה (v. 31), a rare verb used in other heroic poetry; (6) the description of the woman's actions rather than her inner feelings or physical appearance; and (7) the evidence of the valiant woman's wealth and social position which indicates that she belongs to the aristocratic class in which honor and individual initiatives ranked highly. For detailed arguments, See Wolters, "Heroic Hymn," passim.

[22]See Waltke, "Valiant Wife," 25 for additional observations.

[23]For detailed arguments, cf. Wolters, "Heroic Hymn," esp. 453-57; Waltke, "Valiant Wife," esp. 24-25. See also n. 20 here.

[24]See Wolters, "Heroic Hymn," 454; Waltke, "Valiant Wife," 27.

[25]As suggested by Waltke ("Valiant Wife," 26), I see this reading perspective quite appealing as it serves as an interpretive key to make sense of the sequence of her activities as described here.

[26]I shall come back to this in the following section on "The Hebrew Concept of Time."

[27]Note that Waltke takes v. 19 as the janus to stitch the two halves together without showing the seam. See Waltke, "Valiant Wife," 27-28.

[28]See Murray H. Lichtenstein, "Chiasm and Symmetry in Proverbs 31," *CBQ* 44 (1982) 202-211; Waltke, "Valiant Wife," 27-28.

[29]K. C. Hanson, "Alphabetic Acrostics: A Form-Critical Study," (Unpublished Ph.D. Dissertation; Claremont Graduate School, 1984) ii; cited in Waltke, "Valiant Wife," 25.

[30]Kuntz, "Biblical Hebrew Poetry in Recent Research, Part I," 32.

[31]Waltke, "Valiant Wife," 25.

[32]As to the function of the acrostic and emotive response, it is interesting to note that in Pamela Jean Owens's analysis of Lamentation 3, she concludes that the acrostic technique is a highly appropriate form for containing the expression of extreme suffering and grief. The alphabet, as a ready metaphor for totality and completeness, serves as an excellent frame for praising God (Pss 111 and 145), or for describing the just man (Psalm 112), or the "virtuous wife" in Prov 31:10-31. See Owen, "Personification and Suffering in Lamentation 3," *Austin Seminary Bulletin* 105 (2, 1990) 75-90.

[33]Ole J. Thienhaus, "Jewish Time: Ancient Practice, Hellenistic and Modern Habits, Freud's Reclaiming Judaism," *American Jewish Congress* 48 (1999) 442.

[34]Simon John DeVries, *Yesterday, Today and Tomorrow: Time and History in the Old Testament* (Grand Rapids: Eerdmans, 1975) 31.

[35]Ole J. Thienhaus, "Jewish Time: Ancient Practice," 444-45.

[36]Psalm 9 and 10 together has been identified as constituting a single acrostic poem. Based on the socio-economic-political setting of the two Psalms, they can be read as expressing the experience and aspirations of the marginalized poor. See Walter Bruggemann, "Psalm 9-10: A Counter to Conventional Social Reality," in *The Bible and the Politics of Exegesis* (Gottwald Festchrift; ed. David Jobling, Peggy L. Day and Gerald T. Sheppard; Cleveland: Pilgrim, 1991) 3-15.

37 For a survey of biblical acrostics, cf. Will Soll, *Psalm 119: Matrix, Form, and Setting* (Washington, DC: The Catholic Biblical Association of America, 1991) 11-20. See also Paul W. Gaebelein, "Psalm 34 and other Biblical Acrostics: Evidence from the Aleppo Codex," *Maarav* 5/6 (1990) 127-43.

[38]See n. 20. Cf. also Waltke, "Valiant Wife," 25 for additional observations.

[39]I take (תנו־) in v. 31 to be from the root נתן, ("to give") as opposed to תנה (which in the Piel, means "to praise, celebrate"). A number of Old Testament scholars support the latter root meaning. Cf. Waltke's comprehensive treatment of this verb in "The Role of the 'Valiant Wife' in the Market Place," n. 43). My preference is based on two grounds: (1) the latter meaning requires a repointing of the verb form to Piel; and (2) when the imperative (תנו־לה, "give to her") is followed by a Piel in the jussive (יהללוה, with conjunction ן] "and let ... praise her"), it carries the force of a double emphatic.

[40]According to David A. Hubbard, viewing "the book as a collection of collections of wisdom materials" is crucial in the interpretation of Proverbs (*Proverbs* [Dallas: Word, 1989] 18).

[41]See Camp, *Wisdom and the Feminine*, 183-91; also Waltke, "Valiant Wife," 30.

[42]Note the emphatic verb forms used in v. 31.

[43]Cf. v. 23.

[44]Wolters concludes that the use of the heroic poem genre here functions as a polemic against the ancient Near Eastern literature in praise of women, as well as against the intellectual ideals of Hellenism. See Wolters, "Heroic Hymn," 456-57.

[45]In particular, if we read it from the perspective of a 'eulogy,' it means a lot for older women and men as they reflect on the different stages of their life.

[46]Waltke, "Valiant Wife," 29

Chapter 6

Josephus Among His Contemporaries:
Abraham the Philosopher and Josephus' Purposes in Writing the Antiquities of the Jews

Nancy Calvert-Koyzis

The Significance of Josephus for New Testament Research

One may ask why consulting Josephus' works is important for a study of the New Testament. A number of responses might be given. For example, many New Testament scholars have found this Jewish historian's work significant from the early days of Christianity when the church appropriated Josephus' writings. "Two famous church leaders in particular, Origen (d. 254) and Eusebius (d. 340), cited Josephus extensively in their writings and thus popularized his works in Christian circles."[1] In fact it was this appropriation by the church, in part, which led to the preservation of Josephus' work throughout the centuries.[2]

Josephus also gives New Testament scholars a sense of the social and political milieu of the first and second centuries. Considering his perceptions assists us in understanding the perspectives of New Testament authors who shared this milieu. Yet we do not want to fall into the trap of only using a "scissors and paste" method to understand Josephus as he relates to the New Testament because this may lead to a misunderstanding of Josephus' views[3]. In this essay, therefore, I will examine both Josephus' understanding of Abraham, as well as the background and purposes of his *Antiquities of the Jews*.

Because the discussion of Abraham was popular during Josephus' time, we will look at how the latter shapes the figure of Abraham in his own writing. Several Jewish authors roughly contemporary with Josephus also discussed Abraham. For these authors, Abraham in some way represented the ideal person of God. But, as we shall see, the various authors gave Abraham different ideal characteristics depending upon their situation and their message.

Josephus as Apologist

As a member of an aristocratic priestly family, Josephus could trace his roots back to the era of the Hasmoneans under the rule of John Hyrcanus.[4] During his upbringing he studied Jewish law and traditions and probably received "at least the rudiments of Greek learning."[5] Like many prominent Jews of the time, Josephus accepted Roman power and mixed with Greeks.[6]

However he also claimed to be supportive of Jewish law and practice, and as expected of prominent Jewish males, he was involved in the war against the Romans in Galilee with some kind of military assignment. [7] Vespasian defeated the Galileans in the spring of 67 C.E. and any authority that Josephus may have had ended with the fall of the fortress of Jotapata (*B.J.* 3.328).

The motivation behind Josephus' behaviour after the fall of the fortress has been a point of contention for centuries among scholars of Josephus. For two days after the Roman victory, Josephus, along with "forty persons of distinction" *(B.J.* 3. 342) hid in a cave. Believing himself to be an interpreter of dreams and "skilled in divining the meaning of ambiguous utterances of the Deity," Josephus claimed to have remembered nightly dreams in which God had told him of the "impending fate of the Jews and the destinies of the Roman sovereigns" (*B.J.* 3.352). When he announced that he intended to surrender, his compatriots surrounded him and accused him of being a traitor. A suicide scheme was devised whereby they should draw lots for the order in which they would slay one another (*B.J.* 3.387 - 390). The lots were cast in such a way that all others died before Josephus and one other. At that point Josephus persuaded his countryman that they both should remain alive (*B.J.* 3.391).

It was only after the group was betrayed that Josephus faced the Roman tribunes (*B.J.* 3.344). According to Josephus' account when he was led before Vespasian, he predicted the future emperor's elevation to the throne (*B.J.* 3.399 - 408). Because of the prediction Josephus' life was spared. Two years later the prophecy was fulfilled and Vespasian was proclaimed emperor (*B.J.* 4.622 - 629).

As a result of these actions scholars have both maligned and exalted the character of Josephus. For example, writing from the standpoint that Josephus' motivations were less than commendable, Schalit contends that "Josephus artfully cast the lots, deceitfully managing to be one of the two last men left alive, and then persuaded his companion to go out with him and surrender to the Romans . . . To convince the Romans, Josephus attributed to himself the qualities of a diviner . . ."[8]

In more recent years, works on Josephus have given him the benefit of the doubt, if not outright praise. Tessa Rajak presents a more generous appraisal of Josephus' actions: "What happens to him is still, in part, a reflection of his class position and attitudes; but we have also to reckon . . . with individual, personal attributes. Ingenuity, quick thinking, unscrupulousness and good fortune all contributed to the way he came out of the affair."[9] Cohen probably comes closest to the truth when he says that Josephus "considered himself much too important for a death in a cave near an obscure fortress in the country district of a small province."[10]

The Antiquities of the Jews

Josephus' *Antiquities of the Jews* is most germane for our concerns here. Written in 93 - 94 C.E.,[11] the twenty-volume work covers the story of the Jewish people from creation until the administration of the last procurators before the war with Rome. Much of the *Antiquities* bears similarities to literature characterized by a style best described as "rewritten Bible." This term "is used simply to refer to those products of Palestinian Judaism at the turn of the era that take as their literary framework the flow of the biblical text itself and apparently have as their major purpose the clarification and actualization of the biblical story."[12] Many of the non-scriptural details in Josephus' rendition of the biblical text "are paralleled in various re-writings of Scripture from the Second Temple period . . . Josephus may have used such materials or may have relied on oral traditions familiar from his youth in Jerusalem or from Diaspora exegetical traditions."[13]

What were Josephus' purposes when writing the *Antiquities*? Some scholars have focused on Josephus' attempts to provide an apologetic for the Jewish community by whom he was dubbed a traitor even early in his military career.[14] Schwartz, for example, believes that the purpose of the *Antiquities* was "a new defence of Judaism" in which he ultimately aimed to "promote the acceptance of new leadership under the Rabbis, or some group much like the Rabbis in both upper class Jewish and Roman communities."[15]

Others have argued that his main purpose was to provide an apologetic for Judaism for a Gentile audience.[16] One of his stated motives was to publish a history of important affairs for the benefit of the public (*A.J.* 1.3 - 4). A large portion of his reading audience would have been Greek or Roman. He later states in *Against Apion,* "In my history of our *Antiquities* . . . I have . . . made sufficiently clear to any who may peruse that work the extreme antiquity of our Jewish race, the purity of the original stock, and the manner in which it established itself in the country which we occupy today" (*Ap.* 1.1). According to Per Bilde, Josephus' aim was to "prove the age and dignity of the Jewish people apologetically to the Greco-Roman world . . . "[17]

In a recent essay Mason argues that Josephus wrote the *Antiquities* neither as a vague apologetic to Gentiles nor as a work intended for a Jewish readership.[18] Instead he maintains that Josephus wrote for "a Gentile audience in Rome that is keenly interested in Jewish matters . . . the book has a coherent and powerful message . . . his audience desires a comprehensive but readable summary of the Judean *constitution and philosophy:* origins, history, law, and culture."[19]

Mason's main point makes good sense: it is difficult to imagine Gentiles who were only marginally interested in Judaism sitting "patiently through . . . 20 volumes on Judean history and culture."[20] It would seem likely that Josephus aimed for an audience of Gentiles who probably resided in Rome and who were interested in Judaism.[21]

Mason further argues that if the *Antiquities* was written for Jews, Josephus would not need to explain so much about Jewish life and heritage for his audience. [22] But does this necessarily mean that he had no Jewish readers in mind? In this essay we shall see that Josephus' portrayal of Abraham as compared to that of his Jewish contemporaries belies an attempt to reach a Jewish audience as well.[23]

Abraham as Philosopher in Josephus' Antiquities of the Jews

Scholars of Josephus have traditionally seen him in a negative light and have related this judgement to his literary works. His works were considered to be devoid of originality,[24] and his depiction of Abraham as lacking coherence.[25] In contrast to such an approach, I maintain that, using traditions about Abraham from a variety of oral and written sources, Josephus provides his reader with a politically expedient, coherent reworking of the life of Abraham.[26] Due to the limitations of space we will not consider Josephus' entire description of Abraham, a description which includes the latter's adherence to the Jewish constitution. We will instead focus upon Josephus' portrayal of Abraham as the premier monotheist and philosopher.[27] Speaking of Abraham, Josephus states,

> He . . . determined to reform and change the ideas universally current concerning God. He was thus the first boldly to declare that God, the creator of the universe, is one, and that, if any other being contributed aught to man's welfare, each did so by His command and not in virtue of its own inherent power. This he inferred from the changes to which land and sea are subject, from the course of sun and moon, and from all the heavenly conjunctions; for, he argued, were these bodies endowed with power, they would have provided for their own regularity, but since they lacked this last, it was manifest that even those services in which they cooperate for our greater benefit they render not in virtue of their own authority, but through the might of their commanding sovereign, to whom alone it is right to render our homage and thanksgiving *(A.J.* 1.154-156).[28]

According to Josephus' description of Abraham discerning the existence of God from changes in the sea, earth and sky, Abraham is a natural theologian and a superior philosopher.[29] His "proof is in the form of the proofs for the existence of G-d promulgated by the Greek philosophic schools, notably the Stoics. . . who first presented the teleological argument that the orderly state of the universe manifests a design perfected by the rational power of an infinite mind."[30] However, as opposed to most teleological arguments which are based on the regular movements of the stars and planets, Abraham reasons inversely that since their movement is irregular, then there must be a "commanding sovereign" or a God (*A.J.* 1.156). The phrase Josephus uses to describe these celestial phenomena — "those services in which they cooperate for our greater benefit"— sounds strangely like a description of the theory behind astrology, in which the stars and planets cooperated together to determine the steps of human beings.[31]

As found in the biblical account, Abraham later travels to Egypt because of a famine in the land (Gen 12:10; *A.J.* 1.161). But according to Josephus, Abraham's foundational reason for travelling to Egypt was that he "was of a mind to visit them, alike to profit by their abundance and to hear what their priests said about the gods; intending, if he found their doctrine more excellent than his own, to conform to it, or else to convert them to a better mind should his own beliefs prove superior" (*A.J.* 1.161). His journey of inquiry leads him to learn from the priests of the Egyptians like a student in a philosophical school. Feldman points out that one of the "recurrent characteristics of the pre-Socratic philosophers as viewed in Hellenistic times, is that they visited Egypt to become acquainted with Egyptian science and other esoteric lore and to engage in discussions with Egyptian wise men."[33] Abraham is a true philosopher; what he believes about God depends upon which doctrine is superior. As portrayed by Josephus, he apparently would have no problem converting to Egyptian beliefs should their arguments prove superior.

Concerning Abraham's journey into Egypt, Josephus continues:

> Abraham consorted with the most learned of the Egyptians . . . conferred with each party and, exposing the arguments which they adduced in favour of their particular views, demonstrated that they were empty and contained nothing true. Thus gaining their admiration at these conversations as a man of extreme wisdom, gifted not only with high intelligence but with power to convince his hearers on any subject which he undertook to teach, he introduced them to arithmetic and transmitted to them the laws of astronomy. For before the coming of Abraham the Egyptians were ignorant of these sciences, which thus travelled from the Chaldaeans into Egypt, whence they passed to the Greeks (*A.J.* 1.165 - 168).

In the *Antiquities,* Abraham becomes the Hellenistic philosopher without equal. The trip to Egypt ends with Abraham participating in the debate foretold at its beginning (*A.J.* 1.161). Apparently Abraham was not at all convinced by their arguments, and was even able to show how empty they were of truth. Abraham is portrayed as such a convincing teacher that he was able to persuade his hearers on any chosen subject. If we again refer back to the introduction to the trip to Egypt, we find that Abraham intended to discuss their respective doctrines about the gods (*A.J.* 1.161). One would conclude that Abraham was especially convincing regarding his doctrine of monotheism.

According to Feldman, Josephus depicts Abraham as gifted "in the very areas most cultivated by the Hellenistic Greeks, namely logic, philosophy, rhetoric, and science."[33] Through the depiction of Abraham exposing empty arguments and teaching in such a manner that he always convinced his listeners, Josephus portrays Abraham as the supreme logician and rhetorician. His mastery of philosophy was found in his proof for the existence of God (*A.J.* 1.167 - 168).

Obviously Josephus portrays Abraham purposefully. At the end of the section he reminds us that before Abraham, the Egyptians were ignorant of astronomy, which was tantamount to astrology, and arithmetic which were then passed on to the Greeks (*A.J.* 1.168).[34] Not only is Abraham portrayed as a well-educated Hellenist, but he is responsible for important aspects of culture being given to the Egyptians and the Greeks. Ultimately, even Roman readers owe this knowledge to Abraham himself.

Abraham in the Works of Josephus' Contemporaries

Josephus is not the only Jewish author to concentrate upon Abraham's association with monotheism, astrology and philosophy. One of the earliest texts written in the "rewritten bible" genre mentioned above, the *Book of Jubilees,* also describes Abraham's association with monotheism and astrology. Although scholars differ regarding the exact date of its composition, it is usually placed near the middle of the second century, B.C.E.[35] What the text reflects is an ideological tension between those Jews who stood for strict maintenance of the law and separation from Gentiles and those who freely associated with Gentiles and assimilated aspects of Hellenistic culture.

Jubilees' author fits decisively into the first group of non-assimilationist Jews (e. g. *Jub.* 15:31-32). Because of this, in his rewriting of the Abraham monotheist/astrology traditions, he styles Abraham as the first monotheist and an avid anti-idolater (e. g. *Jub.* 11:16-17; 12:2b-5 which includes his denouncing astrology). For example, while living in Haran, Abram sits up "[to] observe the stars. . . so that he might see what the nature of the year would be with respect to rain" (*Jub.* 12:16). One should remember here that "astrology and meteorology were so inseparable in antiquity that *Jubilees* is able to rebuke Abraham for his attempt to forecast the weather."[36] It is at this point that "a word came into his heart, saying, 'All of the signs of the stars and the signs of the sun and the moon are all in the hand of the Lord'"

(*Jub.* 12:17). After rejecting astrology, Abraham reasons and prays, "My God, my God, God most High, you alone are my God. You have created everything; everything that was and has been is the product of your hands" (*Jub.* 12: 19).[37]

Through his mouthpiece Abraham, the author of *Jubilees* is telling his reader the reasons for the worthlessness of idolatry and encouraging the reader to worship the one, true Creator God of Abraham. In his cultural and political milieu, either during the days of Antiochus IV Epiphanes or the early days of Hasmonean control, the author thereby instructs his Jewish readers not to assimilate with Gentile culture or religion.

While *Jubilees* precedes Josephus by over two centuries, *The Apocalypse of Abraham*, dated soon after the destruction of the Jerusalem Temple in 70 C.E. belies an attitude similar to that found in *Jubilees*.[38] The *Apocalypse of Abraham* is composed of two major sections: narrative (chapters 1-8) and apocalyptic (chapters 9 - 32). The author rewrites the biblical account of Abraham portraying him as the son of an idol-maker (Terah). Abraham eventually reasons that one should not believe in idols because one should not believe in the changeable, created, subduable things (*Apoc. Abr.* 7:1-6). In the remainder of chapter seven, Abraham uses an argument concerning the heavenly phenomena: beyond the planets and stars a Creator and God exists. Abraham reasons that although the sun illuminates the whole universe, it is obscured at night by the moon and clouds. But the moon and stars are not gods, since they are also dimmed. Instead, Abraham encourages his father to worship the true God who creates and empowers the universe. In the conclusion of the chapter, Abraham prays for the true God to reveal himself (*Apoc. Abr.* 7:7-12).

This speech made by Abraham to his father is based upon extra-biblical tradition about Abraham and his conversion from idolatry.[39] The depiction of Abraham reasoning that the true God is not contained within the cosmos but created and controls the cosmos is familiar from our previous consideration of *Jubilees* and Josephus' *An-*

tiquities. Furthermore, as in *Jubilees,* the author of *The Apocalypse of Abraham* condemns blatant idolatry and the Greek philosophical arguments concerning the priority and divinity of the elements. Those who read the apocalypse are shown that nothing in the created world is worthy of worship. Only the one God and Creator is worthy of the veneration of the readers.

Yet it is in the apocalyptic section that we find the real significance of Abraham. As the vision continues, the evil of those who can only be understood as Abraham's descendants is described. Abraham sees the "likeness of the idol of jealousy" which is similar to the carpenter's figure which his father had made formerly (*Apoc. Abr.* 25:1). In front of this idol is a man who is worshipping it. Opposite the idol is an altar where boys are being slaughtered in the face of the idol. Abraham asks the identity of the idol and the other elements, and the "handsome temple . . . the art and beauty of your glory that lies beneath your throne" (*Apoc. Abr.* 25:3).

The reader is told that the priesthood and the Temple have deviated from God's idea of what they should be. He became angered by the priesthood. The idol associated with the Temple was described as the "idol of jealousy" (*Apoc. Abr.* 25:1). The description of the statue as "God's anger" in 25:5 represents the "image which provokes God's jealousy or anger."[40] The slaughter of boys on the altar sounds like the offering of children to pagan gods and is reminiscent of the apostasy committed by Manasseh.[41]

Just as the writer of 2 Kings blames the fall of Jerusalem and Judah in 587-86 B.C.E. on Manasseh's apostasy (2 Kgs 21:10-15; *Apoc. Abr.* 25: 5-6) so the author of the *Apocalypse of Abraham* blames the fall of the Temple in 70 C. E. upon the apostasy of the Jewish people, particularly in the form of their priests.[42]

At the end of the apocalypse Abraham finds himself back on earth and God describes the final vindication.[43] The trumpet will sound; God's unnamed chosen one will summon God's people who have been humiliated by the heathen. Those who mocked and ruled over God's people are condemned to Gehenna, a place of punishment. Those who kept the commandments will rejoice at the downfall of those who "followed after the idols and after their murders" (31:5). They are condemned because "they glorified an alien (god). And they joined one to whom they had not been allotted, and they abandoned the Lord who gave them strength" (31:8).[44]

Abraham thus provides a contrast both to the idolatry of Terah and that of his descendants. Unlike Terah, Abraham chose not to worship idols. Similarly, Abraham provides a striking contrast to those who practised the idolatry which led to catastrophic destruction of the Temple in 70 C.E. According to the *Apocalypse of Abraham,* Abraham was known for abhorring idols and manifesting faith in the one, Creator God. In contrast to the priests, Abraham was the example of the true person of God.

Hanson has contended that "since the typical apocalyptic universe develops as a protest of the apocalyptic community against the dominant society, it is concerned . . . with the demands of the immediate crisis, especially those of defining identity within a hostile world, and of sustaining hope for deliverance."[45] The author of the *Apocalypse of Abraham* was concerned with the crisis of the destruction of the Temple by the Romans. He wanted to show that ultimately God would vindicate the people of God over their hostile oppressors. The identity of the people of God and their hope for deliverance rested in their maintaining faithfulness to the one Creator God.

A survey of portrayals of Abraham contemporary with Josephus would not be complete without a consideration of Abraham in the works of Philo of Alexandria.[46] Writing for both Jews and Gentiles near the end of the first century B.C.E. and the beginning of the first century C.E., Philo states that the Chaldeans were

> especially active in the elaboration of astrology and ascribed everything to the movements of the stars . .
> . they glorified visible existence, leaving out of consideration the intelligible and invisible. But while ex-

ploring numerical order as applied to the revolution of the sun, moon, and other planets and fixed stars, and the changes of the yearly seasons and the interdependence of the phenomena in heaven and on earth, they concluded that the world itself was God, thus profanely likening the created to the Creator. In this creed Abraham had been reared, and for a long time remained a Chaldean. Then opening the soul's eye as though after profound sleep and beginning to see the pure beam instead of the deep darkness, he followed the ray and discerned what he had not beheld before, a charioteer and pilot presiding over the world and directing in safety his own work, assuming the charge and superintendence of that work and of all such parts of it as are worthy of the divine care (*Abr.* 68 - 70). [47]

Both Josephus and Philo thus depict Abraham as discerning the existence of God and his care for the world from the phenomena of the natural world around them.[48] But unlike some Stoics who concluded that no God existed outside of reason and fate,[49] or that a variety of gods were responsible for fate,[50] Abraham discerns that one God exists. In Philo it is clear that Abraham had been reared in the practice of astrology. In Josephus, one might not know of Abraham's familiarity with the presuppositions of astrology unless one paid attention to his relatively obscure statement about the celestial phenomena and their "services in which they cooperate for our greater benefit" (*A.J.* 1.156). But in both Philo and Josephus, Abraham infers his teleological argument that the one Creator God exists and acts on behalf of all humankind.

Philo probably wrote for both Jewish and Gentile audiences. Sandmel long ago asserted that the more literal portrayal of Abraham found in *De Abrahamo* may have been written to non-Jews while the more allegorical portrayal of Abraham found in the *Migration of Abraham* may have been written to Jews.[51] One of Philo's reasons for

writing was to prevent Jews who were sympathetic to Hellenism and
on the verge of apostasy from totally forsaking Judaism. From Philo's
accounts, it appears that there were not only Jews in Alexandria who
were opposed to the kind of philosophical allegorizing of the law that
Philo practised, but also those who were so allegorical in their treatment of the law that they rejected the literal sense of the law. In his
work *On Providence* Philo is depicted as debating the belief in divine
providence with his nephew, Tiberius Julius Alexander, whom Wolfson
categorizes as belonging to the class of apostates known as "uprooted
Jewish intellectuals."[52]

Josephus Among His Contemporaries

According to Greg Sterling, ways that Jews responded to the
destruction of the Temple of Jerusalem included writing apocalyptic
and rabbinic literature as well as other literature that offered a new
definition of Judaism.[53] This includes the *Apocalypse of Abraham,* discussed above. Yet even earlier than this, Jewish authors had been responding to encroaching Hellenism in similar ways.

For example the author of *Jubilees* illustrates the themes of adherence to Israel's God and the law especially as it means separation
from Gentiles. In this sense the author of *Jubilees* is a prototype of the
rabbis who will later support comparative isolation from the Greco-
Roman world.

If we contrast the attitude towards Abraham's practice of astrology in *Jubilees* with Josephus' attitude towards astrology in the *Antiquities,* a significant difference of opinion is noticeable. Through
Abraham, the author of *Jubilees* rejects the practice of astrology outright. In the *Antiquities* Josephus does not so much condemn the practice *in toto* but rejects the major presuppositions which exist behind
the practice. It is not the stars which act upon their own power for the
benefit of humankind, but the one Creator God who does so. Astrol-

ogy is not necessarily equivalent to idolatry; idolatry is the lack of recognition from the natural phenomena that one God exists and works for the benefit of humankind.

In regard to their attitude to the surrounding culture, Josephus and the author of *Jubilees* are on opposite ends of the spectrum. Josephus represents the assimilationist Jew. He has no problem portraying Abraham in the garb of an intelligent Hellenistic rhetorician who uses the philosophical proofs of the time to make his own deductions.

Josephus has made Judaism attractive to his readers. The Greco-Roman world was used to a plurality of gods in a variety of forms. "Jewish refusal to accept such gods incurred the charges of atheism and misanthropy (*Apion* 2.14) and sometimes ridicule . . . . Josephus denies the charge of atheism and challenges polytheism by affirming the superiority of Jewish monotheism, the origin of which he attributes to the Jewish patriarch and philosopher Abraham."[54] Thus Josephus simultaneously deflects charges of perceived anti-social behaviour and appeals to philosophically minded readers. In contrast, the author of *Jubilees* portrays Abraham as the explicitly law-abiding separatist Jew. Abraham's slogan is separation from all things Gentile. To the author of *Jubilees,* embracing the attributes associated with Hellenism is tantamount to accepting the idolatry upon which the degenerate Gentile ways are based.

However, the fact that both authors make use of the same traditions to speak to their respective audiences - one from the standpoint of progressive Judaism and one from the standpoint of a more reactionary Judaism - suggests the existence of a collection of either oral or written traditions about Abraham which had developed. It also suggests that each author used traditions about Abraham to speak to particular Jewish communities from a standpoint of power: the ideal Jew will imitate Abraham as he embodies the Jew who deals with the non-Jewish world.[55]

For the author of the *Apocalypse of Abraham*, Abraham represents the faithful one who set aside idolatry, including astrology, as he reasoned that one true God existed. Abraham's abhorrence of astrology served as an anti-type to those who continued to practice their idolatrous ways, particularly the priests who were primarily to blame for God's wrath, as exemplified in the destruction of the Temple of Jerusalem because of their perceived idolatrous practices.

Sterling, among others, has argued that the *Antiquities* were written not only for a Gentile readership but for a Jewish audience as well.[56] One reason is that Josephus himself mentions his fellow Jews that may be reading his book when he apologizes for collecting the laws systematically in the *Antiquities*. He says "I have thought it necessary to make this preliminary observation, lest perchance any of my countrymen who read this work should reproach me at all for having gone astray."[57] Sterling further points out that in the *Antiquities* Josephus responded to the destruction of the Temple, not from an apocalyptic or rabbinic stance (see above), but by offering a definition of Judaism. [58] Given the incredible impact that the relatively recent destruction of the Temple had on Jews in both Palestine and the Diaspora, this definition would be of significance to those Jews who were struggling with their commitment to their faith.

Given that Jews in the Diaspora were highly Hellenized, one can not rule out the idea that Josephus was attempting to make Judaism more attractive to Hellenized Jews in Rome. As we have seen, Philo wrote to both Jews and Gentiles in his highly Hellenized accounts. While it may be that the assimilation of Roman Jews to pagan culture was not as widespread as assimilation among Alexandrian Jews, one can not totally rule out some assimilation.[59] Mason mentions that high-profile Jews like Agrippa II and Berenice may have acted as types of literary patrons for Josephus.[60] But, as Barclay notes, both were probably highly assimilated to the culture around them.[61] One might argue that while supporting Josephus' work they also took the opportunity to consider his views concerning what it meant to be a Jew in a Hellenized world not long after the destruction of the Temple.

Thus, while a major reason that Josephus wrote his *Antiquities of the Jews* may have been his desire to convince interested Gentiles of the superior philosophy of the Jews, this was almost certainly not his only reason. Josephus also seems to have written for his compatriots, some of whom may have dubbed him a traitor in earlier years, but who now attempted to reconcile their own questions about Judaism in light of their own assimilation. In this case Josephus explains aspects of Judaism not only for Gentiles but for his assimilationist Jewish readers as well. In a way similar to some of his literary compatriots, Josephus used the account of Abraham to speak to fellow Jews about the superiority of their faith and its philosophical foundations.[62]

Conclusion

As we have seen, the figure of Abraham played an important role in Jewish literature roughly contemporary with the New Testament. By using the ancient patriarch, Josephus portrayed the ideal Jew for his readers, both Jews and Gentiles.

But these authors were not the only ones who found their ideal in Abraham. Authors whose works are found in the New Testament also discovered that Abraham was a useful tool for their expression. Paul's use of Abraham, specifically in Romans, provides us with a glimpse of such interpretation.

In Romans Paul uses Abraham to portray the ideal person of God in a more inclusive sense than the author of *Jubilees*, in that his example includes Gentiles as well as Jews (Rom 4:10 - 12). Because Paul interprets Abraham as having faith "reckoned to him as righteousness" (Rom 4:5), which was before circumcision (Rom 4:9-12), both Gentiles and Jews who have faith are members of the people of God.

But in another sense Paul's portrayal of Abraham is more exclusive than that of Philo or Josephus, because Abraham is now the one who believes not only in the one God, but in the God who sent Jesus Christ to be crucified and resurrected for their salvation. The ideal person of God is one who believes this as well.

Paul is not a detached observer of Judaism but a participant in Judaism, although now from a Christian perspective. He is not easily pigeon-holed into a "non-assimilationist" or "assimilationist" Jewish category, as we might desire. But like his Jewish contemporaries he finds that Abraham is a useful vehicle for expressing his point of view that just as Abraham was made righteous by faith in the God of the crucified Christ, so may those who follow in his footsteps.

Notes

[1] Steve Mason, *Josephus and the New Testament,* (Peabody, MA: Hendrickson, 1992) 8.

[2] Ibid.

[3] Ibid., 26-30.

[4] While the overview of Josephus' life may be familiar to some I assume that the majority of readers of this essay are not familiar with this information. E. Schürer, *The History of the Jewish People in the Age of Jesus Christ,* (Edinburgh: T & T Clark, rev. ed., 1973) 1.44. See also *Vita* 1-6.

[5] Harold W. Attridge, "Josephus and His Works," *Jewish Writings of the Second Temple Period,* (CRINT 2.2; Assen: Van Gorcum, 1984) 185-232.

[6] Tessa Rajak, *Josephus: The Historian and His Society,* (London: Duckworth, 1983; Philadelphia: Fortress, 1984) 4. See further, M. Goodman, *The Ruling Class of Judaea,* (Cambridge: Cambridge University Press, 1987) 20-21.

[7] He portrays himself an ideal general in *B.J.* 2.568-646 and as a member of a panel of priests sent to Galilee in *Vita* 28-413. For different perspectives on Josephus' commission in Galilee, see Abraham Schalit, "Josephus Flavius," in *Encyclopaedia Judaica,* (ed. Cecil Roth and Geoffrey Widoger; Jerusalem: MacMacillan, 1971); Per Bilde, *Flavius Josephus between Jerusalem and Rome: His Life, his Works, and their Importance,* (Sheffield: JSOT, 1988) 44-45; Attridge "Josephus and His Works," 185-90.

[8] Schalit, "Josephus Flavius"; see also H. St. John Thackeray, *Josephus: The Man and the Historian,* (New York: KTAV, 1967) 19.

[9] Rajak, *Josephus,* 168; see also Bilde, *Flavius Josephus,* 52.

[10]Shaye J. D. Cohen, *Josephus in Galilee and Rome: His Vita and Development as a Historian*, (Leiden: E. J. Brill, 1979) 229-30.

[11]*A.J.* 20.267; Attridge, "Josephus," 210.

[12]Daniel J. Harrington, "Palestinian Adaptations of Biblical Narratives and Prophecies," in *Early Judaism and Its Modern Interpreters* (ed. Robert A. Kraft and George W. E. Nickelsburg; Atlanta: Scholars, 1986) 239.

[13]Attridge, "Josephus and His Works," 212.

[14]Mireille Hadas-Lebel, *Flavius Josephus: Eyewitness to Rome's First-Century Conquest of Judea*, (trans. Richard Miller; Toronto: Macmillan, 1993) 73.

[15]Seth Schwartz, *Josephus and Judaean Politics*, (Columbia Studies in the Classical Tradition 18; Leiden: E. J. Brill, 1990) 16, 216.

[16]For example, see L. Feldman, *Studies in Josephus' Rewritten Bible*, (Leiden: E. J. Brill, 1998).

[17]Bilde, *Flavius Josephus*, 93.

[18]Steve Mason, " 'Should Any Wish to Enquire Further' (*Ant.* 1.25): The Aim and Audience of Jospehus's *Judean Antiquities/Life*," in *Understanding Josephus: Seven Perspectives*, (ed. Steve Mason; JSPSup 32; Sheffield: Sheffield Academic Press, 1998) 95.

[19]Ibid., 101, italics mine.

[20]Ibid., 68.

[21]Many Gentiles were interested in Judaism in Rome and elsewhere. Such individuals could be located on a continuum comprising those who followed a few Jewish laws to those who became full proselytes. For example, see Tac., *Hist.* 5.5; *A.J.* 18.81-85 and the discussion in N. L. Calvert, "Abraham Traditions in Middle Jewish Literature: Implications for Galatians and Romans" (Ph.D. diss., University of Sheffield, 1993), 343-48.

[22]Mason, " 'Should Any Wish to Enquire', " 66-68.

[23]Ibid., 95.

[24]See the good overview of scholarship on Josephus in Bilde, *Flavius Josephus*, 123-71.

[25]Samuel Sandmel, *Philo's Place in Judaism: A Study of Conceptions of Abraham in Jewish Literature*, (New York: KTAV, 1971) 75.

[26]Louis H. Feldman *Josephus' Interpretation of the Bible*, (Berkeley: University of California Press, 1998) 223.

[27]*A.J.* 1.154-68. For a discussion of the entirety of Josephus' depiction of Abraham see Calvert, "Abraham Traditions."

[28]Translations of Josephus are taken from *Jewish Antiquities Books I - IV* (Loeb Classical Library 242; trans. H. St. J. Thackeray; Cambridge, MA: Harvard University Press, 1930). In some places I have adapted Thackeray's translation in favour of less archaic language.

[29]T. W. S. Franxmann, *Genesis and the 'Jewish Antiquities' of Flavius Josephus,* (BibOr 35; Rome: Biblical Institute Press, 1979) 119.

[30]Feldman, "Abraham the Greek Philosopher in Josephus," *T(P)APA* 99 (1968) 146.

[31]Franxman states, ". . . the arguments of Philo against the Chaldaean astrology seem to be echoed in this passage, especially in the emphasis on the good which the heavenly powers are capable of performing." Franxmann, *Genesis,* 119.

[32]Feldman, "Abraham the Greek Philosopher,"151.

[33]Ibid., 153.

[34]*Jewish Antiquities Books I - IV,* 82 n. 2.

[35]J. C. VanderKam, *Textual and Historical Studies in the Book of Jubilees,* (HSM 14; Missoula, MT: Scholars, 1977) 255-57. Those who maintain a pre-Hasmonean date include G. W. E. Nickelsburg, in "The Bible Rewritten and Expanded," *Jewish Writings of the Second Temple Period,* (CRINT 2.2; Assen: Van Gorcum, 1984) 101-3. Those who hold to an early Hasmonean date include O. S. Wintermute, "Jubilees: A New Translation and Introduction," in *The Old Testament Pseudepigrapha,* (ed. J. H. Charlesworth; London: Darton, Longman, and Todd, 1985) 2.44; John C. Endres, *Biblical Interpretation in the Book of Jubilees,* CBQMS 18 (Washington, DC: The Catholic Biblical Association of America, 1987).

[36]Geza Vermes, *Scripture and Tradition in Judaism,* (Leiden: E. J. Brill, 1961) 81.

[37]Translation from J. VanderKam, *The Book of Jubilees,* (CSCO 510-11; Scriptores Aethiopici 87-88; Louvain: Peeters, 1989) 72.

[38]*Apoc. Abr.* 27:1-3; James R. Mueller, "The Apocalypse of Abraham and the Destruction of the Second Jewish Temple," *SBLSP* 1982 (ed. Kent H. Richards; Chico, CA: Scholars, 1982) 341-49.

[39]Although see Joshua 24:2 where Abraham is said to leave idolatry behind.

[40]Box and Landsman, *The Apocalypse of Abraham,* (London: SPCK, 1918) 73 n. 3. Cf. Ezek 8:3-5.

[41]Box and Landsman, *Apocalypse of Abraham,* 73 n. 5.

[42]What precise form this apostasy took is not clear from the text, although it does seem to be related to cultic matters. One possibility may be that he is reacting against the high priesthood especially in regard to their predominant Saduceism. See M. Stern, "Aspects of Jewish Society: The Priesthood and other Classes." in *The Jewish People in the First Century,* (CRINT 1.2; Assen:

Van Gorcum, 1974) 611. Another possiblity is that the author may be reacting against the continual daily sacrifice which was made on behalf of the emperor. See Schürer, *The History of the Jewish People,* 1.379-80; cf. *Ap.* 2.77.

[43]I have purposely omitted a discussion of the man from the "heathen side" of a vision because it is probably a Christian interpolation (*Apoc. Abr.* 29:3-13). See Robert G. Hall, "The 'Christian Interpolation' in the *Apocalypse of Abraham,*" *JBL* 107 (1988) 107-10.

[44]Translation from R. Rubinkiewicz, "The Apocalypse of Abraham: A New Translation and Introduction," in *The Old Testament Pseudepigrapha,* (ed. James H. Charlesworth; Garden City, NY: Doubleday, 1983) 1:681-719.

[45]P. D. Hanson, "Apocalypticism," *IDBSup,* 30; id., *The Dawn of Apocalyptic: The Historical and Sociological Roots of Jewish Apocalyptic Eschatology,* (rev. ed.; Philadelphia: Fortress, 1979) 283.

[46]For a discussion of Abraham in Philo see N. L. Calvert, "Philo's Use of Jewish Traditions about Abraham" in *SBLSP* 1994 (SBLSP 33; ed. Eugene H. Lovering, Jr.; Atlanta: Scholars) 463-76.

[47]See also *Migr.* 178-79; Sandmel, *Philo's Place,* 107; translation taken from Philo, *Philo in Ten Volumes,* (Loeb Classical Library 261; ed. G. P. Goold; trans. F. H. Colson, G. H. Whitaker, and Ralph Marcus; London: Heinemann; Cambridge, MA: Harvard University Press, 1968).

[48]Borgen points out that for Philo "the search for the beyond by the mind could not bring about the encounter with God. God had to reveal himself, as it is said in Gen. 12:7: 'God was seen by Abraham' (*Abr.* 77)." Peder Borgen, *Philo of Alexandria: An Exegete for His Time,* (NovTSup 86; Leiden: Brill, 1997) 218.

[49]H. Koester, *History, Culture, and Religion of the Hellenistic Age,* (Philadelphia: Fortress, 1982) 149, 157-59; see also *Migr.* 179.

[50]*The Manual of Epictetus* in *The Stoic and Epicurean Philosophers,* (ed. Whitney J. Oates; trans. P. E. Matheson; New York: Random House, 1940) 476.

[51]Sandmel, *Philo's Place,* 107.

[52]Harry A. Wolfson, *Philo: Foundations of Religious Philosophy in Judaism, Christianity and Islam,* (2 vols.; Cambridge: Harvard University Press, 1947), 1.57-68.

[53]Ibid., 307.

[54]John R. Bartlett, *Jews in the Hellenistic World: Josephus, Aristeas, the Sibylline Oracles, Eupolemus,* (Cambridge Commentaries on Writings of the Jewish and Christian World 200 BC to AD 200, 1.1; Cambridge: Cambridge University Press, 1985) 146-47.

[55]For a discussion of power and imitation in Paul see Elizabeth A. Castelli, *Imitating Paul: A Discourse of Power,* (Literary Currents in Biblical Interpretation; Louisville, KY: Westmnister/John Knox, 1991).

[56]Gregory E. Sterling, *Historiography and Self-Definition: Josephos, Luke-Acts and Apologetic Historiography,* (NovTSup 64; Leiden: E. J. Brill, 1992) 306.

[57]*A.J.* 4.197; cf. *B. J.* 6.107.

[58]Sterling, *Historiography,* 307.

[59]For example, see John M. G. Barclay, *Jews in the Mediterranean Diaspora: From Alexander to Trajan,* (323 BCE - 117 CE). (Edinburgh: T & T Clark, 1996) 316-19, 320-35; Graydon F. Snyder, The Interaction of Jews with Non-Jews in Rome," *Judaism and Christianity in First Century Rome,* (ed Karl P. Donfried and Peter Richardson; Grand Rapids: Eerdmans, 1998); Michael Grant, *The Jews in the Roman World,* (London: Weidenfeld and Nicolson, 1973).

[60]Mason, " 'Should Any Wish to Enquire,' "78.

[61]Barclay, *Jews in the Mediterranean Diaspora,* 323, 328.

[62]Josephus also uses Abraham to illustrate the superiority of the Jewish constitution, but this will be the topic of a future article.

Chapter 7

Does Yahweh Take Risks?

Terrance Tiessen

*I*met Don Leggett when I joined the faculty of London College of
Bible and Missions as a rookie teacher. We had adjoining offices
and established a friendship which was profitable for my own theological development. We shared a common commitment to the general framework of Reformed theology even though he had done his
work as an Old Testament exegete and I as a systematic theologian.
For this reason, I will examine some Old Testament material in regard
to the pressing theological question of God's providential rule in the
world. This is particularly timely because of the stimulating work which
is being done by proponents of the "Open Model of God." This
term derives from the title of a book in which five evangelical scholars put forward a new understanding of God and his work in the
world.[1]

A more recent book has presented in greater detail the doctrine
of divine providence that is central to the openness model of God.[2]
As the title indicates, the model assumes that God takes risks in creating other beings to whom he gives the freedom to make their own
decisions and to determine the course of much of human history. In

this proposal, God himself is very "open" or responsive to the agency of his creatures. With this proposal before us, this essay will ask whether Yahweh, the covenant God of Israel, as he is portrayed in the Old Testament, puts his own plans and desires for the world at risk by giving to creatures a significant amount of self-determination. I will (1) outline the openness model of providence; (2) present the case that John Sanders and Gregory Boyd[3] make for the model ; (3) briefly assess the openness model; and (4) present a no-risk view of divine providence in the Old Testament narrative, with special reference to Leggett's work.[4]

The Open Model of God as Risk-Taker

Divine self-limitation

Fundamental to the openness model of God is the conviction that God is responsive to his creatures and that he has limited his own control in the world, in order to give them libertarian freedom. "Libertarian" freedom is one in which creatures have the power of contrary choice. Proponents of this view believe that in most situations, we could have acted differently than we did. This is considered to be the essence of authentic freedom, in distinction from the classical Augustinian notion that we are free provided we act voluntarily. In this regard, the openness model is no innovation because libertarian human freedom was the common assumption in the early centuries and has been strongly affirmed by Arminian theology in the Protestant tradition and by most forms of Roman Catholic theology. In general, Arminian theology has taught that God is not able to achieve his wishes in every instance because he has given freedom to his creatures and they are able to thwart his will on occasion. This was particularly stated in regard to salvation, where it was assumed that God wants all people to be saved but that some people reject his provision for their salvation and so God's desire is not fulfilled. The openness model has paid more attention to divine providence than earlier forms of Arminian theology did and it has thus drawn attention to the more general ways in which God's wishes are not achieved in the world.

It is important to recognize that this proposal is not denying God's sovereignty in the world. In the ultimate sense, God's will is done. But, God willed to create free creatures and, given the assumption that genuine freedom is libertarian, God thereby voluntarily limited the extent to which he can always achieve what he wishes. The rise of interest in this divine self-limitation seems to have been prompted especially by the need to defend God's goodness in the face of horrendous evil in the world, such as the holocaust. In the words of Hans Jonas: "not because he chose not to, but because he *could* not intervene did he fail to intervene . . . God . . . has divested himself of any power to interfere with the physical course of things; and . . . responds to the impact on his being by worldly events, not 'with a mighty hand and outstretched arm,' . . . but with the mutely insistent appeal of his unfulfilled goal."[5] This situation is very much God's choice so that his own freedom is not diminished by human freedom. However, God has chosen to restrain himself in order to give the creature room to act and flourish. This entails significant risk on God's part, because it means that there will be occasions when evil will occur which God can not prevent without withdrawing the freedom which he gave to the creature - and this can only very rarely be done or creaturely freedom becomes an illusion.

In the perspective of Peter Baelz, God wills his creation to be free and so he "withdraws a space from the world in order to let it be itself." God gives to the world "a real measure of independence. But he does not cease to care for his world. And he does not cease to work in and for his world. He comes. He calls. He shares. He gives and forgives. He creates and re-creates."[6] Since love creates in and for freedom, we might say that God creates the world by "persuading it to create itself." This involves experiment and risk, the potential for both triumph and disaster, but it is necessary because the loving Creator seeks and awaits the creature's own response. Even boundless love is, by its very nature, self-limiting. Consequently, there are many things that God can not do, though he would like to, yet we know that "God is already doing all that Love can do."[7] So, our trust is not grounded in God's power but in his love.

It is not that God is impotent, claims Hendrikus Berkhof, who does not wish to deny God's omnipotence. But God is "defenceless," not because he is unable to exercise power actively, but because he has chosen this special way to make his power felt.[8] Although God allows himself to be "limited and resisted by the freedom" of the partner he created, "all of salvation history guarantees that ultimately he will not lose his grip on the world and will not rest until he has—no, not conquered and subjugated but—led his human opponent to the true freedom of the sons of God. In his association with the world he is so great that he can remain present in it when he is cast out, and active when he is resisted."[9]

God's Openness to Change

Included in this model of divine responsiveness is the belief that God is open to changing his own plans in response to the will of his creatures, when this is good for them. Such "reciprocal relations between Creator and creature" are deemed to be lost in the traditional risk-free view of providence, where God "has a controlling relationship with the world such that everything works out in exhaustive detail just as God desired."[10] It appears to Vincent Brümmer that, if everything was determined by God in eternity, God would not be the sort of being to whom we could address meaningful petitions because he could not react to what we do or feel or ask. We could not say that God did something *because* we asked him to. In certain respects, God is immutable, particularly in that "we can trust him to remain *faithful* to his character."[11] It is precisely this faithfulness that is the ground of our trust when we bring our desires to God in prayer. But, in other respects, God is able to change, as in instances where he responds to contingent events and human actions.

God has intentions for the world but he does not have plans that are fixed and invariable. He is engaged in a dynamic relationship with his creatures, and the history of the world is the outworking of the combined agency of God and his creatures. God has good purposes for his creation and he does not change these but, in working toward the achievement of those purposes, God must respond to the actions and wishes of his creatures. He may even repent that he has done something because it did not turn out as he wished, and he may act differently than he had originally intended because of the way a situation has developed.

God's Relationship to Time

For centuries, theologians commonly taught that God was an absolutely timeless being who lived in an "eternal now." The idea developed early in the thought-life of the Church, under the influence of Middle-Platonism[12] and it was deemed necessary to God's unchangingness. But, the proponents of the openness of God consider this to be a Hellenized perversion of the biblical perspective. On the contrary, says Richard Swinburne, God "exists throughout all periods of time." This does not make him "time's prisoner, for the reason that although God and time exist together—God is a temporal being—those aspects of time which seem so threatening to his sovereignty only occur through his own voluntary choice. To the extent to which he is time's prisoner, he has chosen to be so. It is God, not time, who calls the shots."[13]

Putting together the belief that genuine creaturely freedom is libertarian and the understanding that God's eternity is everlasting (endless time) rather than timeless, the Open God theologians have arrived at their most controversial conclusion: namely, that God does not know the future comprehensively. If God infallibly foreknew every event and human action, it is argued, petitionary prayer would be meaningless. In the words of Vincent Brümmer, "no event could take place differently from the way it in fact does, and no human agent could act differently from the way it in fact does, for that would falsify

God's infallible foreknowledge, which would be logically impossible."[14] If the everlasting God had always possessed infallible knowledge of all future events in history, "then it would have to be foreknowledge, and we are back with the problem of determinism."[15] It is the conviction of John Lucas that a view of providence in which God foreknows and foreordains the details of the future course of events, though widely held, "is un-Christian. Apart from leaving no room for human freedom, it poses the problem of evil in irresoluble form, and subverts the moral teaching of Jesus."[16]

Richard Swinburne also complains that foreknowledge is impossible because it affirms backward causation, in that the actions of agents cause God's earlier beliefs. "We act freely and God's beliefs are as they are because of how we have acted."[17] Since God is necessarily and eternally perfectly free, he must be ignorant even of his own future actions "except in so far as his perfect goodness constrains him to act in certain ways."[18] God's omniscience concerns the past, which is causally unaffectable, and his omnipotence concerns the future, which is causally affectable. If God's omniscience included knowledge of his own future actions, he would no longer be free.[19] Furthermore, according to David Bartholomew, God's ignorance of the future in detail is a consequence of the role of chance within the world as he has made it.[20]

The denial of divine foreknowledge is not deemed to be a rejection of divine omniscience. God knows everything which can be known, but this does not include the future, which contains various alternative possibilities, any one of which could be actualized.[21] Through God's intimate knowledge of all human beings, he knows "the precise range of alternatives available to every individual."[22] God could have created a deterministic universe in which he knew the one possible course that future events would take. But, "we all know from personal experience that this is not the sort of universe which he has in fact created." Rather, God has created a world with an open future in which various possibilities could be actualized; a world, therefore, where events have two-way contingency and human beings are personal agents who are able freely to decide which of the possibilities presented to them they will realize." Given God's decision to create this sort of world, "he has limited his own possibilities for knowing beforehand which future potentialities will become actual."[23]

Having reviewed the basic features of the open model of God, we are ready to see how such a model has been derived from the Old Testament revelation of God and his activity in the world by proponents of the openness model.

The Old Testament Through the Lenses of a Divine Risk Model

The Risk God Took in Creating Humans

To Sanders, God's creation of humans in his image and his delegation of responsibility to them (Gen 1:26-28) is indication of his willingness to share power with them. "God sovereignly decides that not everything will be up to God."[24] Within the rules that God has established there is freedom for humans to be creative. Early in the narrative, we learn that Adam and Eve broke those rules but the predicted judgment is not realized because God does for the first time what becomes a pattern in his dealings with humans—he relents "from negative consequences in favor of mercy."[25]

In the generations that follow, sin increases, and God "regrets his decision to go ahead with the creation in light of these tragic developments."[26] But, in spite of the deep grief that God experienced, he does not give up hope and he continues his project through Noah's family. Eventually, God makes himself vulnerable by binding up with Abraham the future blessing of the human race, but he wished to find out how completely Abraham trusted him. With the test given to Abraham, God came to know what he had not known (Gen 22:12), and Sanders sees in these words "serious theological problems regarding divine immutability and foreknowledge."[27] There was risk in the incident for both God and Abraham. "God takes the risk that

Abraham will exercise trust" and Abraham "takes the risk that God will provide a way into the future."[28] In his ongoing relationship with Abraham, God then reveals that he is open to his creatures, particularly to their requests in prayer, because he wants "a genuine relationship" with them.[29] In the intercession of Abraham for Sodom, "we see that God sovereignly chooses not to govern the world without our input."[30]

Proponents of a risk-free model of divine providence frequently view the experience of Joseph as paradigmatic of a situation in which God accomplishes his sovereign will even through the sinful deeds of human beings. Sanders grants that "a risk-free reading of the text is possible" but he thinks that it has several problems. Responsibility for the selling of Joseph is ascribed to his brothers (Gen 37:28; 45:4-5) and their deed was sin against Joseph (Gen 42:22), an evil which can not be ascribed to God without problem. Consequently, Genesis 50:20 is best understood as a statement that "God has brought something good out of their evil actions" rather than a description of God's determining everything in Joseph's life.[31]

The story of Israel's deliverance from Egypt is full of problems if viewed from a risk-free model of providence, suggests Sanders, but it indicates that "God works with what is available in the situation" because he has chosen not to "ride roughshod over his creatures."[32] There was no comprehensive divine blueprint for the events and God took significant risk because key people in the deliverance that is recorded might have failed to do what God wished. This would include, for instance, the midwives, the mother and daughter of Moses, and even Moses himself. This would have required God to try other means of liberating his people. It could have been a very different story than the one that we now have. Even divine hardening was not a guarantee of the outcome, "for Pharaoh and his advisers are all hardened and yet they disagree with one another."[33] In the years following the deliverance from Egypt, as Moses becomes an intercessor on behalf of a rebellious people in danger of God's judgment, he does not get everything that he requests. But, "God takes Moses' concerns seriously, even to the point of twice changing the divine plan." What would have happened if Moses had not interceded we do not know but the future was shaped to some extent by Moses himself.[34]

Against the classical theist insistence that the biblical language of divine repentance is anthropomorphic, Sanders argues that a careful analysis of the texts which speak of divine repentance or which deny that God repents reveals the consistent responsiveness of God to human activity while maintaining his prerogative to reject human petitions. It was precisely this prerogative of Yahweh to change his mind that led Jonah to refuse to preach (Jonah 4:2), but Hezekiah took advantage of it and obtained an extension of his life through the changing of God's mind (2 Kgs 20:5).[35] On the other hand, the disobedience of Eli's sons led to a negative change in God's mind and a cutting off of Eli's household from the priesthood which they had been promised in perpetuity (1 Sam 2:30).[36]

These and other incidents of divine responsiveness and suffering lead Sanders and others to conclude "that there is sufficient biblical warrant for affirming that the future is in some respects indefinite even for God."[37] Thus, some predictions in Scripture do not come to pass at all, such as the warning of Jonah to Nineveh (2 Kgs 20) or are not fulfilled exactly, such as the qualification of Jacob's blessing by the blessing on Esau (Gen 27:27-40). Where texts indicate that a future is definite it is either because God determined that it should happen that way or because "God knows the event will result from a chain of causal factors that are presently in place." On the other hand, some texts indicate that God does not know the future because he "has not decided what it will be. The matter is open for both God and creatures."[38] Predictive prophecy is, therefore, no indication of comprehensive divine foreknowledge. Many prophecies are conditional, similar to the prediction Jonah made to Nineveh. What gives us the impression that God knows the future is that the conditions are so often fulfilled that predicted acts of libertarianly free people often do occur as foretold.

Sanders expresses concern about the over reading of some Old Testament texts which refer to God's control of specific situations, extending them to teach that everything is caused by God. Examples cited include the following: Isaiah 45:7 ("I make weal and create woe; I the Lord do all these things) which "pertains to Yahweh's dealings with Israel, not the entire cosmos;"[39] Amos 3:6 ("Does disaster befall a city, unless the Lord has done it?") which likewise has a specific instance in the history of Israel in view; (also Lam 3:38; Prov 16:9; 21:1; and Exod 4:11).[40] These are statements regarding specific and limited instances and not general pronouncements of God's pancausality. "God is indeed a potter and a king but one whose clay and subjects sometimes cooperate with and sometimes rebel against divine initiatives."[41] This is the risk that God took knowingly in giving his creatures authentic freedom. But, God is "involved in a historical project, not an eternal plan." He has a goal but remains flexible, responding to the surprises that occur as his plans fail to be achieved.[42]

The Risk God Runs in His War with Rebellious Beings

Most presentations of the openness model of God have focused on the role of human agents within a world in which God has voluntarily limited his own control by giving them libertarian freedom without giving up his own purposes or his involvement in the world as he works to achieve them. An important new dimension of God's openness to the world has been introduced by Gregory Boyd.[43] He works within the basic framework of the openness model as I have described it, but he is particularly interested in the way in which God's control of the world is limited by the activity of rebellious spiritual creatures, Satan and his demons.

Boyd believes that the basic biblical understanding of the cosmos is a "warfare worldview". In this perspective "the good and evil, fortunate or unfortunate, aspects of life are to be interpreted largely as the result of good and evil, friendly or hostile, spirits warring against each other and against us."[44] The truth attested by both the Old Testament and the varied mythologies found around the world is "that God's good creation has in fact been seized by hostile, evil, cosmic forces that are seeking to destroy God's beneficent plan for the cosmos." God is waging war against these forces and has secured their overthrow through Jesus Christ. The church is "a decisive means by which this final overthrow is to be carried out."[45]

Boyd's quest for a new model of providence is significantly stimulated by the need to address the reality of evil in the world. He posits that the "classical-philosophical theistic tradition" has rightly assumed that God is perfectly loving and good but wrongly assumed "that divine omnipotence entails meticulous control."[46] By contrast, Boyd's own "warfare worldview" works on "the assumption that divine goodness does not completely control or in any sense will evil; rather, good and evil are at war with one another." This means, of course, that God does not now have "exhaustive, meticulous control over the world." Rather, "God must work with, and battle against, other created beings. While none of these beings can ever match God's own power, each has some degree of genuine influence within the cosmos."[47] Boyd believes that this perspective will generate less theologizing *about* evil and more war *against* it. Particular evils "flow from the wills of creatures" and we need not speculate about a divine purpose for them but we should revolt against them.[48]

Theological followers of Thomas Aquinas and John Calvin have believed that God maintains absolute control of the world he has created even though his creatures are genuinely free. The will of God's eternal purpose or decree is always done. That is the "classical theism" against which the openness model is launching its major protest. The openness model functions within the tradition that Protestants frequently identify as Arminianism. However, Boyd and other theologians of the openness model believe that Arminian theologians have generally not carried through their understanding of the nature of creaturely freedom to its logical and biblical conclusion. They have continued to affirm that God's immutability, timelessness, impassibility and other attributes are derived "more from Hellenistic philosophy than from the Bible, and they render genuine freedom on the part of created beings impossible."[49]

The experience of Job offers a good case study for comparing the interpretations of risk and non-risk models of divine providence. Given Boyd's interest in the spiritual opponents of God, this is a particularly significant event for observing God's role in the world where evil occurs. When Yahweh finally appears to Job (Job 38-41), the thrust of his speeches to Job is "to drive home the point—the point of the entire epic poem—that neither Job nor his 'friends' are in a position to understand the goings-on of the vast cosmos Yahweh has created." The speeches reveal "that one aspect of Yahweh's incomprehensible task in creating and preserving order in the world is to contend against the cosmic forces that perpetually threaten it." Running the cosmos "is no easy matter, even for the Creator. There are forces of chaos (to say nothing of the *satan*) to contend with. Unless Job can do it himself, the poem suggests, he ought to refrain from arrogant accusations (38:1-41:34)." [50] From Daniel's delayed answer to prayer (Dan 10) and from Israel's unexpected defeat by the fury of Chemosh (2 Kgs 3:26-27), we learn again that "things go on behind the scenes of the human drama, sometimes thwarting the will of God."[51] Evil does not happen because it is the will of God; "it is rather the mystery of what goes on among the gods in 'the great assembly' and in an incomprehensibly vast cosmos threatened by cosmic forces."[52] Boyd concludes that, "without undermining the sovereignty of God, the Bible generally portrays the cosmos as more like a divinely governed democracy than a divinely controlled dictatorship, and this democracy encompasses, but greatly transcends, free human beings."[53]

A General Assessment of the Openness Model of God

Human Freedom

The openness model of God has been severely criticized in recent years, particularly because of its rejection of comprehensive divine foreknowledge. It can not, however, be easily dismissed. It arises from careful reading of the biblical revelation and a desire to represent Scripture in a coherent manner. It criticizes the philosophy that underlies classical theism from the conviction that the biblical witness forces us in a different direction. Fundamental to the model is the assumption that authentic human freedom is libertarian. In order to give this kind of freedom to his creatures, God has limited his ability to realize his own desires at every moment in history. As an everlasting rather than an absolutely timeless being, God is engaged in history in a way that opens him up to being influenced in a genuinely reciprocal relationship with the creatures. Being unable to predict with complete accuracy what a libertarianly free creature would do in a particular circumstance, God works ceaselessly to bring good out of evil and to move the world toward his purposes for it. Given the premises of the openness model, its conclusions are generally sound. If one is unsatisfied with those conclusions, the premises need to be reexamined. It is not appropriate to affirm the premises while rejecting the conclusion to which they are deemed to lead unless one can show that this conclusion is not necessitated by those premises.

Scripture does not give us a definition of morally responsible creaturely freedom. Theologians like Leggett or myself, who work within the Augustinian tradition, and with a no-risk model of divine providence, believe that moral responsibility only requires the freedom of spontaneity or of voluntariness. People need not have the power of contrary choice to be responsibly free, they only need to be choosing willingly, without external coercion. This understanding of human freedom is not prescribed by particular biblical texts; it is derived from the conclusion that the biblical narrative presents God as meticulously in control in the world of his creation. In God's sovereignty, the will of his eternal purpose is always accomplished. He takes no risks but is always completely in control. Yet creatures (human and angelic) are morally responsible and therefore free, in that they act voluntarily, not under coercion by God or by anything external to themselves.

God, Time and Knowledge

Gerald Bray has wisely observed that "the conceivability of eternity is more a philosophical than a strictly theological issue, but its implications are so great that it can hardly be ignored."[54] Indisputably, God acts in our time. All that he created exists in time relationship to all else that is created; it has an existence that can be measured and that is experienced as a succession of moments. We call "now" the moment which we are presently experiencing but we recollect moments in our past experience and we anticipate that there will be moments which we have not yet experienced. Whether or not God has any personal experience of this succession of moments I do not know, but I know that our experience of such succession is "real" to him as the one who created us in this mode of being. Yesterday may not be the "past" to God, in the way it is to us, but he knows that what we are experiencing (and what he is experiencing with us) today, comes after what we experienced yesterday and before what we will experience tomorrow.[55] For this reason, I doubt that an assertion of timelessness is helpful in our effort to understand how God knows a future which is yet to be effected by our free agency. Even if God does not experience the difference between today and tomorrow in the same way that we do, it is still true (if God has foreknowledge, as we assert) that God knows today what will happen tomorrow. Since his knowledge is "before" *from our perspective*, the perceived problem of the actuality of the future is not avoided by asserting that it is not "before" in God's experience unless that is our way of asserting that God's experience of time is not the same as ours although our experience of it is real and known to him.[56]

It was "when the fullness of time had come" that God sent his Son (Gal 4:4), and it was "at the right time" that Christ died for the ungodly (Rom 5:6); it was not until his "time" came that Jesus went to Jerusalem (John 13:1), and it will be "when his time comes" that the lawless one will be destroyed by Christ (2 Thess 2:6). Jesus did not know when that time would be, when questioned about it by his disciples, although the Father did know (Mt 24:36). In short, whatever God's own experience of time may be, he is not excluded from acting in our own time or from knowing the time-relatedness of all the events of created history. Indeed, he determines the very time at which those events occur, while not negating the agency of creatures which bring events to reality at a time.

The openness model argues that God can not know the future acts of libertarianly free creatures because these do not exist until the decision has been made and the action taken. However, if one thinks of God's omniscience as his knowledge of all true propositions, there is no problem. God can know the truth value of propositions about the future even though that truth value is yet to be effected by the actors who will make the propositions true as statements about the present.[57] At the time that I call "yesterday," God knew that I would write these words today, even though it was not an actuality until today when I chose to do this rather than something else. So, even libertarian freedom and divine temporality do not necessitate limited divine knowledge of the future. What God knows ahead of time (from our perspective) is the future that comes about through the decisions of free human agents (and would be so, even if they were libertarianly free). If people decided differently, God's knowledge would have been different. This does not entail that the future must be undecided; it affirms rather that the future which actually comes to be is determined by responsible agents at that time, that those actual decisions have truth value, and that God knows their truth value.

David Basinger identifies three commonly propounded options regarding God's knowledge: present knowledge, simple foreknowledge and middle knowledge. His own position favors present knowledge, the approach of the openness model. In a recent article, his primary objective is to demonstrate that simple foreknowledge does not have significant advantages over present knowledge, particularly as an aid in God's control over earthly affairs. He does grant, however, that "a God with MK [middle knowledge]—a God who knows before he acts exactly what will occur as a result—is in a better position to ensure his desired ends than is a God without MK."[58] The same is not the case if God has simple foreknowledge. Basinger illustrates with the case of a lottery player who knows the winning numbers ahead of time.

> Our lottery player can beneficially utilize her fore-knowledge of the winning numbers *only if* she has access to this information *before* she decides what numbers she will play. However, if our player has always possessed complete foreknowledge, then there has never been a time at which she foreknew what the winning numbers would be but did not already know at this same time what numbers she would choose to play. Thus if our player has complete foreknowledge, her knowledge of next week's winning numbers cannot influence what numbers she chooses to play and thus is of no practical benefit.[59]

The application of this illustration to the planning of God's eternal purpose or decree is obvious. If God only has simple foreknowledge (i.e. completely knows only the *actual* future), then he can not decide how he will act on the basis of a knowledge of how other creatures would respond. He knows, eternally, his own action and the creature's at the same logical moment, even if God is absolutely timeless.

Following the lead of the 17th century Jesuit theologian, Luis de Molina, some thinkers have attempted to provide God with the necessary opportunity for planning his action, through the concept of middle knowledge. God knows what people *would* do in all the possible situations that never occur (i.e., counterfactuals) and he chooses to actualize the world in which libertarianly free creatures make the choices that serve his purposes. On the matter of God's knowledge of counterfactuals, however, I agree with the proponents of the openness model that it is impossible (even for God) to know counterfactuals of libertarian freedom. *Actual* libertarianly free future events can be known because they have truth value. The same is not true of libertarianly free counterfactuals, events which would have happened if important factors had been different than they were. By definition of the terms, it is impossible to know what a person would decide to do in a given situation if the person's decision is conceived to be indeterministically free. Surely, as William Craig says, there are many future counterfactuals that do have truth value, for example, numerous negative statements concerning the future. One who has God's comprehensive knowledge of the past and present can identify with certainty many things which will *not* happen in the future. Unfortunately, this is not enough to satisfy the requirements of Molinist middle knowledge. For the proposal to work, God must know what a person would do in every possible situation and one can not have such knowledge if the person's decision is ultimately indeterminate, awaiting the apparently arbitrary choice of the free agent when the moment of decision arrives.[60]

In short, for God to accomplish his purposes in the world all the time, creatures must be voluntarily, rather than libertarianly, free and God must have a knowledge of counterfactuals. God's knowledge of the future must be comprehensive, including the acts of free creatures, both actual and possible, so that he is able to plan his own actions and include within the process of history the spontaneous actions of morally responsible creatures without risking failure to achieve his own purposes. I believe that just such a picture is provided by the Old Testament narrative.

The Old Testament Through the Lenses of a No-Risk Model

Leggett's No-Risk View of the Old Testament Narrative

In Leggett's analysis of the message of Habakkuk, he develops a fine overall perspective on divine providence as it is presented in the Old Testament. God's relationship to history is summarized under four points:[61] (1) "History is under divine control," and this is taught and implied in so many texts that "one hardly knows where to begin: Gen 20:6; 45:5; 50:20; Ruth 2:3; 2 Sam 17:4; 2 Chr 36:17; Isa 7:18-20; 10:5-19; 37:26; Jer 25:9; Amos 4:6-11; Hab 1:6"; (2) "History is following a divine plan (Hab 2:44-45; Deut 32:8)"; (3) "History progresses under a divine timetable (Dan 9:24-27)"; and (4) "Events within our world are connected with the divine purpose for the people of God. Cyrus' decree, allowing the Jews to return from exile, is a prudent and strategic political move on his part, but it is part of the divine purpose as well."

In the biblical narrative regarding the exile, Leggett finds "a fascinating interplay between a sovereign God working out his purposes and the freely chosen activities of those agents through whom these purposes are worked."[62] Clearly this is a compatibilist view of human freedom, in which God's will is always done but human "free decisions are the means by which God works out his purpose."[63] It was God who brought the king of the Babylonians against God's people (2 Chr 36:16-17) but this was triggered by the rebellion of Zedekiah against Babylon (Jer 52:3). This is a perspective that runs throughout the Old Testament narrative. "Being sovereign and in control of history, [God] brings Israel out of Egypt, the Philistines from Captor and the Arameans from Kir (Amos 9:7)."[64] Isaiah's vision was very much like Habakkuk's; "the Assyrian king is God's razor hired from beyond the river to shave their heads, legs and beards (Isa 7:20) and is the rod of God's anger and the club of his wrath, dispatched against a godless people (Isa 10:5,6; cf. Deut 28:49-50).'"[65]

Habakkuk struggled precisely because of "his faith in a God who was both holy and righteous, powerful and good."[66] Leggett rejects the answer to suffering put forward by Harold Kushner, in *Why Bad Things Happen to Good People.* In that view, "God would like to do more to overcome suffering but his hands are tied; he can't because he is not omnipotent." Leggett grants that this extricates the Lord from the problem but he believes the price paid to achieve this is too great.[67]

Joseph's Experience

As one who works within the framework of meticulous divine providence which is evident in Leggett's work, I find the words of Joseph to his brothers (Gen 50:20) to be an excellent paradigm for our approach to situations where other people transgress God's moral precepts and we suffer as a result. The distinction between God's intention and the intention of human actors is important; God's intention was (and always is) good. God was acting to realize that intention in and through the very different intention and evil action of Joseph's brothers.[68] In retrospect, Joseph was able to discern God's intention and to understand why God had allowed him to be sold into slavery in Egypt. Joseph could see the good that had resulted, but the text "does not picture God as *post eventu* deflecting the evil action of the brothers and transforming it into something good." Both God and the brothers had intentions in the act itself.[69]

God's Control in the Spiritual World

In my reading of the Old Testament, Satan and the demons are never able to act contrary to God's sovereign purpose. Even in their evil action, they accomplish the will of God. I have significant appreciation for Boyd's treatment of the biblical material concerning spiritual conflict, but I disagree in regard to the risk which Boyd believes God has undertaken and regarding the seriousness of the threat that the rebellious spirits pose to his rule in the world. Satan himself is very powerful and is indeed the enemy, the Satan, the opponent of God, but God is always completely in control.[70] As Stephen Noll puts it, "God has committed himself to rule through the free, and thus potentially wicked, wills of his creatures."[71]

Because of the evident dominion of God, Satan is sometimes represented as God's servant rather than God's opponent. Sydney Page notes that "contemporary biblical scholars do not agree on the Joban conception of Satan."[72] Page and Noll's own conclusion on the matter seems highly plausible. Both of them reject the suggestion that Satan is "a title designating an officer of the divine council, like a prosecuting attorney in a courtroom,"[73] given that "there is no evidence for a legal position of 'the satan' inside or outside of Israel.[74] God is able to use Satan in punishing sin because "his malicious intent is overlapped by the Lord's righteous indignation."[75] In 1 Kings 22:19-23 and 1 Chronicles 21:1, "Satan operates in heaven, not because he occupies a post or wants to serve God but because the repaying of evil in this case is 'an act of God,' that is, not the normal working out of natural justice by which the wicked steps into his own trap (Ps 7:14-16)."[76] Page further observes the difficulty created for the view that Satan was understood as a prosecutor by noting that the initiative in the first meeting comes from God. This "immediately establishes that [God] is in control."[77] Indeed, "Satan implictly acknowledges that Job's fate is in God's hands and that Satan himself has no power to do anything independently of God's will." For Job to be afflicted, "Yahweh must stretch out his hand and strike what the man has (1:11)."[78]

God's use of evil spirits as a form of judgment is exemplified in the experience of Abimelech who murdered sixty nine of his brothers to consolidate his power. Because of this, "God sent an evil spirit between Abimelech and the lords of Shechem" after he had ruled over Israel for three years (Judg 9:23a) and this resulted in much civil strife, war and death. The phrase "evil spirit" that is used here is identical to the term used of the spirit that troubled Saul[79] and that evil spirit is described as "from the Lord" six out of the seven times that it is mentioned (1 Sam 16:14; cf 18:10; 19:9).[80] "The contrast between the Spirit of Yahweh and the evil spirit virtually demands that the evil spirit be understood as an external power that existed independently of Saul" not simply as a psychological problem, but it is best not to view this as an Old Testament counterpart to the demonization encountered in the New Testament. It was periodic, was from the Lord, was judgment for sin, and was relieved by music.[81] Similarly, King Ahab was lured to his death by an evil spirit that is serving God (1 Kgs 22:19-22).

The story of Job is one of the clearest illustrations of God's *permission* relative to Satan. I strongly disagree with Brother Andrew's assessment that Job was guilty of the error of fatalism when he said "the Lord gave, and the Lord has taken away" (Job 1:21).[82] Granted, it was the Sabeans who killed some of his sons and daughters (Job 1:13-15), it was lightning that killed his sheep and shepherds (1:16), it was Chaldeans who raided and stole his camels (1:17), it was a great wind that knocked down the house that killed more of his children (1:19), but Job rightly understood that forces of nature (wind and lightning) and greedy, violent people (on that occasion, Sabeans and Chaldeans) all do their deeds within God's providence. Job did not then realize that he was also under assault from Satan who sought to destroy Job's faith in God. What the narrative tells us, however, is that Satan himself, the most powerful of all evil beings, is restrained or released by God to do what he does (1:6-12).[83]

God repeatedly establishes the boundary within which Satan can work. God first gives Job's possessions and then his body into Satan's hand (Job 1:12; 2:6), but Satan "is not granted the right to seize Job's most important possession, his soul (compare Luke 12:16-23)."[84] God authorizes Satan's action and he takes responsibility for its effects on Job (Job 2:3; 42:11) but then he blesses him even more richly in his later days than in his earlier life. Page aptly sums up his analysis of the Old Testament teaching regarding Satan, in Job, Zechariah and 1 Chronicles. Throughout these passages, Satan "is subordinated to God, and never is Satan portrayed as capable of thwarting God's purposes. Nor is Satan's influence over humanity such as to relieve anyone of responsibility for sin."[85]

Conclusion

This brief look at two different readings of the level of risk that Yahweh took upon himself, according to the Old Testament narrative, demonstrates the inevitable hermeneutical circle with which theologians and biblical interpreters necessarily work. We endeavour to derive from the biblical narrative the major features of our doctrine of providence. On the other hand, the need for theological and philosophical coherence puts certain constraints upon the way in which we read the various aspects of the narrative. A crucial turning point seems to lie in one's definition of the nature of morally responsible creaturely freedom. Those who are convinced that authentic freedom is libertarian inevitably see greater divine risk in God's activity in the world than those who believe that God's sovereignty requires a different definition of creaturely freedom.

Don Leggett and I work within the theological tradition that has been particularly impressed by biblical descriptions of the sovereignty of God. His knowledge is comprehensive because the future that God knows is the future he has chosen. Theologians working within this model have insisted that this complete control of history by God does not eliminate the genuine agency of creatures, human and angelic. I have proposed that the concept of "middle knowledge," although originally developed to preserve God's ultimate control in the face of libertarian creaturely freedom, can only be validly incorporated into a model that defines freedom as voluntary or spontaneous. God's knowledge of what a creature would do in hypothetical situations is only possible if freedom is of this kind. However, it is having this knowledge that enables God to take freely chosen creaturely actions into account when he decides what will actually happen in the process of world history.

The openness model doubts that creatures are genuinely free unless they are libertarianly free. This has always been assumed by Arminian theologies. God has therefore been understood as taking some risk in creating free creatures. He chose not to be able to achieve his will in every instance, including the highly important desire that everyone be saved from sin and its condemnation. Arminian theologies have generally assumed, however, that God knows the actual future comprehensively and some (Molinists) have even believed that he knows all the possible futures that could come about if circumstances were different. The value of the openness model is precisely at this point where it makes classic Arminian theologians nervous. Adherents of the openness model are pressing others within the Arminian tradition to take more seriously the extent to which Yahweh's decision to give creatures libertarian freedom limits his range of control in the world, including a measure of ignorance concerning the future acts of free creatures. This is not a rationalistic move; openness theologians feel compelled in this direction by the seriousness with which the biblical narrative presents God's responsive engagement with his creatures. For this reason, the current discussion is very constructive. It forces all of us to listen carefully to Scripture, to discern the dominant thrust of its narrative, and to construct our understanding of God and his work in the world in a way that is coherent or self-consistent.

Notes

[1] Clark Pinnock, Richard Rice, John Sanders, William Hasker and David Basinger, *The Openness of God: A Biblical Challenge to the Traditional Understanding of God* (Downers Grove, IL: InterVarsity, 1994).

[2] John Sanders, *The God Who Risks: A Theology of Providence* (Downers Grove, IL: InterVarsity, 1998).

[3] Gregory A. Boyd, *God at War: The Bible and Spiritual Conflict* (Downers Grove, IL: InterVarsity, 1997). Another book by Boyd in which he specifically addresses the doctrine of providence has been announced but is not available at the time of my writing.

[4] Portions of this material are adapted from my book, *Providence and Prayer: How Does God Work in the World* (Downers Grove, IL: InterVarsity, 2000).

[5] In "The Concept of God After Auschwitz. A Jewish Voice," *JR* 69 (1987) 109-10, cited by Marcel Sarot, "Omnipotence and Self-Limitation," in *Christian Faith and Philosophical Theology: Essays in Honour of Vincent Brümmer Presented on The Occasion of The Twenty-fifth Anniversary of His Professorship in The Philosophy of Religion in The University of Utrecht* (ed. Gijsbert van den Brink, Luco J. van den Brom and Marcel Sarot; Kampen: Kok Pharos, 1992) 175.

[6] Peter Baelz, *Does God Answer Prayer?* (London: Darton, Longman & Todd, 1982) 26.

[7] Ibid., 28.

[8] Hendrikus Berkhof, *Christian Faith: An Introduction to the Study of the Faith* (rev. ed; trans Sierd Woudstra; Grand Rapids: Eerdmans, 1986) 141.

[9] Ibid., 223.

[10] Sanders, *The God Who Risks*, 39.

[11] Vincent Brümmer, *What Are We Doing When We Pray? A Philosophical Enquiry* (London: SCM, 1984) 40.

[12] Alan G. Padgett, *God, Eternity and the Nature of Time* (New York: St. Martin's Press, 1992) 42.

[13] Richard Swinburne, *The Christian God* (Oxford: Clarendon, 1994) 140.

[14] Brümmer, *When We Pray*, 41. In regard to knowledge concerning true propositions, Richard Swinburne states this point succinctly: "if humans are sometimes free in the sense that sometimes their choice at a time as to how they will act is not determined by any prior cause (nor does reason make it inevitable how they will act), then they are sometimes in a position to make false any belief that some person has about how they will act. Whatever proposition I believe in advance about what you will do, if you act freely in this sense, you have it in your power to make my belief false. Hence no one can be guaranteed to have true beliefs in advance about the actions of free agents" (*The Christian God* [Oxford: Clarendon, 1994], 131).

[15] Brümmer, *When We Pray*, 42.

[16] J. R. Lucas, *The Future: An Essay on God, Temporality and Truth* (Oxford: Basil Blackwell, 1989) 227.

[17] Swinburne, *The Christian God*, 132.

[18] Ibid., 134.

[19] Ibid.

[20]David Bartholomew, *God of Chance* (London: SCM, 1984) 148.

[21]As Swinburne puts it, God's omniscience must be defined "not as knowledge at each period of time, of all true propositions, but as knowledge of all propositions that it is logically possible that he entertain then and that, if entertained by God then, are true, and that it is logically possible for God to know them without the possibility of error" (*The Christian God*, 133).

[22]Richard Rice, *God's Foreknowledge*. Revised ed. (Minneapolis: Bethany House, 1985) 56; citing 1 Sam 16:7; Ps 94:11; 139:2-4; Matt 10:30; Heb 4:2.

[23]Brümmer, *When We Pray*, 43-44.

[24]Sanders, *The God Who Risks*, 44.

[25]Ibid., 48.

[26]Ibid., 49.

[27]Ibid., 52.

[28]Ibid., 53.

[29]Ibid.

[30]Ibid., 54.

[31]Ibid., 55.

[32]Ibid., 57.

[33]Ibid., 59.

[34]Ibid., 64-66.

[35]Ibid., 69-71.

[36]Ibid., 71.

[37]Ibid., 73. In this regard, Sanders recommends Terence Fretheim's book *The Suffering of God: An Old Testament Perspective* (OBT; Philadelphia: Fortress, 1984).

[38]Sanders, *The God Who Risks*, 75.

[39]Ibid., 82.

[40]Ibid., 82-85.

[41]Ibid., 87.

[42]Ibid., 88.

[43]Boyd, *God at War*.

[44]Ibid., 13.

[45]Ibid., 19.

[46]Ibid., 20.

[47]Ibid.

[48]Ibid., 22.

[49]Ibid., 49.

[50]Ibid., 148.

[51]Ibid., 148-49.

[52]Ibid., 149.

[53]Ibid., 165.

[54]Gerald Bray, *The Doctrine of God* (Contours of Christian Theology; Downers Grove, IL: InterVarsity, 1993) 83.

[55]As Paul Helm says, God understands what it is like for a person to have had a birthday "ten days ago." (*Eternal God: A Study of God Without Time* [Oxford: Clarendon, 1988] 25).

[56]Paul Helm suggests that "the concept of foreknowledge applies not to a timeless knower's knowledge of certain events or actions, but to a temporal agent's recognition of timeless knowledge under certain temporal conditions" (*Eternal God*, 98).

[57]Helm: "The propositions are true now, but what the propositions are about has not yet occurred" (*Eternal God*, 117).

[58]David Basinger, "Can an Evangelical Christian Justifiably Deny God's Exhaustive Knowledge of the Future?" *CSR* 25, no. 2 (1995) 136. Cf. also David Basinger, "Simple Foreknowledge and Providential Control: A Response to Hunt," *FP* 10 no. 3 (July 1993) 421-27.

[59]Basinger, "Can an Evangelical Christian Justifiably Deny?", 136-37.

[60]John Feinberg rightly asks: "how can God *know*, even counterfactually, what *would* follow from anything else unless some form of determinism is correct?" ("God Ordains All Things," in *Predestination and Free Will: Four Views of Divine Sovereignty and Human Freedom,* ed. David Basinger and Randall Basinger; [Downers Grove, IL: InterVarsity, 1986] 34).

[61]Donald A. Leggett, *Loving God and Disturbing Men: Preaching from the Prophets* (Burlington, ON: Welch, 1990) 122.

[62]Ibid., 122-23.

[63]Ibid., 123.

[64]Ibid., 96.

[65]Ibid.

[66]Ibid., 119.

[67]Ibid.

[68]As D. A. Carson observes, Joseph's statement "so it was not you who sent me here," is hyperbolic. *Divine Sovereignty and Human Responsibility: Biblical Perspectives in Tension* (Marshalls Theological Library 7; London: Marshall, Morgan and Scott, 1981) 10.

[69]Carson, *Divine Sovereignty*, 10, taking issue with G. C. Berkouwer.

[70]Cf. Clinton Arnold, *Powers of Darkness: Principalities and Powers in Paul's Letters* (Downers Grove, IL: InterVarsity, 1992) 101.

[71]Stephen Noll, *Angels of Light, Powers of Darkness: Thinking Biblically About Angels, Satan and Principalities* (Downers Grove, IL: InterVarsity, 1988) 106.

[72]Sydney H. T. Page, *Powers of Evil: A Biblical Study of Satan and Demons* (Grand Rapids: Baker, 1995) 25.

[73]Noll, *Angels*, 103, rejecting the proposal of Gerhard von Rad in *TDNT*, 2.73-75.

[74]Noll, *Angels*, 103; cf. Page, *Powers*, 26. Both cite Peggy Day's failure to discover an office of prosecuting attorney that could have provided a model (*An Adversary in Heaven: 'Satan' in the Hebrew Bible* [HSM 43 Atlanta: Scholars, 1988] 34-43).

[75]Noll, *Angels*, 104-5.

[76]Ibid., 104.

[77]Page, *Powers*, 27.

[78]Ibid.

[79]Arnold, *Darkness*, 60.

[80]Page, *Powers*, 76.

[81]Ibid, 76-78.

[82]Brother Andrew and Susan De Vore Williams, *And God Changed His Mind Because His People Prayed* (London: Marshall Pickering, 1991) 19-20.

[83]Commenting on the intent of Job's statement, H. H. Farmer notes that it was not a denial "that viewed from within the dimension of the temporal series, it was a human procreative act that 'gave', and the activity of a diphtheric germ from a bad drain that 'took away.' The two statements do not contradict one another, for they are incommensurables, as relations in different dimensions are, and supremely so when one of the dimensions is that which stands over all other dimensional distinctions whatsoever, namely the dimension of God" (*The World and God: A Study of Prayer, Providence and Miracle in Christian Experience*. [Second ed; London: Nisbet, 1936] 104-5).

[84]Noll, *Angels*, 106.

[85]Page, *Powers*, 37.

Chapter 8

"The Most Moved Mover":
Abraham Heschel's Theology of Divine Pathos

Dennis K.P. Ngien

Introduction

J ewish and Christian theologians have traditionally assumed divine impassibility to be "the fundamental principle" in their doctrine God![1] The notion of divine impassibility, however, is more philosophical than biblical.[2] "If God is a being of absolute self-sufficiency, then the entire world outside Him can in no way be relevant to Him."[3] This abstract God stands "aloof from the affairs of man," existing in transcendent calm and having no contact with a world external to himself. The deity is thus an apathetic God, the Wholly Other. He is distant, shrouded in his unfathomable darkness, and essentially irrelevant and unrelated to humanity. However, in the prophetic corpus of the Hebrew Bible the question of divine relatedness to humanity is paramount. "The supreme issue," Abraham Heschel argued, "is not the question whether in the infinite darkness there is the ground of being which is an object of man's ultimate concern, but whether the reality of God confronts us with a pathos."[4] The nearness of God permeates the Hebrew Bible. It is precisely in divine pathos that God and humanity meet, and that the chasm between them is overcome.

The purpose of this essay is to expound Heschel's theology of divine pathos and defend it against the idea of divine impassibility, accentuating it as "a more plausible view of ultimate reality."[5] I shall first examine the basis of traditional theology's rejection of the suffering God, and then explore Heschel's doctrine of divine pathos, showing that the God of Israel is not the "Unmoved Mover" of traditional theism, but rather in Fritz Rothschild's salient description, "the Most Moved Mover."[6] The God whom the prophets face is a God of compassion, a God of concern and involvement, and One who is most moved by the actions and fate of humanity. Next, I will present the biblical basis Heschel uses to advance his position. Finally, I will explore the contemporary relevance of Heschel's concept of divine pathos.

The Greek Doctrine of Divine Impassibility (Apatheia)

Christianity's embrace of impassibility stemmed from two Greek metaphysical concepts: apathy (*apatheia*) and sufficiency (*autarkeia*).[7] Apathy denotes incapacity of experiencing passion or feeling. For Aristotle, that which characterizes God's nature is immateriality and pure reason. This immaterial God of pure reason is insensitive to passion or feeling. To experience passion means to be acted upon from without. Aristotle therefore assumes God to be, by nature, apathetic. Divine apathy similarly undergirds the Christian denial of divine passibility. The Christian concept of divine sufficiency builds upon the Greek conviction that no external agent affects or moves God. Furthermore Aristotle's self-sufficient God lacks or needs nothing. "Satisfying conditions of insufficiency requires that some being affect or move the individual who experiences deficiency."[8] Furthermore Aristotle's God is a completely actual God, and thus has no potential for change. Aristotle excluded his self-sufficient God from movement, and he thus understood God's nature as immutable.

Aquinas, following the Aristotelian tradition, saw potentiality as a kind of imperfection. Any potentiality in God's being would detract from his perfection. God is pure act. While God can act, he cannot be acted upon; God moves us, while remaining unmoved. God is the "Unmoved Mover," and "the first cause of all things."[9] The attributes of immutability and impassibility are closely related, but not equivalent. Immutability suggests that God does not change in any way, even from within, while impassibility affirms the impossibility of God's being affected by any other realities, even in the emotional sense. Because the Greeks pursued pure reason as an ideal for humanity, they did not view emotions positively. The Stoic Zeno, for example, regarded emotions as "diseases of the soul," irrational experiences by which the mind is passively swayed, resulting in sin and suffering.[10] Emotions ought to be subject to the rational mind, thus safeguarding its undisturbed rational operation. This idealization of apathy governs the way in which both Greek philosophy and the Christian theology influenced by it conceive of God. What is disapproved of in humanity cannot be attributed to God. Therefore suffering and passion, which are characteristics of humans, are both inapplicable to the nature of a God who never becomes, but eternally is.

In traditional theism, accepting any one of the attributes mentioned above, logically or necessarily implies accepting the entire package.[11] Governed by this basic assertion, divine impassibility is closely linked with other aspects of the Greek understanding of God.

> Suffering is connected with time, change and matter, which are features of this material world of becoming. But God is eternal in the sense of atemporal. He is also, of course, incorporeal. He is absolute, fully actualized perfection, and therefore simply is eternally

what he is. He cannot change because any change (even
change which he wills rather than change imposed on
him from outside) could only change for the worse.
Since he is self-sufficient, he cannot be changed. Since
he is perfect, he cannot change himself.[12]

The Greek understanding of divine "unconditionedness" thus
undergirds the concept of divine impassibility.[13] Greek thought argued that because God is unconditional, he must be incapable of suffering, for suffering is always caused by something. God is perfect, so
he cannot suffer from some aspect of his being. If God were to suffer, he would have to suffer from or under an outside force. But this
would make him contingent upon something outside of himself. God's
benevolent will cannot be swayed by passions nor can his eternal bliss-
fulness be interrupted.

It was mainly the influence of Greek metaphysics that prompted
early Christian theologians to adopt the notion of divine impassibility.[14] Philosophers such as Plato, Aristotle, Parmenides and the Stoics
developed an understanding of God as the Absolute Monad, self-
sufficient, immutable, impassible and static. These categories, which
continued through the patristic and medieval periods, were assumed
by early Christian theologians to describe God. More specifically, the
idea of divine impassibility frequently served as a grid regarding what
may or may not be said of the Christian God. It erected, as Moltmann
noted, "an intellectual barrier against the recognition of the suffering
of Christ, for a God who is subject to suffering like all other beings
cannot be God."[15] Philo, the Hellenistic Jewish theologian, assumed
this in his understanding of Israel's God.[16] Virtually all the early church
Fathers took it for granted, denying God any emotions because they
would interrupt the divine tranquillity.[17] For example, Gregory of
Nazianzus, even though constrained by the Alexandrian Christology
to ascribe the sufferings of Jesus to the Logos, could speak of God's
suffering only by a paradox, that "by the sufferings of Him who could
not suffer, we were taken up and saved."[18] This usually means the

Logos, though aware of the sufferings of his human nature, is untouched by them. The Council of Chalcedon (A.D. 451) declared "as vain babblings" the idea that the divinity could suffer, and it condemned those who believed it.[19] Jaroslav Pelikan goes so far as to maintain that divine impassiblity was "a presupposition of all Christological doctrine."[20] Like most theologians of Chalcedonian and earlier times, Calvin and Reformed theology after him assumed divine impassibility. The Westminster Confession of Faith explicitly asserted that God is "without body, parts, or passions, immutable."[21]

Beyond Theism: Heschel's Theology of Divine Pathos

Heschel sought to emancipate the biblical understanding of God from the categories imposed on it by Greek philosophy. In order to move beyond theism's idea of divine *apatheia*, he developed a theology of divine pathos from the Old Testament prophets. He affirmed that divine pathos is "the central idea in prophetic theology," and is "the summary of Jewish theology."[22] By pathos he meant God's passionate and intimate "concern" for humanity, even to the point of being stirred and affected by human activity and conditions in which humanity dwells. He called this concern "transitive concern."[23] Divine pathos constitutes "the unity of the eternal and the temporal...It is the real basis of the relation between God and man, of the correlation of Creator and creation, of the dialogue of the Holy One of Israel and His people."[24] Divine pathos referred to God's outward relationship with his people, to the "situation" in which God involves himself in sharing the history of his people. The Hebrew Bible reveals a God who earnestly desires fellowship with humanity. "God's dream is not to be alone," but "to have mankind as a partner in the drama of continuous creation."[25] It is in this context that Heschel said that God "needed" human beings.[26] Heschel explains this divine-human intimacy:

To the prophet, ... God does not reveal himself in an

abstract absoluteness, but in a personal and intimate relation to the world. He does not simply command and expect obedience; He is also moved and affected by what happens in the world, and reacts accordingly ... Quite obviously in the biblical view, man's deeds may move Him, affect Him, grieve Him or, on the other hand, gladden and please Him. This notion that God can be intimately affected, that He possesses not merely intelligence and will, but also pathos, basically defines the prophetic consciousness of God.[27]

Heschel recognized the static idea of Greek deity to be the outcome of two major presuppositions: "the ontological notion of stability and the psychological view of the emotion as disturbances of the soul."[28] He repudiated each of these strands of thought, seeing them as contrary to the "Most moved mover" of Israel.

Pathos and Ontology

The Greeks assumed Parmenides' static view of ultimate reality, and this influenced their concept of God: "according to Greek thinking, impassivity and immobility are characteristic of the divine."[29] Any movement in God's being is illusory. Change is viewed as a sign of imperfection. God's true being is "that which 'always is' and 'never becomes': it is 'ever immutably the same.'"[30] Responding to the "Eleatic" ontology of Parmenides and to theology influenced by it, Heschel wrote:

The Eleatic premise that true being is unchangeable and that change implies imperfection is valid only in regard to being as reflected in the mind. Being in reality, being as we encounter it, implies movement. If we think of being as something beyond and detached from beings, we may well arrive at an Eleatic notion. An ontology, however, concerned with beings as involved in all beings or as the source of all beings, will find it impossible to separate being from action or movement, and thus postulate a dynamic concept of divine being... Biblical ontology does not separate being from doing. What *is*, acts. The God of Israel is a God who acts, a God of mighty deeds... Here the basic category is action rather than immobility. Movement, creation of natures, acts within history rather absolute transcendence and detachment from the events of history, are the attributes of the Supreme Being.[31]

Divine pathos, said Heschel, is "not a name for God's essence;"[32] it is "functional" rather than "substantial."[33] It belongs to the realm of God's relatedness.[34] His emphasis is on how God acts in relation to his creatures, not on how God may be in himself. "The Bible does not say how He is (in Himself), but how He acts (towards us)."[35] "God in Himself, His Being, is a problem for metaphysics."[36] Classical metaphysics speculates upon God's "inmost" essence apart from God's pathos in history. For prophetic theology, being as an ontological category is to be apprehended in relation, not in essence. Heschel made a distinction between God's essence, into which one cannot pry, and God's pathos, in which God and humanity meet most intimately. This distinction poses a limit for a proper discourse about God. God as he is in himself was not the God with whom we have to do because this God was not preached, not revealed, and not worshipped. God in essence, in his own nature and Supreme Majesty, is beyond us, and theology must observe this limit. He warned against any speculative incursion into God as he is in himself, but pointed rather to God's functional relatedness to humanity where he is to be apprehended. Because God chose to be found in his outward relation with humanity, the prophets dwell on "a dynamic modality," on the actual concrete relationship that God has towards them.[37]

The prophets did not discuss God "as He is in Himself, as ultimate being."[38] God in essence is "above and beyond all revelation."[39] "God cannot be distilled to a well-defined idea. All concepts fail when applied to His essence."[40] What God discloses is not his "essence." "He communicates only His pathos, His will."[41] Here Heschel's terminology seems to drive a wedge between God's "inmost" essence and his "outward" actions, pushing God into a realm from which no revelation ever proceeds. It would appear that Heschel failed to reach clarity in this area.[42] Despite this, he expressly affirmed that God's being can be known through his acts: "For of God we know only what He means and does in relation to man." "God as turned toward man" is known to the prophet.[43] God's being is known through his intentionality and his interaction with humanity. He firmly stated that the object of prophetic revelation is not God's impenetrable "essence," but God's revealed "pathos." And yet it is really "God Himself" who relates to humanity. This is in line with biblical ontology which does not drive a wedge between being and act. Speculative ontology based on pure being is thus given up in favour of biblical ontology.

The identity of God is inseparable from his operations. As Heschel put it, "What *is*, acts." God's being corresponds to God's acts. God's being is found in his acts of pathos, in his covenantal participation and involvement with humanity. Who God is, is the result of what he does, and what he does is to act lovingly towards the objects of divine concern. To put it in Heschel's terms, God's concern, not God's rule, motivates his activity. God is truly involved in human history and experience to the extent that human actions truly affect his being. "Whatever man does affects not only his own life, but also the life of God insofar as it is directed to man."[44] In divine pathos the Almighty goes out of himself, and in the fellowship of his covenant with Israel, God becomes capable of suffering. Thus the prophets could speak of the "history in God," and "of an event in the life of God."[45] Suffering action is taken up into God's very being. Critics have argued that Heschel, for all his efforts to avoid describing God's essence, seems to have done just that.[46] "God's participation in human history," he argued, "finds its deepest expression in the fact that God can actually suffer."[47]   God is so thoroughly woven into history that he allows himself to suffer under it. This motivated Berkovits to argue that in spite of Heschel's reluctance to think of God's innermost essence, suffering, a function of God's concern, is thus carried into the life of God. Heschel's theology did not admit a duality of the impassible essence and suffering action in his doctrine of God. Berkovits explained: "The life-giving significance of God's relatedness to the world is not in the act of relatedness but in the fact that it is God who relates himself to it. It is the very essence of God, God as he exists in his absoluteness and perfection, that determines the value of his care for man."[48] Heschel informed us of this: "For all the impenetrability of His being, He is concerned with the world and relates Himself to it."[49]   It is in divine pathos that the gulf between God and humanity is overcome.

Heschel's understanding of God as self-moving or as moved by concern for others inevitably distinguishes him from the unmoved mover of theism. The divine pathos which the prophets expressed in many ways constitutes "the modes of His reaction to Israel's conduct which would change if Israel modified its ways."[50] This does not mean that God changes as it relates to his essential nature. Heschel clearly distinguishes between a changeless essence and a changing intentionality. Divine pathos is "not a name for His essence." What changes then, is the structure of divine pathos, not God's being. For fear of limiting God's sovereignty and freedom, Heschel refused to attribute God's passion to God's ultimate being. Divine pathos is "not an essential attribute of God;" it is "an expression of God's will."[51] If it were God's essential attribute, then God would be coerced to act in certain ways based on his pathic nature. "God Himself is not pathos," but is a "subject of pathos."[52] Yet being this "subject" who involves himself in human life, God must be passible. Given that "biblical ontology does not separate being and act," God must be capable of

being affected or moved, and thereby capable of varied modes of
reaction depending upon human situations. In Merkle's reading of
Heschel:

> Pathos may not be an 'essential attribute of God,' but
> Heschel would have to admit that passibility is. For
> pathos is only possible in a being that is in essence
> passible. But this does not mean that the divine es-
> sence is changeable. The fact that God's modes of
> reacting to the world are changeable does not mean
> that God changes in essence. To be in essence passi-
> ble is not the same as to have a passible essence. To
> be in essence passible is to be by nature a being who
> may change modes of action and reaction; to have a
> passible essence is to have a changing nature - for
> example, now human, now divine, or now living, now
> inanimate. God's nature may be immutable while the
> modes of God's being-in-relation may change.[53]

Philosophically, a suffering God is an imperfect being who necessarily seeks his perfection and tries to overcome his deficiency through
actions. The Hebrew concept of God, in contrast, consists of a passionate God who is infinitely charged with "transitive concern." God
is so eager to express his concern for the people of his covenantal love
that he suffers under their actions. And yet God suffers not out of any
lack in himself, but out of his will to express his inexhaustible pathos
for people. The immutability of God is understood not in terms of
the divine perfection of Greek metaphysics; rather it is understood in
terms of a belief in the constancy of God's faithfulness to his covenant, a key concept in the Hebrew Bible. The notion of self-sufficiency, that is, his being unaffected or unmoved by external realities, is
not an ideal in Hebrew thought. "Not self-sufficiency, but concern
and involvement characterize His relation to the world."[54] God's concern generates his activity on behalf of humanity. God is secure and
trustworthy enough to be most moved by human situations. Biblically,

God suffers change not because of any imperfection, but because different situations require different responses. This means that there is potentiality in God. God has the potential to be moved and to elicit responses not yet actual. This by no means implies that God's being is thereby perfected or enhanced or in the process of becoming more divine. Change is no sign of imperfection. It is rather an aspect of God's transitive concern for the world, the expressions of which are always subject to change.

Pathos and Psychology

In addition to Greek ontology, Greek psychology is also responsible for the rejection of the idea of divine suffering. Theists in the Aristotelian tradition, such as Maimonides or Thomas Aquinas, did not deny God's concern for humanity. What they denied was that God could be moved by the world. They conceived of God's concern merely as an intellectual act and benevolent attitude. This kind of concern, Heschel argued, does not signify a real genuine relationship because it is cold and remote. God's involvement with humanity is not merely a benevolent attitude, but "a feeling of intimate concern."[55] "He is a lover engaged to His people, not only a king. God stands in a passionate relationship to man."[56]

Heschel made a distinction between two kinds of concern: "transitive" and "reflexive." The former focused on others, whereas the latter focused on the self.[57] The Pagan gods had only a reflexive, self-centered concern, a love dominated by self-seeking desires. The Israelite God had a selfless concern, a "pure concern," sharing his boundless goodness without thought of return.[58] Pathos, which Heschel also characterizes as "absolute selflessness" and "undeserved love," is more divine than human. It is "theomorphic."[59] In discussing divine pathos, Heschel stressed the freedom of God. Israel's God gladly bestows his goodness, and does so only for the sake of the ones he loves. God determined within himself to be divinely loving, sharing his pure concern for humanity. Divine passion is an act which God brings to himself, thus allowing himself to be most moved by the actions of humanity. This involves "no inner bondage, no enslavement to impulse, no subjugation by passion."[60] Human deeds do not necessitate divine pathos, but only occasion it. Divine pathos is not an "unreasoned emotion," but "an act formed with intention, depending on free will, the result of decision and determination."[61] It is God's glory to give, to act, and to love freely. In Heschel's schema, the immutability of God's freedom must be affirmed alongside the possibility of God's pathos. In so doing he avoided attributing to God the unbridled and selfish passions which characterize humanity.

Insofar as God is not subject to creaturely passions, God is impassible. But the Greeks were wrong to conclude from this that God has no passion. Greek psychology regarded pathos, an emotion implying change, as an imperfection. Since pathos is an emotional reaction aroused by an external agent rather than an intellectual act, it was viewed as a sign of weakness. "The dignity of man" lies primarily "in the activity of the mind, in acts of self-determination."[62] Thus the Greeks radically dissociated reason from emotions, viewing them as sharply opposed to each other. To attribute emotion to God would be to introduce change, and therefore to ascribe weakness to him, which, for them, would have seemed blasphemous. "Such preference for reason," Heschel wrote, "enabled Greek philosophy to exclude all emotion from the nature of Deity, while at the same time ascribing thought and contemplation to it."[63]

> The perfect example of an impassive deity is the God of Aristotle. By identifying the Deity with the First Cause with something which, while it has the capacity of moving all things, is itself unmoved, Aristotle's Deity has no pathos, no needs. Ever resting in itself, its only activity is thinking, and its thinking is thinking of thinking. Indifferent to all things, it does not care to contemplate anything but itself. Things for it and thus are set in motion, yet they are left to themselves.[64]

Hebrew thought, on the contrary, had a positive evaluation of emotion. In Heschel's terms: "the mind is not a member apart, but is itself transformed into passion."[65] "Thought is part of emotion. We think because we are moved...Emotion may be defined as the consciousness of being moved."[66] "Emotion can be reasonable just as reason can be emotional."[67] Emotion is basic to the life of reason; it is also important to the life of action, because great acts are usually performed by those who are filled with passion.[68] Divine pathos, though an emotional response, is never devoid of God's reason and will, but informed by them.[69] Given this positive view of emotion in the Bible, Heschel rejected the dualistic framework of Greek metaphysics, that God could think but could not feel, that God could move, while remaining unmoved. Therefore, "to the biblical mind the conception of God as detached and unemotional is totally alien."[70]

Divine Pathos in the Prophetic Texts

Heschel gave priority to biblical texts rather than to the presuppositions of Greek philosophy. This section offers a synthesis of Heschel's understanding of the texts, showing how he found biblical justification for his view that God could fully experience the range of emotions.[71] A detailed analysis of the texts is beyond the scope of this paper.

Amos

Amos' proclamation does not consist of "an impersonal accusation," but proceeds from a living God who cares, "a Redeemer who is pained by the misdeeds, the thanklessness of those whom He has redeemed."[72] The iniquities of God's people had aroused divine wrath against them. God cried out and roared in excitement and pain (Amos 1:2; cf. Isa 42:13-14). Amos' contemporaries were condemned because they had rejected the Torah, and had not kept Yahweh's statutes (Amos 2:4). Israel's election was not to be "mistaken as divine favoritism or immunity from chastisement."[73] On the contrary, God's chosen ones are more seriously exposed to God's judgement. Divine justice in Amos's message is divine concern, not a "stern mechanical justice."[74] If the God in whose name Amos preached were a God of stern, mechanical justice, then long ago he would have nullified his covenant and abandoned Israel. What transpires between God and his people is the expression of God's deepest affection for those whom he has known more intimately than any other people. Though Israel proved faithless, God called out to her hoping that she might see her own failure and repent. Numerous times, God sent warning portents, that Israel might take heed and return to him. And yet she did not return to God. Amos 4:6-13 conveys the sense of both God's mercy and his disappointment over Israel's faithlessness, with its recurrent refrain, "yet you did not return to Me". Having been shown in a vision the imminent destruction of Israel by locust or fire, Amos does not question divine justice. He appeals to divine mercy: "O Lord God, forgive, I beseech Thee! How can Jacob stand? He is so small! The Lord repented concerning this; It shall not be, said the Lord" (Amos 7:2-3). At the heart of the covenant lies God's everlasting love. God's wrath is less final than God's mercy. God's mercy will ultimately triumph over his wrath; God's compassion prevails over justice (Amos 5:15). Mercy is a "perpetual possiblity,"[75] and will ultimately conquer the "contingency and non-finality" of wrath.[76] Thus the prophecy of Amos, which began with a message of doom, ends with an affirmation of hope (Amos 9:11ff).

Hosea and Jeremiah

Both Hosea and Jeremiah affirm that God could be wounded. God grieved over his people even amidst his anger with them. For instance, God cries out concerning wayward Israel: "How can I give you up, Ephraim? How can I hand you over, O Israel? My heart recoils within me; I will not again destroy Ephraim; for I am God and no mortal man, the Holy One in your midst, and I will not come in wrath" (Hos.11:8-9; cf. Jer.31:30).[77] Humanly speaking, in such a situation a complete abandonment is expected. But God's love is such that it eternally attaches itself to his people. Hosea speaks of the modulation of divine feelings toward repentance, expressed most movingly by the words: "My heart is turned within me" (Hos11:8; cf. 12:6). Yet he also said: "Compassion remains hid from Me" (Hos.13:14). How does one reconcile the antinomy between the tenderness of divine love and the severity of divine judgement? True love, Hosea saw, is not a love that overlooks easily the wickedness of the beloved, forgiving carelessly every sin. Rather it is "a love grown bitter with the waywardness of man."[78] Israel's God also "has passionate love of right and a burning hatred of wrong."[79] God's anger against sin is "a tragic necessity, a calamity for man and grief for God."[80] God is moved into wrath by human sin. The wrathful opposition against sin is not generated by some abstractly conceived justice of God, which demands retribution for the broken law; rather it is generated by God's burning desire for reunion, a pure, simple and undefiled relationship with Israel. God suffers the pain of a broken relationship with his beloved. Yet this pain springs from God's resolve to love the object of his own wrath. The mingling of sorrow and love in God prevents the final ruin of his beloved. God's being is revealed in the way in which, amidst all the sorrow and anger, his redeeming love endures forever. Heschel captured this crucial point: "Over and above the immediate and contingent emotional reaction of the Lord we are informed of an eternal and basic disposition" already indicated at the beginning of the passage: "I loved him" (Hos.11:1).[81] The pathos of love, expressed first in the pain of distress, reaches its climax in the final triumph of reconciliation. "I will heal their backsliding, I will love them freely, for Mine anger has turned from him" (Hos 14:4). As such God's judgement is not final, but only a disciplinary means of leading people to repentance. Anger is a mode of God's responsiveness to humanity, showing that he cares.

Though divine anger is aroused by human sin, it is subject to God's will. Divine anger is not a childish loss of temper nor is it a frustrated love turned sour or vindictive. Rather, it is an expression of God's pure love, that does not allow him to stand by idly in the face of unrighteousness. Wrath is the purity of God's love burning hot in the face of wickedness. God's pure love expresses itself in a wrathful opposition against anything that stands between God and humanity so that their unity might not be severed. As a mode of pathos, God's wrath is to be understood as "suspended love, as mercy withheld, as mercy in concealment."[82] Hidden in a severe 'no' is an assuring 'yes'. Anger generated by love is only "an interlude," awaiting compassion to resume in its fullness. God's long-suffering love waits eagerly to overcome the contingency and non-finality of terrifying anger. Jeremiah 12: 14-15 confirms this: "I will pluck them from their land... and after I have plucked them up, I will again have compassion on them, and I will bring them again each to his heritage and each to his land" (cf. Jer 26:13). Heschel grasped the mysterious paradox of Hebrew faith:

> Jeremiah had to be taught that God is greater than His decisions. The anger of the Lord is instrumental, hypothetical, conditional, and subject to His will. Let the people modify their line of conduct, and anger will disappear. Far from being an expression of "petulant vindictiveness," the message of anger includes a call to return and to be saved. The call of anger is a call to cancel anger. It is not an expression of irrational, sudden, and instinctive excitement, but a free and deliberate reaction of God's justice to what is wrong and evil. For all its intensity, it may be averted by prayer. ... Its meaning is ... instrumental: to bring about repentance; its purpose and consummation is its own disappearance.[83]

Isaiah

The opening speech of Isaiah, using parental imagery, contains a mixture of lament and accusation (Isa 1:2-3). It sets the tone for the subsequent utterances of the prophet. It deals not primarily with divine anger but with the divine sorrow in anger. The prophet pleads with his hearers to identify with the plight of a father whose children have abandoned him.[84] The focus here is not on Israel's disobedience to an external moral code, but on a broken relationship between parent and child. The rebellion occurs, even in the face of the best fatherly care possible. The prophet expresses divine anguish over Israel's rebellion in the form of rhetorical questions, powerfully expressed in the song of the vineyard: "What more was there to do for my vineyard, that I have not done in it? Why did it yield wild grapes?" (Isa 5:1-7; cf. Jer 2:21). There is sorrow in divine anger. Commenting on 30:18, "Therefore the Lord waits to be gracious to you;" Heschel wrote that anger is not God's "disposition, but a state He waits to overcome."[85] God's anger, which is instrumental in purification, lasts only for a season. For when the Lord smites, He is both "smiting and healing" (Isa 19:22). In anger, God's mercy is not abandoned, but merely suspended. God's mercy will finally triumph over his own wrath.

> In a very little while My indignation will come to an
> end ...
> Come, My people, enter your chambers,
> And shut your doors behind you;
> Hide yourselves for a little while
> Until the indignation is past.   (Isa 10:25; 26:20)

"The allusion to the Lord as 'a woman in travail,'" Heschel wrote, is "the boldest figure used by any prophet (to) convey not only the sense of supreme urgency of His action, but also a sense of the deep intensity of His suffering"[86] (Isa 42:14). Of God's involvement in human pain, the prophet declares affirmatively: "In all their affliction He was afflicted" (Isa 63:9).[87]

Conclusion

In the Bible, God is revealed not as an onlooker but as a participant. God is concerned for and moved by humanity. What are the implications of recognizing the "Most Moved Mover" as Israel's God?

First, this concept has profound implication for ethics. God seeks a response from humanity that corresponds to the divine pathos. This response is sympathy. Heschel wrote:

> The nature of man's response to the divine corresponds to the content of his apprehension of divine. When the divine is sensed as mysterious perfection, the response is one of fear and trembling; when sensed as absolute will, the response is one of unconditional obedience; when sensed as pathos, the response is one of sympathy.[88]

"The prophet not only hears and apprehends the divine pathos; he is convulsed by it to the depths of his soul."[89] He is "inwardly transformed: his interior life is formed by the pathos of God."[90] He, by sympathy with the divine pathos, is himself intimately involved in divine concern for his people. In this way, the prophet is a partner or associate rather than a mouthpiece or instrument of God. Just as divine *apatheia* has its anthropological corollary, so does divine pathos: "The ideal state of the Stoic sage is apathy, the ideal state of the prophets is sympathy."[91] As opposed to *homo apathetikos* (apathetic man), the individual becomes *homo sympathetikos* (sympathetic man). His involvement in social justice, the passion with which he condemns injustice, is rooted in his sympathy with the divine pathos. Sympathy moves him out of the narrow confines of self-centeredness. Sympathy is emotion, in the sense of motion, of movements, which motivates him to act on behalf of others. Thus sympathy is a precondition of moral actions. The church and the Christian life should be patterned after sympathy, which necessarily involves risk, pain, and loss. The church of a passionate God must exist in and for this world, accepting suffering itself as it cares for the needy, the sick, and the poor and seeks the liberation of the oppressed. In its moral behaviour, the church must reflect the person and righteous actions of God. This is what it means to live a life oriented towards "the living reality of God."[92]

Second, God's pathos should govern the life of the preacher. The tension between God's love and God's wrath ought to awaken a corresponding tension in the heart of the prophet. God feels anguish for his people, but he also feels anger for them. Likewise, the prophet feels it, and lives it. These two opposing currents of intense emotion felt by Jeremiah are attributed to God. Commenting on Jeremiah 23:9, "My heart is broken within me, all my bones tremble; I am like a drunken man, like a man overcome by wine, because of the Lord and his holy words," Heschel wrote: "What convulsed the prophet's whole being was God. His condition was a state of suffering in sympathy with the divine pathos."[93] The preacher must learn to identify both with God and with his people. This double sympathy inevitably leads to a painful conflict within the preacher's inner existence. Impassioned with the reality of divine wrath, Jeremiah, for one, pronounced judgement with a vehement indignation, while at the same time his heart was filled with tenderness and sensitivity to human suffering. His calling as a prophet required that he preach with severity; but at the same time he pitied his people. Heschel would concur with Calvin's remarks on this dual sympathy:

> Let then all teachers in the Church learn to put on these two feelings - to be vehemently indignant whenever they see the worship of God profaned, to burn with zeal for God and to show that severity which appeared in all the prophets, whenever due order decays - and at the same time to sympathize with miserable men, whom they see rushing headlong into destruction, and to bewail their madness and to interpose with God as much as is in them; in such a way, however, that their compassion render them not slothful or indifferent, so as to be indulgent to the sins of men.[94]

Furthermore, the preacher's anger must truly reflect the divine pathos. He must have enough discernment to be angry about the right things, and yet have enough control to hold his anger in check. The task of the preacher is not to recommend that God should depart from his merciful forbearance, but that he test and purify his people (Jer 5:1, 4ff.; 6:9ff). When Jeremiah's anger became stronger than God's anger, God had to correct him and remind him about the non-finality of anger. In response to Jeremiah's prayer, "Avenge me on my perse-cutors" (15:15), the Lord said to him: "If you return, I will restore you, and you shall stand before Me. If you utter what is precious, and not what is base, you shall be as My mouth" (15:19).[95] Bearing in mind that God is concerned about the disciplining, not destruction, of his adversaries, the preacher must avoid a hypertrophy of sympa-thy for God's wrath.

Prophetic suffering, in various kinds, results from this two-fold sympathy for God and for his people. Suffering is constitutive of the life of the preacher. However the world must observe that he or she suffers not because of public scandal or vice, but because of a dedica-tion to preaching and living the Word of God.

Third, prayer would lose its meaning if God were not respon-sive to human cries. If God remains unmoved by whatever we do, there is really very little point in doing one thing rather than the other. An apathetic God would be unable to transform human hearts due to an inability to react or respond to human behaviour. However the prophetic faith assumes a God whose attitude towards his people changes when his people repent and turn to him. Thus prayers make a difference not only in human lives but also in God's life. God desires humanity to be his conversation partner, and this provides a strong incentive for loving devotion. Prayer is not so much a duty under-taken to please God as a delight at the heart of relationship. To pray is to enter into a living and loving relationship in which both parties influence each other. The reciprocal relationship of love into which God enters with humanity entails that God gives and receives from humanity. The interaction between God and humanity does not occur simply in the intellectual level, nor in a law court; it occurs at the emotional level. God relates to humanity as "a lover," who eagerly "waits for (humanity) to seek Him."[96] God takes human cries seriously, allowing them to affect his being and change his mind. Petitionary prayers may have a contributive, though not determinative, effect on the outcome because they have an effect on God himself. In Heschel's schema, petitionary prayer is not the cause of God's response, but rather is the reason for his response.[97] God is not under obligation to answer human requests, otherwise he would not be the One who acts from free choice. However, because God is responsive, humanity can pray with confidence that he will be moved by human cries.

Finally, Heschel's analysis provides an appropriate entry point for sharing the gospel. Divine pathos discloses "the extreme pertinence of man to God."[98] Divine concern moves God to come to humanity, thus abolishing his distance from humanity. God does not conceive of humanity as an idea in his mind but as a concern, as "a divine secret" (Ps 139:7-18). This means that humanity lives in the "perpetual awareness of being perceived, apprehended, noted by God, of being an object of the divine Subject."[99] An apathetic God, who dwells in the transcendent and lonely splendour of eternity, strips humanity of "dignity and grandeur," striking us with a sense of "poverty and emptiness."[100] What consolation could such a God offer if he is too sublime to be moved by events on this earth? Of what help to wounded humanity is a God who knows nothing of pain himself? Furthermore this conception of God could easily give rise to atheism. On the contrary, Israel's God is not remote from human struggles in history. God takes humanity so seriously that he attaches himself to human situations. God, in Whitehead's famous phrase, is "the great companion - the fellow-sufferer who understands."[101] When God is understood as a suffering participant in human history, he is less likely be criticized as a deceiver, executioner, sadist and despot. This notion could reduce the intensity of the atheistic objections to belief in God and enable the unbelievers to hear the gospel, and eventually to find faith. God feels for humanity; he cares! God is most supremely divine in his intimate concern for human agony. And that, surely, is news worth sharing.

Notes

1 Abraham Joshua Heschel, *The Prophets* (New York: Harper and Row, 1962) 254.

2 See Jürgen Moltmann, *The Crucified God* (trans. R.A. Wilson and John Bowden; New York: Harper & Row, 1974) and his *History and the Triune God* (trans. John Bowden; New York: Crossroads, 1992). While writing his noteworthy book *The Crucified God*, Moltmann observed that Jewish writers had already been discussing the theme of God's suffering (267). In *History and the Triune God*, he acknowledged the impact the Jewish theologian Abraham Heschel had had upon his theological understanding of the suffering God: "My first discovery was the Jewish concept of the pathos of God with which Abraham Heschel has interpreted the message of the *Shekinah*, the indwelling of God in the persecuted and suffering people of God..." (172). See also John Jaeger, "Abraham Heschel and The Theology of Jürgen Moltmann," *Perspectives on Religious Studies* 24 (1997) 167-178, where he focused on the apparent parallels between Heschel and Moltmann.

3 Heschel, *The Prophets*, 232.

4 Abraham Heschel, "The Jewish Notion of God and Christian Renewal," *Renewal of Religious Thought* (Theology of Renewal I; ed. L. K. Shook; New York: Herder and Herder, 1968) 107; also cited in Merkle, "Heschel's Theology of Divine Pathos," 74.

5 Heschel, *The Prophets*, 247.

6 Fritz A. Rothschild, ed., *Between God and Man: An Interpretation of Judaism from the Writings of Abraham J. Heschel* (rev. ed; New York: The Free Press, 1975) 25, 89.

7 John Russell, "Impassibility and Pathos in Barth's Idea of God," *ATR* 70(1988) 222. See also Francis House, "The Barrier of Impassibility," *Theology* 83 (1980) 410-11; Colin Grant, "Possibilities for Divine Passibility," *Toronto Journal of Theology* 4 (1988) 6-8; T. E. Pollard, "The Impassibility of God," *SJT* 8 (1955) 353-64; Richard Bauckham, " 'Only the Suffering God can Help': Divine Passibility in Modern Theology," *Themelios* 9 (1984) 7.

8 Ibid., 233.

9 *Summa Theologia* 1.13.5 in *Basic Writings of Saint Thomas Aquinas* (2 vols; trans. Anton C. Pegis; New York: Random House, 1945) 8-25.

10 Marcel Sarot, "Divine Suffering: Continuity and Discontinuity with the Tradition," *ATR* 78 (1996) 226.

[11]See David Griffin, *God, and Power and Evil: a Process Theodicy* (Philadelphia: Fortress, 1976) 73. He identified at least eight logically connected attributes in the writings of Aquinas, which constitute "the essential core of theism."

[12]Bauckham, " 'Only the Suffering God can Help', " 7-8. See also R. B. Edwards, "The Pagan Doctrine of the Absolute Unchangeableness of God," *RelS* 14 (1978) 305-13.

[13]Sarot, "Divine Suffering," 226.

[14]For further studies on the influence of Greek ideas upon classical Christianity, see Charles Hartshorne and William L. Reeve, *Philosophers Speak of God* (Chicago: University of Chicago Press, 1953) 104-6; Marcel Sarot, *God, Passibility and Corporeality* (Kampen: Kok Pharos, 1992) 32-35; Edwin Hatch, *The Influence of Greek Ideas and Usages upon the Christian Church,* (London: William and Norgate, 1892) 3-4; 114-15; Wolfhart Pannenberg, "The Appropriation of the Philosophical Concept of God as a Dogmatic Problem of Early Christian Theology," in *Basic Questions in Theology*, vol.2., (trans. George H. Kehm; Philadelphia: Westminster, 1971) 119-83.

[15]Moltmann, *The Crucified God*, 228.

[16]Bauckham, " 'Only the Suffering God can Help', " 7.

[17]For further discussions of the early Church fathers on the impassibility-passibility debate, see John Mozley, The *Impassibility of God: A Survey of Christian Thought* (Cambridge: Cambridge University Press, 1926); Joseph Hallman, *The Descent of God: Divine Suffering in History and Theology* (Minneapolis: Fortress, 1991); Warren McWilliams, *The Passion of God: Divine Suffering in Contemporary Theology* (Macon: Mercer University Press, 1985); Dennis Ngien, *The Suffering of God According to Martin Luther's 'Theologia Crucis'* (Bern: Peter Lang, 1995).

[18]*Theological Oration* 4:5 as cited in Pollard, "The Impassibility of God," 359.

[19]J. Stevenson, *Creeds, Councils, and Controversies: Documents Illustrative of the History of the Church A.D. 337-461* (London: SPCK, 1966) 336. Also quoted in William C. Placher, *Narratives of a Vulnerable God* (Louisville: Westminster John Knox, 1994) 5.

[20]Jaroslav Pelikan, *The Emergence of the Catholic Tradition (100-600)*, vol. 1 (Chicago: University of Chicago Press, 1971) 270-71.

[21]Westminster Confession of Faith, chap. 2, *Book of Confessions*, Presbyterian Church (U.S.A.) 6.011 as cited in Placher, *Narratives of a Vulnerable God*, 6.

[22]Abraham Joshua Heschel, "Teaching Jewish Theology in the Solomon Schecter Day School," *The Synagogue School* 28 (1969) 4-33. See John C. Merkle, "Heschel's Theology of Divine Pathos," in *Abraham Joshua Heschel: Exploring His Life and Thought*, ed. John. C. Merkle (New York: Macmillian; London: Collier Macmillan, 1985) 67.

[23]Abraham Heschel, *Man is Not Alone. A Philosophy of Religion* (New York: Farrar, Straus, and Young, 1951) 245.

[24]Ibid., 231.

[25] Abrham Heschel, *Who is Man?* (Stanford: Stanford University Press, 1965) 119.

[26] Heschel, *The Prophets*, 235.

[27] Ibid., 223-24.

[28] Ibid., 260.

[29] Heschel, *Man is Not Alone*, 65.

[30] Heschel, *The Prophets*, 261.

[31] Ibid.

[32] Ibid., 231.

[33] Ibid.

[34] For further discussions of whether duality exists in Heschel's doctrine of God, see Paul Fiddes, *The Creative Suffering of God* (Oxford: Oxford University Press, 1988) 111-12; Lawrence Perlman, *Abraham Heschel's Idea of Revelation* (Atlanta: Scholars, 1989) 91-101; Eliezer Berkovits, "Dr. A. J. Heschel's Theology of Pathos," *Tradition: A Journal of Orthodox Thought* 6 (1969) 67-104, and *Major Themes in Modern Philosophies of Judaism* (New York: Ktav, 1974) 192-224; Merkle, "Heschel's Theology of Divine Pathos," 75-81.

[35] Heschel, *The Prophets*, 262.

[36] Ibid., 484.

[37] Ibid., 229.

[38] Abraham Heschel, "Prophetic Inspiration: An Analysis of Prophetic Consciousness," *Judaism* 11 (Winter 1962) 7.

[39] Ibid.

[40] Heschel, *Man is Not Alone*, 108.

[41] Heschel, *The Prophets*, 485.

[42] Ibid., 484-85. "It is improper," Heschel informed his readers, "to employ the term 'self-revelation' in regard to biblical prophecy." He argues that "God never reveals Himself." Heschel did not like the term "self-revelation;" he called it a revelation of divine pathos. Heschel's phraseology such as "God never reveals himself" seems to push God to a realm from whence no revelation ever proceeds. Did he mean that there really is no direct revelation from God to humanity? And must we, on the other hand, understand him to say that this same God who is hidden in himself ("beyond and above all revelation") is also so wrapped up in history that we may speak of "history in God," and of "an event in the life of God?" Heschel would have rendered us a great service had he elaborated upon these questions.

[43] Ibid., 485.

[44]Ibid., 226.

[45]Ibid., 277, 437; cf. Heschel, *God in Search of Man* (New York: Crossroads, 1955) 174-75.

[46]See note 34.

[47]Heschel, *The Prophets*, 232.

[48]Berkovits, *Major Themes in Modern Philosophies of Judaism*, 204.

[49]Heschel, *The Prophets*, 228.

[50]Heschel, *Man is Not Alone*, 245.

[51]Heschel, *The Prophets*, 231. See Perlman, *Abraham Heschel's Idea of Revelation*, 93-94.

[52]Ibid., 485.

[53]Cf. John C. Merkle, *The Genesis of Faith: The Depth Theology of Abraham Joshua Heschel* (New York: Macmillan;London: Collier Macmillan, 1985) 133.

[54]Ibid., 235.

[55]Heschel, *Man Is Not Alone*, 244.

[56]Ibid.

[57]Ibid., 245; cf. his *The Prophets*, 225-26.

[58]Heschel, *Man is Not Alone*, 245.

[59]Heschel, *The Prophets*, 271.

[60]Ibid., 254.

[61]Ibid., 224.

[62]Ibid., 248.

[63]Ibid., 250.

[64]Ibid., 251.

[65]Ibid., 257.

[66]Ibid., 316

[67]Ibid., 256.

[68]Ibid., 258.

[69]Merkle, *The Genesis of Faith*, 131.

[70]Heschel, *The Prophets*, 257.

[71]For an Old Testament study of God's suffering, see Terence E. Fretheim, *The Suffering of God: An Old Testament Perspective* (Philadelphia: Fortress, 1984).

[72]Heschel, *The Prophets*, 32.

[73]Ibid.

[74]Ibid., 35.

[75]Ibid., 35-36.

[76]Ibid., 285.

[77]Ibid., 48.

[78]Ibid., 50.

[79]Ibid.

[80]Ibid., 294.

[81]Ibid., 48.

[82]Ibid., 295.

[83]Ibid., 286.

[84]Ibid., 80.

[85]Ibid., 83.

[86]Ibid., 151.

[87]Ibid.

[88]Ibid., 307.

[89]Heschel, *Between God and Man*, 125.

[90]Heschel, *The Prophets*, 319.

[91]Ibid., 258.

[92]Ibid., 322.

[93]Ibid., 118.

[94]John Calvin, *Twelve Minor Prophets*, vol. 2 (Grand Rapids: Eerdmans, 1950) 329-30; also quoted in Donald A. Leggett, *Loving God and Disturbing Men* (Grand Rapids: Baker, 1990) 47.

[95]Heschel, *The Prophets*, 126.

[96]Heschel, *God in Search of Man*, 39. Cf. his *Man is not Alone*, 244.

[97]For further discussions of prayer, see Terrance Tiessen, *Providence and Prayer* (Downer's Grove, IL: InterVarsity, 2000); Richard Foster, *Prayer: Finding the Heart's True Home* (New York: HarperCollins, 1992); Peter R. Baelz, *Prayer and Providence: A Background Study* (New York: Seabury, 1968); David Basinger, "Why Petition an Omnipotent, Omniscient, Wholly Good God?" *RelS* 19 (1983) 25-41.

[98]Heschel, *The Prophets*, 483.

[99]Ibid.

[100]Ibid., 258-59.

[101]Alfred North Whitehead, *Process and Reality: An Essay in Cosmology* (New York: Macmillan, 1929) 532.

Chapter 9

"Reading with the Spirit":
Interpreting Scripture in the Light of Word and Spirit

Mark Husbands

Introduction

> …all else is God's work…because he taught us what to
> do and the Holy Spirit whispered to us what we should
> say—of which I am personally convinced, because fre-
> quently I went to gatherings without a prepared con-
> cept. In fact, I always did so, with the exception of
> three or four historically important meetings. I partici-
> pated in most gatherings in accordance with the gospel
> teaching. 'Do not worry what you will say. The Spirit
> alone will tell you what should be said.'[1]

*I*f these words had been spoken by the Apostle Paul, St. Augustine,
Luther, or perhaps even Bonhoeffer, our sensibilities would remain
largely intact. Once we realize however, that the one confessing belief
in the presence and inner witness of the Spirit, is himself thought to
be directly responsible for acts of genocide and crimes against humanity, our sense of both justice and truth is set on end. How is it

possible that one responsible for a program of 'ethnic cleansing' in the Balkans, leaving more than 100,000 dead, may claim to have been led by the Spirit? Should we not simply dismiss this claim as an utterly spurious understanding of the Christian faith? Or, alternatively, is there something in the way we have come to think and speak of the Holy Spirit that has prepared the ground for such a telling abuse of Christian language? Radovan Karadzic's putative faith in the leading of the Spirit raises the issue of our own claim to understand what is meant by the work of the Spirit.[2] At issue, it seems, is the question of whether there is a relationship between hearing God speak and a corresponding shape to the Christian life. Radovan Karadzic's appeal to an unmediated, private, experience of the Spirit presses in upon us with such force that we are left with no alternative but to re-examine *our* own use and understanding of language about the identity and work of the Spirit.

In this paper, I present an account of the way in which the practice of reading the Bible as Christian scripture follows from a theology of Word and Spirit. The argument is set within the context of what is deemed to be an essential relation between the Spirit and Gospel. This insight is informed by the conviction that the relation between Word and the biblical text is most adequately understood in terms of the ongoing transformative work of the Spirit. I wish to advance the claim that when we speak of 'hearing' God's address, in and through scripture, we are at one and the same time speaking of the present and effective work of the Spirit. This is not, as perhaps many readers will recognize, a view of the Bible that has commanded centre stage. Its eclipse, if you will, stems in part from a failure to recognize the essential relation of Spirit, Word and scripture. At issue is a judgement about the role of the Spirit in relation to hermeneutical practice. Wesley Kort has captured this point with remarkable clarity in the following remark:

> At one time people knew what it meant to read a text as scripture, but we no longer do, because this way of reading has, since the late medieval and reformation periods, been dislocated and obscured. This dislocation has been so thorough that it is difficult today to know

how to raise the prospect of reading a text as scripture,
to regain a sense of what such a practice would be like,
why it should be engaged, and what difference it would
make.[3]

The question of the "difference" such a practice of reading would make is crucial, because it underscores the eschatological character of reading scripture. The kind of practice I have in view is one that recognizes the *eschatological* tenor of what takes place in attending to the biblical witness. Reading scripture is a practice fundamentally shaped by an ongoing encounter with God's disruptive grace and action. In reading *this* text, we come face to face with the reality of the Gospel: "Behold, I make all things new" (Rev 21:5). This approach to the practice of reading scripture admits that 'reading' has at least as much to do with God's *use* of the Bible as it does with our hermeneutical skill and insight. Reading scripture, therefore, is a creaturely activity predicated upon the prior movement of the Spirit.

Our task then, is to rediscover what it means to read *with* the Spirit. To do so is to be drawn within the compass of divine action.[4] As John Webster states, "A Christian theological construal of the church's reading of the Bible is a theology of the Word of God."[5] The following paper is to be understood, therefore, as a modest contribution to the task of working out in detail that which Webster has stated in elegantly laconic form. In order to do this, I will first provide an account of the Spirit as the giver of life. This will be followed by a consideration of the way in which the Spirit, as the Spirit of Christ, constitutes the concrete presence of the risen Lord among us. Finally, this paper will address the issue of what it means for the Word to be set before us in scripture, and so, consideration will be given to Calvin's understanding of the 'inner witness' of the Spirit. I also shall provide a brief reflection upon the relationship among Spirit, Word and tradition. All of this sets the stage for a number of final comments intended to draw out the implications of my argument in the service of articulating the way in which the Church may recover what it means to read scripture with the Spirit.

The 'Life-Giving' Spirit

Christian theology can proceed quite a distance when it seeks to follow, as David Yeago puts it, 'patterns of judgement' which emerge from within scripture.[6] When theologians undertake their work in such a manner, it soon becomes clear that an account of the Church's reading of scripture as Word requires a correspondingly sound doctrine of the Spirit. To this end, part of what this paper seeks to do, is to follow patterns of judgement within the biblical text which bear upon an understanding of the Spirit as—to use the language of the Nicene-Constantinopolitan creed—the 'giver of life'. Let us begin, then with the Old Testament, for it represents a particularly rich resource for coming to terms with the relation between Spirit and God's gift of life.

Spirit as the *ruach* and breath of God

The Old Testament begins with an account of the movement of the *'ruach elohim'* (Spirit or wind of God) over the face of the waters at creation (Gen 1:2). The immediate difficulty we face at this point pertains to the fact that *'ruach'* may very well be understood in instrumental rather than personal terms. It would be unwise, therefore, to suggest that the *ruach elohim* of Genesis 1:2, may be unequivocally likened to 'Spirit' as the third person of the Trinity. What we may claim, however, is this: that as Yahweh's chosen instrument, *ruach* is essential to God's act of creation. For this reason, it is essential to distinguish the *ruach elohim* from all other winds. As Michael Welker notes: "in the majesty of passages this 'wind' is anything but an event to be defined in solely meteorological terms. The 'wind' sent by God is a power that defines and changes history and representative destinies."[7] Even here, therefore, at the beginning of the canon, *ruach elohim,* is distinct and essential to God's creative act.

In Genesis 2:7 the identity of the Spirit as the giver of life comes into sharper focus. As the breath of God, the Spirit is found to be essential to the animation of life. Later portions of the Old Testament, such as Isaiah 42:5 may be profitably read as an extended commentary on this earlier conception of the Spirit as the breath of Yahweh. As Edmond Jacob comments: "the book of Isaiah shows that in the eighth century the spirit and Yahweh denote the same reality," to which he adds:

> The prophet does not go so far as the New Testament affirmation that God is spirit, but he implies—and everything suggests that he is not the first to do so—that spirit characterizes all that is contained in the word "god" and that Yahweh, once he has become the only God, is alone capable of giving it perfect fulfillment.[8]

The importance of this growing identification of the Spirit with Yahweh is telling. Given the development within the Old Testament pertaining to the identity of the Spirit, and the extent to which *ruach* and the breath of God occur with corresponding degrees of symmetry, it becomes clear that the Spirit plays a crucial role in the divine creation and animation of life.[9]

In the book of Job, Elihu's discourse indicates the relation between the Spirit and the ongoing *possibility* of life:

> Of a truth, God will not do wickedly,
> and the Almighty will not pervert justice.
> Who gave him charge over the earth
> and who laid on him the whole world?
> If he should take back his spirit to himself,
> and gather to himself his breath,
> all flesh would perish together,
> and all mortals return to dust. (Job 34:12-16)

Not only does this discourse connect the Spirit (in a way that perhaps we are unaccustomed to recognizing) with God's justice, but it denotes the extent to which the Spirit is responsible for the continuation of the good order of God.[10] It is this insight which informs our sense that the Spirit must be understood within the larger setting of God's action. Yet as the example of Job demonstrates, hunger for the justice and good order of God is that which is only met by divine action, and so we find ourselves in the position of waiting for the coming of the Spirit.

In Isaiah 63, for example, we find a stark contrast between the recognition of the grace and mercy of the God, on one hand, and the rebellion of the nation of Israel on the other (evident in the rhetorical juxtaposition of the verses 7-9 and 10-13). Israel's infidelity takes the form, quite notably, of forgetfulness. As a result of failing to remember the way in which the Spirit of God had been present in the course of their deliverance out of Egypt, God turns against Israel: "...they rebelled and grieved his holy spirit; therefore he became their enemy; he himself fought against them"(Isa 63:10). The connection between Spirit and divine justice is implicit in the Psalmist's confession—a confession which is identified in the Psalm's title with David's taking of Bathsheba:

> Create in me a clean heart, O God,
> and put a new and right spirit within me.
> Do not cast me away from your presence,
> and do not take your holy spirit from me.
> Restore to me the joy of your salvation,
> and sustain in me a willing spirit. (Ps 51:10-12)

While this stands as a negative example of what it means to speak of the Spirit as the 'giver of life'—and yet, as such, functions as a witness nonetheless—it underscores a rather important point: that God's presence and activity of the Spirit is independent of the exercise of our will or discretion.

One way of coming to understand this point is to speak of the Spirit of God in terms of divine 'gift'. It is this locution which indicates both the *eschatological* character of God's action and, correspondingly, the way in which God is not "available" to us. To say that the Spirit, as the giver of life, is both gift and promise is to point to the fact that the Spirit never becomes our *possession*. For we are always, as such, no more than subsequent agents within the *telos* of God's action. While we are indeed given the responsibility and freedom to act, this creaturely action is always, and quite properly so, an activity that is called into being by God. Returning to our discussion of Gen. 2:7, just as *ha-adam* (the man) is brought into being by virtue of God's breath (the Spirit), our existence is formed or given shape in terms of *our relation* to the Spirit of God. To speak of 'gift' here, is to denote something quite specific: that the presence, justice and mercy of God, come to us in a decidedly *gracious* manner. Our encounter with God, therefore, is to issue in a life of thankfulness and acknowledgment.

It is for this reason, that the gift of the Spirit is also promise. This point will become somewhat clearer when, at the end of this paper, I turn our attention to the specific question of the relation of Word and Spirit in the practice of reading scripture. What our present examination of the Spirit indicates, however, is this: that our devotion to God, moral accomplishment or perhaps even exegetical skill, has no imperatival or necessary force before God. Our human activity does nothing to place God under the burden of having to correspond to us. That God is effective and present to us in the power of the Spirit, speaks to the surfeit of his grace and love. This, of course, bears directly upon the question of what we may or may not bring to the text. But what of this second category, the notion of promise?

The entire aspect of 'promise' receives considerable attention in the Old Testament. Yahweh's promise was understood not only in terms of the nation's restoration, divine protection and deliverance from enemies or slavery, but also spoke to the question of the eschatological reconciliation between Yahweh and his people. In several prophetic texts it becomes increasingly clear that the dominant issue is one of disobedience in light of the profound need for salvation from sin. In the book of Ezekiel, for example, we find the following account of the shape of God's promise: "A new heart I will give you, and a new spirit I will put within you; and I will remove from your body the heart of stone and give you a heart of flesh. I will put my spirit within you, and make you follow my

statutes and be careful to observe my ordinances. Then shall you live…"
(Ezek 36:26-28a). Likewise, the connection between promise and
eschatological hope is clearly stated in the Isaianic account of the suffering servant of God: "The righteous one, my servant, shall make many
righteous, and he shall bear their iniquities" (Isa 53:11). The link between
God's justice, salvation, promise and the Spirit of God comes into view
in the recognition that the self-same servant of whom is said "he shall
bear their iniquities" is also, according to the author, the one who God
identifies as: "…my servant, whom I uphold, my chosen, in whom my
soul delights; I have put my spirit upon him; he will bring forth justice to
the nations" (Isa 42:1).

What has emerged out of this brief examination of Spirit in the
Old Testament is this: the Spirit, as the 'giver of life', is active within
and for the world. The Spirit is not only present in creation, but present
precisely as eschatological gift and promise. I have sought to bring us
to the point at which it is possible to begin to recognize the kind of
interest we have in the presence and ongoing work of the Spirit. What
this means in practice will become evident as we turn our attention to
the Christologically focused account of the Spirit in the New Testament.

Given the link between the Spirit of God and divine justice, promise and salvation, our examination of the New Testament calls for some
attention to the task of identifying the one who exists as the messianic
bearer of the Spirit. While the Synoptic tradition in general identifies
Jesus of Nazareth as the bearer of the Spirit, the gospel of Luke provides us with one of the clearest depictions of the way in which the New
Testament account of the Spirit is focused Christologically. In Luke 4, we
find a dramatic account of Jesus as the messianic bearer of the Spirit.
Opening up the scroll of the prophet of Isaiah, Jesus is depicted as
reading the following:

> The Spirit of the Lord is upon me,
> because he has anointed me to bring good news to
> the poor.

> He has sent me to proclaim release to the captives
> and recovery of sight to the blind,
> to let the oppressed go free,
> to proclaim the year of the Lord's favour.
> (Luke 4:18-19; cf. Isa 61:1-2b)

The significance of this narrative does not end however at this point. While all of the synoptic gospels narrate Jesus' teaching in the synagogue (Matt 13:54-58; Mk 6:1-6a; Luke 4:16-30), only Luke offers us a detailed narrative account of the event. Subsequent to reading the words of Isaiah 61:1-2b, Jesus rolls up the scroll, hands it back to the attendant, and then offers this stunning declaration: "Today this scripture has been fulfilled in your hearing." (Luke 4:21). This act represents one of the most poignant *self-declarations* of Jesus as the messianic bearer of the Spirit, the one in whom the kingdom of God has come. Yet, on what basis, may *we* come to know this? How is it that we find ourselves enclosed by the reality and truth of this event? How can we, in other words, become present to Jesus? The short answer is certainly this: by reading the Bible *with* the Spirit; and yet the task of coming to understand precisely what *this* means requires considerable effort.

The Spirit as the 'Spirit of Christ'

The analytical coherence of the Christian faith follows a particular path. One way of coming to terms with the essential shape of Christian belief it seems, is to pursue the way in which the New Testament characterizes the proximity of Son and Spirit. In its most terse form, for example, we have Paul in his first letter to the church at Corinth expressing a basic rule for language about the identity of Jesus Christ: "no can say 'Jesus is Lord' except by the Holy Spirit" (1 Cor 12:3). This it seems, sets things on a quite distinct path. For the very possibility of being able to know the reality of Jesus as the messianic bearer of the Spirit does not rest upon a *natural* footing of any kind. It requires, first and foremost, the prior action of God. It is this action which, according to Paul, constitutes the witness of the Spirit of Christ.

To speak of the Spirit in such a fashion rules out, it seems, a common understanding in which language about Spirit is quickly reduced to anthropological reflection, reflection upon what we might otherwise believe to be an innate hope or capacity for self-transcendence. This form of discourse is reflected in the mistaken belief that the 'image of God', or for that matter, creation, may represent a prevenient or *natural* basis for relation with God. The issue here concerns the degree to which such an approach readily lends itself to an understanding of innate human capacity as an *a priori* basis for relation with God apart from the prior movement of God *pro nobis* in the power of the Spirit. To follow this route would be to suggest that the eschatological reach of the Spirit towards us is met, or somehow anticipated on our part, by a prior (albeit unformed or pre-thematic) natural orientation to God. It is difficult to reconcile this approach with Paul's understanding of the "leading" of the Spirit (cf. Rom 8:14 and Gal 5:18) in which the preceding action of God the Spirit constitutes the basis of the freedom of the Christian life.

One of the primary reasons for the remarkable way in which the New Testament tradition understands the proximal relation of the second and third persons of the Trinity, follows from the nature of the Spirit's work. The Holy Spirit, as the Spirit of Christ, is not only the mode of God's presence, but as God, works to carry out the prophetic office of Christ. On the basis of the present and ongoing work of the Spirit, we are drawn into the reality of the Word. For the risen Christ is present in and through the work of the Spirit. As Barth states:

> The power of the Holy Spirit in which Jesus Christ is already near and present is not merely awakening and quickening but illuminating power in the fact that already, as the first glow of eternity, He shows and promises the dawn of this day, proclaiming it in His opera-

> tion and already being to him the pledge and earnest of
> its coming (Rom 8:23) and therefore of the nearness of
> His redemption.[11]

This 'illuminating' is, as we shall see, an interruptive work. It is for this reason that Barth, following the biblical witness, characterizes this work in terms of an "illuminating *power.*" This interruption, awakening and gathering is an outgrowth of the illuminative work of the Spirit. It is in the power of the Spirit that we encounter the Word of God, Jesus Christ and in this encounter are awakened to freedom and brought to life. The work of the Holy Spirit takes place *pro nobis*, in the following manner: the Spirit "thus wills that the human creature should believe and love and hope. He wills his hope as his own spontaneous act. He awakens us to this hope." What is more, according to Barth, is that the "Holy Spirit is God in the power of His eternal and incarnate Logos, of His Word spoken in Jesus Christ."[12]

But what of this "illuminating power" of the Spirit? Have we simply fallen victim to Amy Plantinga Pauw's foreboding that to speak of the Spirit as the 'Spirit of Christ' is to consider the Spirit as nothing more than simply a "girl-Friday for the Father and the Son"?[13] I do not think so, for we have already seen that the Spirit carries out a distinct mission: to make manifest the concrete presence of Christ in and for the world. The Spirit is thus present and active in such a manner as to draw us into relation with the risen Lord (cf. Luke 1:35 and Matt 1:18,20). As Barth states: "There is only one Word of God and that is the eternal Word of the Father which for our reconciliation became flesh like us and has now returned to the Father, to be present to His Church by the Holy Spirit."[14]

One way of gaining further insight on this issue is to ask, what does it mean to speak of the 'concrete presence' of Jesus? How is it, for example, that the risen and ascended Lord can be legitimately spoken of as *present* among us?

The Holy Spirit as the
'Concrete Presence' of Jesus

What does the Spirit do to bring about the concrete reality and presence of Christ in our midst? Careful attention to the New Testament depiction of the Spirit, as the 'Spirit of Christ' sustains an understanding of the way in which the transformative work of the Spirit constitutes the presence of the risen Lord. While the relation between the Spirit and Christ arises at a number of places within the New Testament, most notably perhaps in the Luke/Acts tradition (where Pentecost can be seen as the point at which the Holy Spirit 'arrives' as both the gift and promise of Luke 11:13), the "farewell discourses" of John's gospel (John 14:16-16:15) provide us with arguably the most compelling account of the Spirit as the 'concrete presence' of Christ. This Johannine tradition offers us a terse and concentrated glimpse into the identity and work of the Spirit.

One of the most striking facets of this tradition is the degree to which the *'Paraclete'* (*parakletos*) is, as the one sent by the Father at the request of the Son, of the same order as Jesus.[15] Our earlier consideration of the relationship between the Spirit and the rule and justice of God has provided us with a context out of which we can immediately grasp the significance of *this* characterization. The *Paraclete*, as "another advocate" carries out God's work in a determinate manner. Which is to say, that the Spirit comes to carry out a particular task, with concrete eschatological goals. The evangelist identifies the Spirit as the one who will "abide" with and "indwell" the disciples (for Jesus will no longer "be" with them in the manner to which they have become accustomed). The mission of the Spirit, as the one *sent* by the Father and the Son, is to draw people into relation with the reality and presence of the ascended Christ in order they may be the gathered people of God. In all of this, there is an unmistakable correspondence between the unity and fellowship enjoyed by the Trinity, and the life that Christians come to share with Christ in the fellowship of the Holy Spirit (John 14:20, cf. 2 Cor 13:14). Earlier I suggested that it is the presence of the Spirit which enables us to be present to Christ. It is important to recognize that this activity and transformative work does not eclipse *our* reality. For however disruptive may be the work of the Spirit, it does not take us over, but comes as grace in order that the Word, Jesus Christ, may be present amongst us (John 16:7). Quite remarkably then, the distinct mission of the *Paraclete* is to come alongside and share the fellowship of God *with us*. The Spirit comes in order that we might have communion with God.

To suggest that the mission of the Spirit has a particular shape, as I have done, is to simply note what the evangelist states in full. It is now apparent that we cannot, in fact, conceive of the Spirit in purely instrumental terms, for rather than being depicted as simply elemental to creation or existence, the Spirit is now to be regarded as the vital or constitutive means of the Christian life. As the concrete presence of Christ in our midst, the *Paraclete* comes to "teach," "remind," "testify," "guide," "speak," "hear," "declare," "prove" and "glorify". Taken together, what we have here is an effectively disturbing account of the Spirit's action.[16]

The Spirit does not come simply as a peaceable and gracious "counsellor" (as some translations appear to suggest), but comes rather, as the one sent to enact the eschatological judgement of the risen and ascended Lord. As John states: "and when he comes, he will prove the world wrong about sin and righteousness and judgment: about sin, because they do not believe in me; about righteousness, because I am going to the Father and you will see me no longer; about judgment, because the ruler of this world has been condemned" (John 16:8-11). The eschatological disclosure of God's judgment *is* central to the way in which God shall bring about peace. This judgement and corresponding peace is by no means unrelated to the identity and action of the Spirit as the "Spirit of truth" (cf. John 14:16; 15:26; 16:13).

While it may be tempting to draw a sharp distinction between the eschatological disclosure of God's judgement by the Spirit, and the Spirit's ongoing activity of 'teaching' (to refer to one of many activities of the Spirit), to do so would be to miss the point entirely. Judgement and teaching are two related aspects of the one work of the Spirit. In this, the kingdom of God breaks in upon us. The Spirit comes, according to the evangelist, to *teach:* to "guide you into all the truth...for this reason I said that he will take what is mine and declare it to you" (John 16:13-15). Yet 'teaching' here is by no means separate from the disclosure of judgement and the promise of peace and reconciliation. To force apart these two corresponding aspects of the Spirit's work is to fail to recognize the centrality of the kingdom of God in Jesus' proclamation and prayer. For this reason, the eschatological 'teaching' which the Spirit brings is co-extensive with the message and reality of the kingdom of God.

The 'illuminating power' of the Spirit is interruptive precisely for this reason: the work of the Spirit pertains to the eschatological rule and actuality of the kingdom of God. It is crucial, therefore, not to empty the evangelist's words of their eschatological force. While it is undoubt-edly true that in the promise of God, the Spirit will come to "guide you into all truth," this 'truth' is of neither a purely representative or expressivist kind. For the 'truth' which the Spirit illumines concerns the much larger, and I would argue, constitutive question of the reality and mission of God. Thus, to speak of the Spirit as the revealer of God, is to lay claim to a profound understanding of divine action. To speak of God in *this* way is to stand at quite a distance from those who might imagine that the work of the Spirit is simply to furnish us with a substantive epistemo-logical argument in favour of the possibility of knowing or experiencing the divine. The Spirit comes to illumine the Word so that we who are unrighteous and at a distance from God, may be reconciled: that we who are apart from God may, through the work of the giver of life, be drawn into the orbit of the incarnate and risen Lord. In the end, the eschatological work of the Spirit is disturbing precisely because this move-ment towards us—and the nature of our corresponding response—comes as sheer grace. In the hearing and witness of scripture, the incar-nate and risen Lord accosts us in the power of the Spirit, and does not permit us to remain as we are. It is in this sense that the illuminative work of the Spirit is accurately characterized as interruptive and disturbing. What remains to be seen, however, is the link between Spirit and reading the Bible.

The Word 'Set Before us in Scripture'

One cannot really begin to make sense of the relation between Word and Scripture apart from an account of the Holy Spirit. For, as Calvin indicates, the actuality of God's Word being "set before us in Scripture"[17] is predicated upon the work of the Spirit. When stated in this fashion, the need to understand the nature of the relationship between the Word and the Spirit is unmistakable.

Calvin and the 'Inner Witness' of the Holy Spirit

Calvin's theology provides us with one of the most significant dogmatic accounts of the work of the Spirit. Early on in the *Institutes,* for example, Calvin speaks of the 'inner witness' of the Spirit as a crucial way of getting at the question of how we become the objects of divine discourse:

> …the testimony of the Spirit is more excellent than all reason. For as God alone is a fit witness of himself in his Word, so also the Word will not find acceptance in men's hearts before it is sealed by the inward testimony of the Spirit. The same Spirit, therefore, who has spoken through the mouths of the prophets must penetrate into our hearts to persuade us that they faithfully proclaimed what had been divinely commanded.[18]

A number of things here demand our attention. It is clear, for instance, that Calvin understands Word and Spirit to be co-extensive realities (with no apparent subordination of the Spirit to the Son). Likewise, while the testimony of the Spirit is indeed "inward", there is little evidence to suggest that Calvin understood this in terms of the discrete personal experience of an autonomous individual. Just as the fourth evangelist depicts the eschatological work of the *Paraclete* within the context of the early Christian community, Calvin depicts the 'inner witness' of the Spirit in much more expansive terms than would be the case had his interest been fixed upon the issue of the free and autonomous experience of the subject. This is not to rule out the view that the 'inner witness' of the Spirit is a reality experienced by individuals. The essential point is this: what ought to occupy our attention is not the matter of *experience* but the teleological trajectory of the movement of God. Given that it concerns a shared text, whose use and interpretation is closely tied to the communal life and faith of the people of God, the illuminative work of the Spirit occurs in order that individuals may gain a share in a reality which extends beyond the limits of discrete identity. The Spirit sets the Word before us in order that we might become the Church and so bear faithful witness to the kingdom and rule of God. Calvin states: "Let us, then, know that the only true faith is that which the Spirit of God seals in our hearts."[19] A final comment on Calvin's notion of the inner witness of the Spirit is perhaps in order.

It is important to see that—contrary to customary ways of mapping out Calvin's doctrine of inspiration—this inner witness is not principally concerned with epistemology. Calvin's language about the inner witness of the Spirit is largely focused upon the divine action of the self-declaration of God. In this, Calvin precludes the possibility that we might wish to accord to the Bible the status of 'Word' independent of God's *use*. In the illuminative power and action of the Spirit, God speaks. For as Calvin states: "those whom the Holy Spirit has inwardly taught truly rest upon Scripture, and that Scripture is self-authenticated; hence, it is not right to subject it to proof and reasoning. And the certainty it deserves with us, it attains by the testimony of the Spirit."[20] We must be particularly alert here in resisting the temptation to understand Calvin's use of the term "self-authentication" apart from its centre in God. This is to say, that scripture is not self-authenticating or, for that matter, perspicuous, *per se*. It is rather, 'self-authenticating' in the event of God's use of this text as divine discourse. As an event of profound grace, human words and witness are 'bent' by the Holy Spirit in such a way as to become the vehicle of God's speech. In the illuminative power and corresponding inner witness of the Spirit, the Bible is a fitting and genuine witness to the concrete action of God. Through the work of the Spirit, divine discourse is seen to be genuinely and finally *effective*. In God's use of the

Bible, we not only hear God speak, but encounter the person and reality of the Word made flesh. In the presence of the Spirit, we come to possess a share in the promise given to Israel: the salvation and reconciliation of God. No longer as a distant and past figure, the risen and ascended Lord is manifest as the most real actuality there is, as the one in whom "we live and move and have our being" (Acts 17:28). It is in this sense that the Spirit *constitutes* the community of the people of God. Let us now follow what all of this means for the Church's reading of the Bible. How does the Spirit work in the midst of the people of God?

Spirit, Word and Tradition

A theology of Word and Spirit is predicated on the recognition that God is the primary author of scripture. This belief does not, however, stand over against a responsible and necessary attention to the question of the human authorship of the Bible. Attention to critical scholarship has demonstrated, with considerable force, the value offered to us in the use of literary and historical-critical methods of inquiry. What a theology of Word and Spirit must affirm, however, is that the task of hearing God speak simply demands *more* than our historical, analytical and hermeneutical skills can provide. To believe that God is the primary author of scripture—notwithstanding complex issues related to the question of *how* God speaks in and through the human words of the biblical canon—is to stand within the Christian tradition.

The force of the term 'tradition' here is important. For as Paul Achtemeier indicates, tradition provides the essential framework within which each new generation may begin to find their bearings. Tradition(s), on this account, comes to represent the historical shape and reality of the present community.[21] Too often we simply fail to grasp the nature and operative force of tradition and even when we do, we commonly understand 'tradition' in entirely negative terms. Part of our anxiety with respect to tradition stems from its potential for *ideological* use in the appeal to historical precedent as a justification for the present exercise of power or force. While this kind of appeal is indeed one which we ought to resist as strongly as possible, it ought not to stand in the way of a faithful appropriation of tradition. For tradition properly understood, stands in clear opposition to such patently ideological ends.

Traditions are, as Achtemeier suggests, dynamic rather than static constructs. As dynamic constructs, traditions can in fact offer us a necessary context out of which we may faithfully appropriate and carry forward our sense of reality in the very midst of an ever-changing present.[22] Our task then, is one of determining how the work of the Spirit is tied to the faithful re-appropriation of tradition. We have within the Bible itself, a number of examples of what it means for there to be a dynamic reappraisal of received tradition. Time and time again Israel is faced with the task of having to reinterpret the meaning of its existence in light of changing circumstances and events. The prophets, in a remarkable fashion, come to represent what it means to faithfully interpret tradition in the face of the exigencies of contemporary existence:

> The prophets warn a people grown complacent on the basis of election and promised land that the God who gave the land can also take it away, and summon that community grown listless in the faith to realize that they depend solely on God's decision to allow them to remain a people. The very traditions on which they depended and from which they gained confidence in their nationhood were the ones used by the prophets to announce exile and an end to such a nationhood.[23]

A not insignificant part of what it meant for Israel to live as the people of God entailed precisely this kind of extended conversation with tradition as a way of remaining faithful to God.

In the course of his work, *Engaging Scripture*, Stephen Fowl demonstrates that understanding the movement of the Spirit is an activity of *discernment* proper to the community of faith. Fowl comments: "...this debate and discernment is itself often shaped both by prior interpretation of scripture and by traditions of practice and belief" to which Fowl lucidly adds, "experience of the Spirit shapes the reading of scripture, but scripture most often provides the lenses through which the Spirit's work is perceived and acted upon."[24] Attention to the way in which the movement of the Spirit is related to our responsible and faithful discernment of a complex of communal structures, practices and beliefs—what I am calling here 'tradition'—is instructive indeed.

Fowl's exegesis of Acts 10-15 attends, with particular care, to the Church's understanding and practice of reading with the Spirit. The Apostolic Council in Jerusalem, for example, was faced with the challenge of having to resolve the question of how and on what basis were Gentile Christians to be permitted entry into fellowship with Jewish believers. Was it necessary, in other words, for Gentile converts to be circumcised and to adopt the religious practices of Jewish Christians in order to be regarded as full participants? The climax of the narrative of this dispute is, as Fowl notes, an agreement reached by "the apostles and the elders, with the consent of the whole church" (Acts 15:22). This agreement is given its clearest identity in the principal statement "for it has seemed good to the Holy Spirit and to us to impose upon you no further burdens than these essentials..." (Acts 15:28). The importance of this example can be readily seen in the fact that the decision reached by the Council was understood to be one in *agreement with* the Spirit. It is important to note that this "leading" was by no means discrete or private. The decision undertaken by the Council involved debate pertaining to the question of what constitutes a faithful discernment and understanding of tradition (cf. James' reference to Amos 9:11-12). The nature of deliberation was such that explicit attention was given to the force of Peter's testimony regarding the work of the Spirit among the Gentiles (traditions of practice and belief). All of this represents the basis upon which the Jerusalem Council, hearing testimony and exercising hermeneutical responsibility, came to learn and demonstrate what it means to read scripture *with* the Spirit. As Fowl indicates: "It is perhaps not surprising to claim that both the practice of testifying and bearing witness and the practice of listening wisely to such testimony are essential to the community's ability to 'read with the Spirit'."[25]

It is this *dynamic*, rather than static, form of practice which ought to stand at the very centre of the Christian faith. We begin to see here what is required of us should we wish to engage in a faithful reading with the Spirit. Just as the cross and resurrection of Jesus stand as the central problematic of the gospels, the 'inner witness' of the Spirit stands at the centre of what it means to have the Word set before us in scripture. In the practice of reading with the Spirit, the people of God encounter and come to understand their identity and vocation in the reality and life of the Word made flesh. In and through this work, God is present among us. Having come to recognize the immense value and promise offered to us by the inner witness of the life-giving Spirit, let us now turn to the specific question of what it means for the Church to read scripture "with the Spirit".

The Church's Reading With the Spirit

Having drawn attention to the work of the Spirit as the means by which the risen Lord is present and active among us, I now wish to speak to the question of the relationship between divine action and a corresponding practice of reading with the Spirit. The claim here is that through the ongoing work of the Spirit, the community of faith finds itself in the presence of the risen and active Lord, Jesus Christ.

The church's reading of the Bible is only truly profitable (for salvation) when it is taken up in the movement of God. The specific shape which this movement takes is concretely tied, as David Demson's reading of Barth reminds us, to the "event of the gathering, upholding and commissioning of the apostles" as witnesses to the coming of Jesus.[26] The Church becomes present to Jesus, in the "gathering, upholding and commissioning" of the apostles. In the grace and action of God the Spirit, we are included in this apostolic gathering, upholding and sending. Demson states: "The power by which Jesus Christ encloses the story of men and women into his story, the power by which he includes later men and women into his relationship with the apostles', is the Holy Spirit.'[27] In the movement of God's gathering, upholding and sending, the Christian community knows itself to have been brought into being through an encounter with the risen Lord in the power of the Spirit. The Christian community, as the community which hears the apostolic witness of the Word, is awakened by the Holy Spirit, gathered and sent into the world. It is in this sense then, that the people of God both read and are 'read' by the Bible. For the Bible is both a fitting and disturbing witness to the reality of the Gospel, the Word made flesh:

> It is a witness and as such it demands attention, respect and obedience—the obedience of the heart, the free and only genuine obedience. What it wants from the Church, what it impels the Church towards—and it is the Holy Spirit moving in it who does this—is agreement with the direction in which it looks itself. And the direction in which it looks is to the living Jesus Christ. As Scripture stirs up and invites and summons and impels the Church to look in this same direction there takes place the work of the Spirit of Scripture who is the Holy Spirit.[28]

The work of the Spirit is constitutive of the awakening, gathering and sending of the people of God as the Church. For not only is the Christian community "stirred up", "invited" and "summoned" to Christ through the hearing of the Word, but in the movement of the Spirit, the Church is awakened, equipped and impelled to follow the witness of Scripture. The Spirit, according to Barth, uses the apostolic witness in such a way as to enable the human words of the Bible to be become a fitting witness to the reality of God: "His Holy Spirit acts and works in the concrete form of the power and truth of their word....Jesus Christ makes use of them. Their authority, power and mission consists in the fact that He does this."[29] Our consideration of what is entailed in the task of 'reading with the Spirit' has, therefore, enabled us to comprehend the disarmingly subtle meaning of the claim that "a Christian theological construal of the church's reading of the Bible is a theology of the Word of God."[30] The contribution that this paper brings to this insight, is its focus upon the constitutive and ongoing work of the Spirit as the basis of our faithful reading of scripture.

Conclusion

In the work of the Spirit, scripture becomes a fitting witness to the reality and presence of the risen and ascended Lord. By virtue of our inclusion in the event of God's gathering, upholding and commissioning of the apostolic witness in the power of the Spirit, we are awakened, gathered and sent into the world. The Church's reading with the Spirit, has therefore, much more to do with human action corresponding to God's divine initiative than it does with interpretive practice *per se.* In recognizing that the 'truth' which the Spirit illumines bears directly upon the reality and mission of God, we have been able to see that there is, contrary to the witness of Radovan Karadzic, an exacting and necessary relation between the message of "the gospel teaching" and the corresponding shape of the Christian life. Our proper task then, is to see that our learning to read with the Spirit has a far greater end in sight than we might have otherwise imagined. As the awakened, gathered, and sent community of faith, we engage in the practice of faithfully reading with the Spirit in order to hear God speak. The promise of the Gospel is this: that as we become hearers of the Word, we may be transformed by the Spirit and become the people of God. The promise of God engenders, therefore, the recognition that as we learn to read with the Spirit, we may truly become the people of God and may enter the world with the hope and witness of Christ. *Veni creator Spiritus,* Come Holy Spirit!

Notes

1 Paul Mojzes, "Confessions of a Serb leader," *Christian Century*, August 16-23 (1995) 766. In this article, Mojzes offers a valuable summary and translation of an interview titled "The Resurrection of the Crouching Soul: A Conversation with Mr. Radovan Karadzic". This interview originally appeared in *Svetigora*, a monthly magazine of the Cetinje Orthodox Metropolitanate.

2 Although Karadzic does not clarify the source of his understanding of the "gospel teaching", his confession bears a family resemblance with the synoptic tradition of Mark 13:11 (Matt 10:19 and Luke 12:11). The social and literary setting of this tradition—in which the promise of the Spirit is set within the context of Jesus' instruction to the Apostles concerning persecution that would come their way as a result of preaching the gospel—indicates the extent to which Karadzic's confession is at a profound distance from the explicative sense of the biblical text. The recognition, for example, that the Apostles were instructed to carry out their ministry without the provisions of tunics, sandals, or even a staff, demonstrates how very different was the life they were to lead from the 'mission' undertaken by Radavon Karadzic. The specific literary and social setting of this tradition ought to stand as a critical hermeneutic by which to judge subsequent interpretations of the leading of the Spirit. This is particularly germane when interpretation is pressed into the service of an ideology at such a profound distance from the 'teaching of the gospel'.

3 Wesley A. Kort, *"Take, Read": Scripture, Textuality, and Cultural Practice* (Pennsylvania: Pennsylvania State University Park, 1996) 1.

4 The approach to reading the Bible which I have in view here is not one in which the emphasis is placed upon the interpretive capacity or skill of an individual. Attention is given, rather, to the communal forms of practice shaped by the desire for a faithful 'hearing' and 'reading' of scripture. To say this, is to recognize the complex relation between text and audience, divine and human action. While this entire question certainly demands a much fuller account than can be provided here, the final section of this paper indicates briefly what such an approach would look like should it be worked out in detail.

5 John Webster, "Hermeneutics in Modern Theology: Some Doctrinal Reflections" *SJT* 51/3 (1998) 323.

6 This locution occurs very early on in the context of what proves to be a very helpful consideration of the relationship between classical creedal statements and a theological reading of the New Testament: cf. David S. Yeago, "The New Testament and the Nicene Dogma: A Contribution to the Recovery of Theological Exegesis" *The Theological Interpretation of Scripture: Classic and Contemporary Readings* (Cambridge: Blackwell, 1997) 88.

7 Michael Welker, *God the Spirit* (Minneapolis: Fortress, 1994) 99.

8 Edmond Jacob, *Theology of the Old Testament* (London: Hodder and Stoughton, 1958) 124.

[9] One may profitably refer to Hans Walter Wolff's discussion of the meaning of *ruach* in relation to breath as the life and activity of the human creature in his classic work, *Anthropology of the Old Testament* (Philadelphia: Fortress, 1981) 32-34.

[10] An illuminative consideration of the function of the Elihu discourse may be found in Jean Lévêque, *Job et son Dieu: Essai d'Exégèse et de Théologie Biblique*, tome II (Paris: LeCoffre, 1970) 573-575.

[11] Karl Barth, *Church Dogmatics*, IV/3.2 (Edinburgh: T. & T. Clark, 1962) 916.

[12] Ibid., 942 (revised).

[13] Amy Plantinga Pauw, "Who or what is the Holy Spirit?" *Christian Century* (January 17, 1996) 49. Plantinga Pauw correctly identifies a tendency within contemporary Western theology that fails to accord equal status to the Spirit. She credits Karl Barth with having provided us with an influential but entirely false characterization of the Spirit as the 'Spirit of Christ'. Theologians who follow Barth in this are, according to Plantinga Pauw, likewise culpable of having committed this reductive move. In arriving at this judgement however, she has apparently failed to recognize that it is Barth, among perhaps all other contemporary theologians of the 20th century, who is most responsible for the renewed attention Western theologians have given to the rich tradition and significance of trinitarian theology (cf. for example, Barth's discussion of 'person' and equality with respect to the Trinity early on in the *Church Dogmatics*, I/1, 2nd ed. [Edinburgh: T. & T. Clark, 1990] 351-53. A close reading of the Barth corpus demonstrates the extent to which Barth's doctrine of the Spirit does not in fact fall victim to critique raised by Plantinga Pauw. Therefore, while largely correct in her identification of a tendency among Western theologians, Plantinga Pauw is incorrect in imputing this error to Barth. A more helpful reflection on the matter is offered by Kilian McDonnell ("The Determinative Doctrine of the Holy Spirit," *Theology Today*, 39 [July 1982] 142-161), who argues that the task of clarifying the nature of the relationship between the second and third article, Son and Spirit, requires a high degree of acuity, for "If trinitarian doctrine is normative, one cannot say that, because in the inner-trinitarian life the spiration of the Spirit is no less than the procession of the Son. Nor can the Spirit's mission in history be less. Even so, the Spirit reveals the true reality of Jesus (John 14:26), and in no sense does this imply a subordinationist diminishing of the Son." (154).

[14] Karl Barth, *CD* I/2, 513.

[15] Cf. 1 John 2:1 where Jesus is identified as our "advocate with the Father."

[16] One way of coming to terms with the 'disturbing' nature of the Spirit, is to closely follow the New Testament's depiction of what happens in the wake of the Spirit's action. As Stephen Fowl (*Engaging Scripture: A Model for Theological Interpretation* [Malden: Blackwell, 1998] 107) indicates, the response on the part of religious Jews to the gift of the Spirit in Acts 2:1-4 is one of 'amazement' and 'astonishment'. Their astonishment did not follow simply from the 'gift of tongues', but from the fact that the Spirit had apparently come upon a most unlikely people, the uncircumcised *Gentiles*. The significance of the Spirit's work in Acts 2 extends considerably beyond the gift of "speaking in tongues" (as important as this is for many), in denoting a new stage in the eschatological

expansion of the kingdom of God, evident in the hearing of the disciples' proclamation among "devout Jews from every nation," including "visitors from Rome, both Jews and proselytes" (Acts 2:11). The implications of the remarkable unfolding of the kingdom of God in the New Testament—as the locus and reign of Christ—become clear as soon as one begins to acknowledge the connection between the Spirit and justice of God, present in the life and work of the messianic bearer of the Spirit. It is this perspective which permits a determination of a context out of which it is possible to begin to articulate the social and political implications of the Gospel. It is for this reason that the freedom we are to enjoy in the Spirit (2 Cor 3:17) is co-extensive with a re-ordering of the social relations of the people of God. This means, in the end, that the divisions of ethnicity, race, culture, status and gender are called into question by the reality of the Gospel (Gal 3:28). A focus on the proclamation and teaching of the kingdom of God does not, accordingly, offer an escape from social and political responsibility, for it focuses the shape of Christian moral responsibility in a concretely Christological fashion. The work of the Spirit and the kingdom of God concern the reality of Jesus Christ in our midst, and we are not permitted to decide in advance, where, when and to whom, the Spirit of God will speak.

[17] John Calvin, *Institutes of the Christian Religion,* vol. 1 (Philadelphia: Westminster, 1960) I,13,7.

[18] Calvin, *Institutes,* I,7,4.

[19] Calvin, *Institutes,* I,7,5

[20] Calvin, *Institutes,* I,7,5

[21] Paul Achtemeier, *Inspiration and Authority: Nature and Function of Christian Scripture* (Peabody MA: Hendrickson, 1999) 111.

[22] Ibid.

[23] Ibid., 112-13.

[24] Fowl, *Engaging Scripture,* p. 114.

[25] Ibid., 115.

[26] David Demson, *Hans Frei and Karl Barth: Different Ways of Reading Scripture* (Grand Rapids: Eerdmans, 1997) 22.

[27] Ibid., 48-49.

[28] Karl Barth, *CD* IV/1, 723.

[29] Ibid., 718.

[30] Webster, "Hermeneutics in Modern Theology: Some Doctrinal Reflections" 323.

Chapter 10

The Significance of Scripture in Christian Formation

Jeffrey P. Greenman

Renewal through Rediscovery

One of the most important trends in recent theology is an eagerness to explore the relevance of ancient Christian thought for the contemporary church. Voices from various points on the theological spectrum are suggesting that "classical Christianity" may provide a particularly valuable resource for revitalizing faith and witness in an increasingly post-Christian culture. In this regard, a programmatic statement has come from a leading Methodist theologian, Geoffrey Wainwright: "The greatest need of our North American mainline Protestant churches is for a reappropriation of evangelical, catholic, orthodox Christianity."[1]

An example of this trend is the resurgent interest in what is being called "the theological interpretation of Scripture." While there is no incontestable definition of what "theological interpretation" means, clearly it involves an effort to take seriously premodern biblical interpretation. A number of thinkers are seeking to develop constructive alternatives to reductionistic or rationalistic trends in modern exegesis, and to overcome the baleful effects of scholarly fragmentation and sub-specialization that routinely segments off biblical studies from matters of doctrine, ethics, and spirituality. According to Stephen Fowl, "premodern scriptural interpretation should be seen as a conversation partner providing insights and resources for reading scripture theologically in the present."[2]

Premodern theologians also are the conversation partners for Ellen Charry, who has drawn deeply upon the classical Christian tradition in her exposition of the "pastoral" function of Christian doctrine.[3] Through an analysis of New Testament materials and major patristic and medieval texts (by figures such as Athanasius, Augustine, Anselm, Aquinas, and Calvin), Charry suggests an outline for the renewal of theology. She contends that historic Christian orthodoxy, particularly in the patristic period, understood theology as "an aid in cultivating a skilled and excellent life."[4] Theology was "sapiential" and "aretegenic". Sapiential theology was understood as a practical discipline that seeks to convey wisdom about God—increasing the **knowledge and love of God was its central focus, not merely setting** forth correct information about God. "Sapience" (wisdom) is necessary for Christian virtue. Charry stresses the "aretegenic" dimension of this approach, and finds that a key trait of classical Christian teaching is a "virtue-shaping function" focused on character formation and spiritual maturation. She concludes that "as these major shapers of the Christian tradition formulated, reformulated, and revised Christian doctrine, its moral, psychological, and social implications were uppermost in their minds."[5]

In the area of spirituality, philosopher Diogenes Allen has attempted to redress what he perceives as "a widespread theological amnesia in the church" by discussing key themes drawn from major (but "utterly neglected") spiritual writers of the early church. He argues against the common notion that spiritual writings are basically non-theological or merely "devotional" literature. For classical Christian thinkers, spiritual theology was theology *per se*: probing the nature of God as triune or the meaning of the Incarnation, and explaining the dynamics of spiritual warfare or liturgy, were part and parcel of the same basic task. Precisely for this reason, a careful reading of spiritual writers can help to reconnect our everyday lives with the Bible and with central Christian doctrines. Allen's concern for practical guidance and pastoral insight is clear from his book's sub-title: "The Theology of Yesterday for Spiritual Help Today".[6] In addition, Roberta Bondi, a church historian, has pursued "conversations" with the early monastics and "desert fathers" concerning topics such as prayer, worship, Scripture, friendship, and the virtues.[7]

This brief survey suggests that "renewal through rediscovery" is a major movement with broad representation across the Christian spectrum. A popular manifestation is the associated trend toward Christian books, lectures, sermons and conferences with the prefix "re-" appearing in their titles: rethinking, renewing, revisiting, revisioning, reengaging, reappropriating, reimaging, and so on. Amidst times of momentous cultural and religious change, such as our rapid transition into a post-modern, pluralistic, multicultural society, it seems natural to look to history. In various ways, these "re-" terms indicate a desire to look backward, to examine where we have been, and to learn from sources in the past about what directions are needed in the future. There is a growing recognition that "without memory, our intellectual life is impoverished, barren, ephemeral, subject to the whims of the moment."[8]

While some "renewal through rediscovery" thinkers may show tendencies toward a romantic yearning for a golden era in the distant past, this theological agenda is neither naively nostalgic or simplistically uncritical. It would be utterly inappropriate to assert that simply because a given thought was affirmed by an esteemed church father (or mother), it is therefore worthy of our acceptance. The quest is for thoughtful engagement with fresh sources of enrichment. In the words of Bradley Holt, "a living tradition is a self-critical developing stream, not a moribund repetition of the past."[9] The historical enterprise— the exploration of neglected ideas and practices from the early church— has a normative goal: fostering faithful Christian thinking and living in the contemporary context.

Trends in Recent Evangelical Theology

For the purposes of this essay, we note with particular interest the involvement of evangelical Protestants in the "renewal through rediscovery" movement. A number of significant projects by evangelicals testify to the importance of this phenomenon. Among the prominent evangelical authors who typify this intellectual direction are Richard Foster and James Houston, whose writings have sparked widespread interest in ancient spiritual disciplines, traditional forms of prayer, and reading devotional classics.[10] Foster and Houston appear to have followed C. S. Lewis' advice: "It is a good rule, after reading a new book, never to allow yourself another new one till you have read an old one in between" so that we might have "the clean sea breeze of the centuries blowing through our minds."[11]

Flowing from this movement, evangelical thinkers are producing a growing body of biblical, theological and historical scholarship. This literature takes a variety of forms, as the following examples illustrate. The title of a monograph by patristics expert D. H. Williams indicates his ambitious and far-reaching goal: *Retrieving the Tradition and Renewing Evangelicalism*.[12] Thomas Oden, who abandoned liberal theology in favor of a "post-critical orthodoxy" focused on the church fathers, characterizes his three-volume systematic theology as an effort that "wishes nothing more than to identify and follow that ancient ecumenical consensus of Christian teaching of God."[13] Books of daily readings from spiritual classics have appeared.[14] A good indicator of the seriousness with which evangelicals are pursuing premodern biblical interpretation is the fact that two leading evangelical publishing houses have committed themselves to major series that make texts of patristic and medieval exegesis readily accessible to pastors and students.[15]

Another noteworthy contribution has been made by a recent volume of essays, *Reclaiming the Great Tradition*, that features leading evangelical, Roman Catholic and Orthodox theologians. The authors champion the vitality of "ecumenical orthodoxy".[16] In that volume, J. I. Packer has delineated the contours of "the great tradition" of Christianity as "the authentic biblical and creedal mainstream of Christian identity."[17] This common heritage of core Christian belief is expressed in Protestant, Roman Catholic and Orthodox "versions." Packer's "great tradition" is highly reminiscent of what C. S. Lewis called "mere Christianity." In principle, diverse adherents of the "great tradition" occupy common ground that provides the basis for a "unified Christian witness" in the face of impending cultural meltdown and widespread moral decline.[18]

Among evangelicals, one of the most zealous and persistent advocates of a whole-hearted embrace of the "great tradition" is Robert Webber. His *Ancient-Future Faith: Rethinking Evangelicalism for a Postmodern World* is a preliminary attempt to generate a dialogue between classical Christianity and postmodern thought.[19] Webber argues not only that historic orthodoxy is a "transcultural framework of faith" with relevance in every era, but that premodern and postmodern outlooks have a great deal more in common than we usually realize. For example, with regard to attitudes toward education (religious or otherwise), both classical Christianity and postmodernity emphasize the passing down of wisdom through experience in community context, rather than the transfer of objective information expressed in propositional truths.[20]

The Classical Christian Approach to Scripture

Christians are "people of the Book," in David Jeffrey's phrase.[21] Classical Christianity endorses the preeminent place of Scripture in shaping the Church's theology and affirms its guiding authority in the moral and spiritual life. If the Bible was "the great textbook of the ancient church," what might we learn from looking back at the way the early Christians understood the Bible?[22] How did they perceive the Bible to shape their spiritual lives?

Charles Kannengiesser observes that the early Christian writers began with the assumption that Scripture is divine: "Holy Writ provided an access to God, a way of communicating with God, which was in itself a divine disposition. There was no question that God ultimately was the source of the Book, deciding about its content and authorizing its relevance."[23] They believed that Scripture "was not only exempt from error but contained nothing superfluous."[24] On account of their emphasis upon Scripture's divine nature, they viewed it as "the living word of God in a written form" and saw that its purpose was to change the lives of its readers. The Bible was seen as "a powerful presence of the inspiring Spirit, ready to operate in the midst of the faithful community."[25]

The case of Antony, the great figure of Egyptian monasticism in the fourth century, is instructive. Antony was once asked what someone must do in order to please God. He replied: "Wherever you go, always have God before your eyes; whatever you do, have before you the testimony of the holy Scriptures." Douglas Burton-Christie comments that such a statement indicates that "having the testimony of the Scriptures constantly before one is equivalent to being always in the presence of God. Scripture has that kind of power."[26] Desert monasticism acknowledged the practical value of Scripture as a God-given text that provided for the discovery of salvation and spiritual growth. "Holiness in the desert was defined, finally, by how deeply a person allowed himself or herself to be transformed by the words of Scripture."[27]

The classical approach to Scripture emphasizes the Bible as a God-given provision for human encounter with God in and through the pages of the sacred scriptures. This emphasis is seen clearly in Gregory the Great's letter of pastoral advice addressed to Theodorus, physician to the emperor. Gregory (c. 540-604) is troubled because the reader "neglects to read daily the words of his Redeemer." Gregory appeals to the distinctive nature of Scripture in order to provide motivation for serious engagement with the Bible. He asks Theodorus: "What is sacred Scripture but a kind of epistle of Almighty God to His creature?"[28] It is striking that the Bible is understood as addressed personally and directly to each reader. Gregory goes on to use an analogy with a letter from the emperor himself: if Theodorus had received letters from "an earthly emperor, you would not loiter, you would not rest, you would not give sleep to your eyes, till you had learnt what the earthly emperor had written." Therefore, how much more should he read "ardently" and meditate daily on the epistles of "the Emperor of Heaven". Gregory exhorts Theodorus: "Learn the heart of God in the words of God."[29]

Recent Evangelical Approaches to Scripture

Some evangelical theologians, digging deeply into the depths of the Christian spiritual tradition, are attempting to articulate a contemporary theology of Scripture which has many affinities with the classical conception sketched above. To illustrate, we can look at the writings of Robert Webber and M. Robert Mulholland.

Webber seeks an alternative theological approach that would avoid what he sees as a strong tendency toward evangelical rationalism. First, he is wary of a propensity to gravitate toward a dangerous kind of biblicism, namely, replacing faith in Christ with faith in the Bible. Strictly speaking, the problem here is idolatry. After all, the Bible itself is "not the object of our faith or belief."[30] Rather, the function of the Bible is to "take us to Christ."

Second, evangelical rationalism often denigrates the validity of symbolic speech, preferring the abstract/conceptual language inherited from Enlightenment thought. Webber claims that this preference engenders a view that reduces the Bible to "a book of words" and that such a view causes a "loss of understanding" since so much of the Bible precisely consists in symbolic speech and imagery (such as poetry, proverb, or parable). Anyone who doubts Webber's analysis should consider, for example, how frequently evangelical sermons force New Testament parables into three-point messages driven by abstract theological categories or doctrinal frameworks that are actually far removed from the passage at hand. Webber decries the loss of a sense of mystery and transcendence in contemporary evangelicalism, especially in worship, and in its understanding of Scripture. His account of the Bible aims for a balance between objective and subjective elements: "Scripture is beyond full comprehension and therefore mystical, but also within the realm of understanding and therefore reasonable."[31]

Webber points us in a promising direction, but does not develop a detailed alternative. M. Robert Mulholland, a New Testament scholar from a Wesleyan background, echoes similar concerns when he contends that we, as Bible readers, deal with the text primarily in an "informational mode." Often we bring our critical, analytical capacities to bear upon the Bible, using rational techniques that serve, generally unwittingly, to maintain our "cognitive, rational control of the text." We approach the text with a problem-solving mentality, and carry with us the assumption that information is to be managed or manipulated according to our desires. Mulholland's point is simple: if this is our view of the Bible, it can have little formative impact on our spiritual lives. Spiritual formation is far more comprehensive (and difficult) than mere "mental agreement with abstract propositions."

His theological alternative emphasizes what he calls the "iconographic" nature of Scripture, a notion that bears a strong resemblance to the patristic perspective on Scripture already described. For Mulholland, the Bible uses ordinary language to speak of spiritual realities, becoming a "verbal window into the reality of life shaped by the Word."[32]   This suggestion about the Bible's "literary iconography" draws an analogy with the traditional understanding of icons, those ornate pictorial representations of Christ (or some other religious scene) which occupy a central place in the liturgical art of the Eastern church. Icons draw the reader "into a reality, a mystery, which opens out in front of you. Instead of being an independent, objective observer who retains control of the picture, you find that the icon conveys an independent, objective reality that encounters you, addresses you, and draws you into its order of being."[33]   According to Kallistos Ware, an icon acts as "a point of meeting, a place of encounter" so that the worshipper is "brought into a living, effectual contact with the person or mystery depicted."[34]   In this way, the icon "serves not as a mere reminder only but as a means of communion."

Mulholland realizes that many Protestants might be "uncomfortable" about using the language of "iconography" to describe Scripture. Whatever we may conclude about the propriety of icons in the Eastern church, the analogy is helpful for two reasons. First, it focuses our attention on the fact that the language of Scripture points beyond itself to another order of reality. Second, the analogy assists us in realizing that the purpose of Scripture is to draw us into an encounter, a participation in communion with God.

At this juncture I would note that Mulholland's account needs to give greater attention to the Trinitarian nature of God's self-revelation. In particular, the ministry of the Holy Spirit is not given adequate weight. Mulholland accentuates the point that we do not come into an encounter with God by means of techniques under our control, but he should emphasize more strongly that any human encounter with God is always through the gift of the Holy Spirit. The natural or unspiritual person does not perceive the things of the Spirit of God (1 Cor 2:14). Because no human eye or ear or heart is adequate to grasp God's self-revelation, the Word must "create its own hearers."[35]   The work of the Spirit, who inspired the Scriptures (2 Tim 3:16), is to make God's Word contemporary with us, to re-present

God to us, and bring us into dynamic relationship with Him. According to Helmut Thielicke: "The presence of the Lord is a sovereign gift. Without this gift we have only a dead past and historical distance."[36]

Discovering Classical Christian Lectio

Kathleen Norris testifies vividly to the lived experience of "renewal through rediscovery" in her bestseller *The Cloister Walk*. The author describes her "immersion into a liturgical world" as a Benedictine oblate. Norris is a married, Protestant poet, a self-confessed "doubter" who only rarely had attended church as an adult, and someone who "hadn't read the Bible in years."[37] She took an "abbreviated but powerful profession of monastic vows" by attaching herself to a particular monastery and by promising to live according to the sixth-century Rule of St. Benedict to the fullest extent that her situation in life allowed.[38]

During two extended periods of participation in Benedictine communal life, Norris discovered the power of the Bible, especially the Psalms, to draw her into communion with God. Life in Benedictine communities is organized around a daily rhythm of corporate worship—consisting of services of morning, noon, and evening prayer, as well as daily eucharist—and manual labour. The focal point of Benedictine spirituality is hearing and praying the Bible. The liturgy is the medium through which the Bible is received, as Jean Leclerq has observed.[39] The Rule of St. Benedict spells out in great detail the schedule for corporate worship in order to ensure that the entire Psalter is read every week. During mealtimes, the Scriptures are read aloud while the community eats in silence, listening to the text. "The purpose of reading at meals is a reminder of the whole purpose of life that Benedict is laying before us: it is so that we should be listening to God at all times."[40] The daily liturgy and mealtime readings involve the practice of *lectio continua*, reading through whole books of the Bible, section by section, often with long silences between selections. Norris notes that during her eighteen months in the abbey, she listened to Genesis, Ruth, Tobit, Esther, Job, the Song of Songs, Hosea, Jonah, large portions of Exodus, Samuel, Kings and Isaiah.

This systematic pattern enables an "immersion" into the world of the Scriptures. Norris suggests that she was attracted to the Benedictines "because of the hospitality I've encountered in their communal *lectio,* a hospitality so vast that it invites all present into communion with the text being read."[41] She observes that "monastic worship is essentially Hebraic; every day you recite the psalms, and you listen, as powerful biblical images, stories, and poems are allowed to flow freely, to wash over you."[42]

The term *lectio* is simply the Latin word for "reading" but in monastic tradition, it carries a rich series of associations. What is called *lectio divina* refers to "divine reading" which is one of the primary activities of the monk. It involves not merely reading the text silently, but hearing the text read aloud. Ancient readers typically used their lips and ears, not merely their eyes, to receive the words. Readers were said to "murmur" the words, often in a quiet tone (and sometimes compared with the buzzing of a bee!). What results is "more than a visual memory of the written words. What results is a muscular memory of the words pronounced and an aural memory of the words heard."[43] Norris comments that "to say or sing the psalms aloud within a community is to recover religion as an oral tradition, restoring to our mouths words that have been snatched from our tongues and relegated to the page, words that have been privatized and effectively silenced."[44]

Lectio divina in the classical Christian tradition includes not only reading, but what we call "meditation" on the words read. The Latin term *meditari,* both in secular and Christian uses, Leclerq explains, "implies thinking of a thing with the intent to do it; in other words, to prepare oneself for it, to prefigure it in the mind, to desire it, in a way, to do it in advance, briefly, to practice it."[45] This practice sometimes has been compared with the process of rumination, repeating, "chewing over" the text to release its flavour. In this way, the process of biblical meditation referred to by *lectio divina* involves audible reading, the exercise of memory, and intellectual reflection. Leclerq points out that to speak, to remember, and to think are "three necessary phases of the same activity."[46] A crucial point here is that biblical meditation engages the capacities of the whole person. Leclerq explains:

> To the ancients, to meditate is to read a text and to learn it 'by heart' in the fullest sense of this expression, that is, with one's whole being: with the body, since the mouth pronounced it, with the memory which fixes it, with the intelligence which understands its meaning and with the will which desires to put it into practice.[47]

Over the course of her months in the monastery, Norris is shaped by the transforming power of Scripture through her engagement in the communal practices of *lectio continua* and *lectio divina*. She says she is surprised to discover this tradition, and that it gives her a "new appreciation for the contemplative potential of the reading process." Norris notes that the reader's relationship to the text of Scripture in the *lectio* tradition is quite different from our modern approaches to reading. "One does not try to 'cover' a certain amount of material so much as surrender to whatever word or phrase catches the attention."[48] This difference—"covering" material as opposed to "surrendering" to it—echoes the warning by Mulholland about our characteristic mentality of maintaining "cognitive, rational control of the text." By contrast, Norris stresses that an approach emphasizing "surrender" is one which "respects the power of words to resonate with the full range of human experience."[49] For Norris, *lectio* means "encountering the words of scripture in such a way that they become as alive as the people around me."[50]

One of the greatest surprises for Norris is finding "personal relevance" in the ancient poetry of the Psalms. She describes how constant reading of the Psalms has changed her perception of God, herself, and the world. Raised in a church context where "one had to be dressed up, both outwardly and inwardly, to meet God", reading the Psalms enables Norris to "let go of that childhood God who had set an impossible standard." She discovers that the men and women of the Psalms come before God in all states and conditions of spiritual-moral-emotional life, only very rarely "all dressed up." Reared in a culture where girls were expected to be "good" by "not breaking the rules, not giving voice to anger or resentment, and not complaining," and where women are expected to "deny their pain, and to smooth over or ignore the effects of violence," Norris finds that the Psalms "do not deny your true feelings but allow you to reflect on them, right in front of God and everyone."[51] The Psalms act as "good psychologists" by revealing "our most difficult conflicts" and "our deep desire." Amidst an American culture whose "true religions" are "optimism and denial" and where "we want to conquer evil by being nice," Norris finds that the world depicted by the Psalms "is not really so different from our own" – a world marked by violence, vengeance, harsh words, and injustice. For this reason, the Psalms are not "comfortable" reading, going "against the American grain." Her insight is that the "psalms demand that we recognize that praise does not spring from a delusion that things are better than they are, but rather from the human capacity for joy."[52] She notes that both lamentation and exultation are forms of *praise*, since both call directly upon God and express a desire for God. By providing "images and stories that resonate with our lives," she suggests that "the psalms mirror our world but do not allow us to become voyeurs."[53]

Athanasius on the Psalms

When Norris refers to the Psalms as a mirror, in fact she is quoting from a short but influential work by Athanasius, Bishop of Alexandria from 328 to 373, called the *Letter to Marcellinus on the Interpretation of the Psalms*.[54] It provides pastoral guidance for a layperson named Marcellinus, who is recovering from an illness. Athanasius begins by noting that Marcellinus maintains "a studious attitude toward all the holy Scripture," reading the Psalms most frequently, and that he strives "to comprehend the meaning contained in each psalm."[55] Athanasius' approach is oriented theologically and pastorally by his understanding of the distinctive nature of the Psalter, especially certain features which make them particularly significant for Christian spiritual transformation. Rather than providing an exegetical treatment of the Psalms, the author focuses upon the personal benefits that result from continually reciting and singing the text.[56]

Athanasius begins by highlighting the peculiar nature of the Psalter: all Scripture is inspired and profitable for teaching, but the Psalms "possess a certain winning exactitude for those who are prayerful."[57] After summarizing how the Psalms recapitulate the teachings of the Old Testament law and prophets, Athanasius mentions that the Book of Psalms "has a certain grace of its own, a distinctive exactitude of expression."[58] What precisely is this "exactitude"? Athanasius believes that in the other books of Scripture "one hears only what one must do and what one must not do," whereas the Psalms offer something more.

> But in the Book of Psalms, the one who hears, in addition to learning these things, also comprehends and is taught in it the emotions of the soul, and consequently, on the basis of that which affects him and by which he is constrained, he also is enabled by this book to possess the image deriving from the words. Therefore, through hearing, it teaches not only not to disregard passion, but also how one must heal passion through speaking and acting.[59]

It is worthwhile examining the key concepts in this passage. The "marvel" of the Psalms is that they contain "the emotions of each soul," and so provide teaching that addresses not merely the reader's mind or will, but also their desires. The Psalms, more directly than any other portion of Scripture, provide specific guidance about "how one must heal passion through speaking and acting." Two points need to be made here. First, we need to be aware that Athanasius is work-ing with a distinction between *emotions* and *passions*. In common with many early Greek fathers and monastics, Athanasius believes that pas-sions are inherently bad. For example, pride, anger, gluttony, and lust were widely considered to be passions. As Roberta Bondi explains, these thinkers held that passions were entirely negative, since they were always destructive of love—love for God and love for neigh-bour—and destructive of authentic human freedom.[60] Such passions are understood as "wounds" that must be "healed" through "speaking and acting." A major focus of the Christian life is the healing of our passions through prayer and the pursuit of Christian virtues.

Second, Athanasius understands the centrality of the affections in the Christian life. He sees that the Psalms speak directly to the affective aspects of the human person. They give expression to the whole range of human experiences. But he is insistent that we must seek to cultivate godly or virtuous affections, rather than being held captive by godless or vicious passions. In this regard, it is important to recognize that Athanasius is drawing an inseparable connection between the cultivation of the godly *desires*, and the resulting *action* that flows from a conversion of the heart with its reorientation of desires. For Athanasius, as for many early Christian thinkers, renewed desires or emotions are the hidden springs of faithful Christian action in the world. In this context, "disregarding passion" is not the same thing as seeking to escape from our human embodiment into a suspi-cious form of intellectualism. While it is clear that Athanasius' lan-guage reveals the influence of the Platonic philosophical tradition, in my opinion, Athanasius should not be accused of holding an overly negative account of human desire, nor devaluing the material realm. Rather, his nuanced description of the competing dynamics of the harmful passions and virtuous affections in the Christian life provides a window for understanding the strongly emotive language of the Psal-ter. There is a realism here about the struggles of the Christian life, which aims to conform to the Bible's "perfect image for the soul's course of life." Scripture conveys an "image" in the sense of a form, or pattern, for the Christian life, and the Psalms are the means through which Christians may attain that "image" by being conformed to its pattern in word and deed.

Athanasius emphasizes the way in which the Psalms uniquely furnish readers with a vocabulary suited to living the Christian life, which necessitates a certain way of "speaking and acting". The stress on *action* is worth noting: Athanasius is very far from suggesting that mere enlightenment, or correct cognition, is sufficient for a life glorifying God. As in Alexandrian Christianity in general, *knowledge* of God and *love* for God go hand in hand.[61] Love describes the shape of a Christian's life in the world, lived in obedience to God, in which the Christian virtues are operative. The supreme virtue is love.

Word and deed belong inseparably together in Athanasius's reading of the Psalms. The words of the Psalms, to borrow a phrase from George Lindbeck, supply "the interpretive framework within which believers seek to live their lives and understand reality."[62] Christians should look to the Psalms to learn what Lindbeck calls "a set of skills that one employs in living one's life."[63] For example, Athanasius mentions that the Bible commands us to repent, but the Psalms prescribe "how to repent and what one must say in the circumstances of repentance." Likewise, "we are asked to bless the Lord, and to acknowledge him. But in the Psalms we are instructed how one must praise the Lord and by speaking what words we properly confess our faith in him."[64] Moreover, Athanasius finds that if a reader would allow the words of the Psalms to shape our speaking and acting in such specific ways, each person "would find the divine hymns appointed for us and our emotions and equanimity."

The author emphasizes the remarkable manner in which the Psalms become a personal word addressed to each individual, a word for *us*, in our particular circumstances. Also, they are words that speak to our hearts and our particular emotional composition. As readers we literally find ourselves in the words of the Psalms, since we come to recognize their words "as being [our] own words. And the one who hears is deeply moved, as though he himself were speaking, and is affected by the words of the songs, as if they were his own songs."[65] This is one of the paradoxes of the Psalms: the reader utters them as the "words of the saints," but at the same time perceives them "as his own words, and each sings them as if they were written concerning him," and therefore "handles them as if he is speaking about himself."[66] In this way, the words "become like a mirror to the person singing them, so that he might perceive himself and the emotions of the soul, and thus affected, he might recite them."[67] This work of direct application of the text to the soul is not a merely human achievement, but the result of the activity of the Holy Spirit. Athanasius very briefly mentions the role of the Spirit facilitating the "mirroring" function of the Psalms, and then later in the epistle provides a fuller account of the Spirit's work, as we will see below.

Athanasius proceeds to provide Marcellinus with a handy reference tool, a succinct classification of the content of the Psalter. He bases his analysis on its various themes and literary forms: "those expressing praise are such and such" or "those in the mode of appeal and thanksgiving are…" Next, in a lengthy section (chapters 15-26 of the *Letter*), Athanasius goes on to provide pastoral advice about which specific Psalms Marcellinus might most profitably read in individual situations. This advice stems from the belief that each Psalm speaks to an individual at a particular time, in a certain situation, and that taken together, they encompass the full range of emotions experienced in the Christian life. He is convinced that "the whole of human existence, both the dispositions of the soul and the movements of the thoughts, have been measured out and encompassed in those very words of the Psalter."[68] For this reason, his approach is to say, "if you have such and such a need, then read this…" For instance:

> When you think of temptations as a testing for you,
> if you want to give thanks after trials, you have the
> one hundred and thirty-eighth psalm. You might find
> yourself beleaguered once more by the enemies. Do

> you want to be rescued? Recite Psalm 139. Do you
> want to offer up supplications and prayers? Chant
> Psalms 5 and 42.[69]

The reference here to chanting the Psalms is important, perhaps more important than we might assume at first glance.[70] The practices of the early church, especially its monastic expressions, as we noted, emphasized the literal hearing of the words of Scripture, as texts were both read aloud and sung. Athanasius gives us an account of why this practice is so valuable in spiritual formation.

For him, music is neither an end in itself nor a mere decoration. Melodies are not "rendered musically for the sake of the ear's delight." Rather, noting that Scripture itself enjoins us to sing praises to God, he suggests there are two reasons for this, both of which refer to the "benefit to the soul" that comes from singing. First, because it is "fitting" for the Scripture to praise God "not in compressed speech alone, but also in the voice that is richly broadened."[71] He has in mind the difference between "psalms, odes and songs," and other types of literature in the Bible. Because psalms are poetic songs with expansive phrases, as opposed to the "close sequence" of words in narrative, they are properly expressed not with mere recitation, but with singing.

Secondly, and more importantly, Athanasius associates the necessity of singing with his theological convictions about human personhood. He claims that the Lord "ordered" that the odes be "chanted tunefully" and the Psalms "recited with song" as a symbol the spiritual harmony in the human soul. The idea here is that singing actualizes the harmonious activity of the soul, employing the body, mind, and affections in a unified manner. Thus, a person becomes like a "stringed instrument and devoting himself completely to the Spirit may obey in all his members and emotions, and serve the will of God." Such a "harmonious" reading of the text is a "symbol of the mind's well-ordered and undisturbed condition."[72] The beneficial effect of singing the Psalms is found in bringing "rhythm to his soul" and leading a person from "disproportion to proportion" and resulting in inner transformation. The harmonious soul, shaped by the whole being's engagement with the words of the Psalms, is marked by transformed desires, a renewed imagination, and a mental outlook "in accordance with the mind of Christ." By reciting the words of the Psalms, unchanged and "without artifice," Athanasius states that "the Spirit who speaks in the saints, seeing words inspired by him in them, might render assistance to us."

Here we see again the seriousness with which an ancient Christian thinker took the *divine* nature of the Scriptures: the Holy Spirit speaks through the historical authors of the Psalms ("the saints"). Athanasius understands the Spirit's ministry as bringing us into personal communion with these words of the text so that we might be reshaped toward the harmonious integration of our lives in Christ. That integral selfhood is the "image" or pattern of Christian life to which Athanasius refers at the outset of his letter. The notion of the Spirit's work through God's word leads Athanasius to his conclusion: "You, too, practicing these things and reciting the Psalms intelligently in this way, are able to comprehend the meaning in each, being guided by the Spirit. And the kind of life the holy, God-bearing men possessed who spoke these things—this life you also shall imitate."[73] The Spirit enables us as readers to find our own lives mirrored in the Psalms, and animates an imitation of the lives of the saints. There is no thought here of imitation as a mechanical copying. Instead, Athanasius has in mind a richer pedagogy: as Christians walk the path of faithfulness, they gain from the saints the skills of speaking and acting which are necessary for the pursuit of holiness.[74]

Conclusion

The Christian tradition, throughout its great variety of forms, not least in its evangelical Protestant expression, has consistently emphasized the importance of Bible reading in the life of discipleship. This essay has attempted to reintroduce some themes from the classical Christian tradition, ones with notable potential to enrich the Church's encounter with God in prayerful meditation upon the Scriptures. In particular, I have emphasized what can be gained from a contemporary recovery of the ancient practice of *lectio divina*, and more specifically, how the an in-depth exploration of the world of the Psalms might shape our Christian lives.

In Christian circles, including theological seminaries, there is a widespread and growing concern for what is being called "spirituality" or "spiritual formation." At its best, a resurgent interest in spirituality seeks fresh insight and guidance from the resources of the classical, orthodox Christian theological tradition. The foremost resource of the "great tradition" is Scripture. The *lectio* tradition of the ancient church—the progressive reading of the whole Bible in *lectio continua*, and its meditatively prayerful reading in *lectio divina*—has much to offer the contemporary church. There is nothing more important for spiritual vitality, corporate or individual, than an ability to hear the Bible as God's word addressed to *us*. And there is no better means of listening to Scripture, opening ourselves to its message, and to its power, than a rediscovered practice of the traditional discipline of *lectio*.

However, it is important to emphasize that it is not necessary to join a monastery, nor even to become a Benedictine oblate, to engage in *lectio continua* and *lectio divina*. The experience of Kathleen Norris is vivid testimony to the depth of personal transformation that can flow from a thorough immersion in the world of the Bible, especially the Psalms. Her life story illustrates a central truth of classical Christianity: encounter with God in the prayed reading of Scripture is a profound catalyst for spiritual growth and Christian maturity. Just as Norris followed the Bendictine tradition to the extent that her particular situation allowed, so we, too, may adopt and adapt the ancient practices within our contemporary context. Norris' encounter with *lectio* reminds us that if we are seeking "to learn the heart of God in the words of God" (Gregory the Great), then we must be prepared to embrace a deeply counter-cultural pattern of life. In our fast-paced, restless, faddish, information-overloaded, trivia-cluttered, 24/7 culture, there are few commitments in the Christian life so strange as spending large quantities of time upon the words of the Bible. A "ruminating" on the words of the biblical text must be regular, ongoing, gradual, unhurried and unharried. Although some in our churches appear to be seeking short-cut techniques for growth in spirituality, or yearning for instantaneous maturity, there is no substitute for the unspectacular practice of patiently, humbly seeking communion with God through communion with the words of Scripture.

Norris' encounter with God through an encounter with the Psalms led us to consider the particular benefits of meditation upon the Psalms. We turned to Athanasius to glean insights about how the Psalter might be approached for maximum benefit, and why the Psalms are such a valuable resource in the pursuit of Christian formation. We saw that he highlighted the fact that the Psalms have a capacity to speak to our lives so deeply that we encounter them as if they were our own words, an insight that Norris echoes. As the words of the Psalter become our words, we learn the language of faith from those who have gone before us. The Psalms teach us what we should say and how to praise God rightly. What Norris describes autobiographically, Athanasius analyzes theologically. Athanasius depicts the "harmonious" Christian life as a transformed personhood in Christ that flows from praying the Scripture. It is a life in which, Norris suggests, our lives *become* a psalm in praise to the glory of God's name.[75]

Notes

[1] Geoffrey Wainwright, *For Our Salvation: Two Approaches to the Work of Christ* (Grand Rapids: Eerdmans, 1997) 119.

[2] Stephen Fowl, "Introduction," *The Theological Interpretation of Scripture: Classic and Contemporary Reading,* (ed. Stephen E. Fowl; Cambridge, MA: Blackwell, 1997) xvii. Among the more significant figures who have stimulated interest in theological interpretation are Brevard Childs, George Lindbeck, and Francis Watson.

[3] Ellen T. Charry, *By the Renewing of Your Minds: The Pastoral Function of Christian Doctrine* (New York: Oxford University Press, 1997).

[4] Charry, *Renewing,* 225.

5 Ibid., 233. A similar argument is developed by C. FitzSimons Allison, *The Cruelty of Heresy* (Harrisburg, PA: Morehouse, 1997).

6 Diogenes Allen, *Spiritual Theology: The Theology of Yesterday for Spiritual Help Today* (Boston: Cowley, 1997).

7 See Roberta Bondi, *To Pray and to Love: Conversations on Prayer with the Early Church* (Minneapolis: Fortress, 1991) and *To Love as God Loves* (Minneapolis: Fortress, 1987).

8 Robert L. Wilken, *Remembering the Christian Past* (Grand Rapids: Eerdmans, 1995) 179.

9 Bradley Holt, *Thirsty for God* (Minneapolis: Augsburg , 1993) 7.

10For example, see Richard J. Foster, *Celebration of Discipline* (San Francisco: Harper San Francisco, 1978); *Prayer* (San Francisco: Harper San Francisco, 1992); *Streams of Living Waters: Celebrating the Great Traditions of Christian Faith* (San Francisco: Harper San Francisco, 1998). Also, see James M. Houston, "A Guide to Devotional Reading" *Crux* 22/3 (1986) 2-15; *The Transforming Power of Prayer: Deepening Your Friendship with God* (Colorado Springs: NavPress, 1996); *The Heart's Desire: Satisfying the Hunger of the Soul* (Colorado Springs: NavPress, 1996); *In Pursuit of Happiness: Finding Genuine Fulfillment in Life* (Colorado Springs: NavPress, 1996); "Toward a Biblical Spirituality," in *The Act of Bible Reading*, (ed. Elmer Dyck; Downers Grove, IL: InterVarsity, 1996) 148-173.

11C.S. Lewis, "Introduction," in *St. Athanasius on the Incarnation*, (trans. and ed. by a Religious of C.S.M.V; Crestwood, NY: St. Vladimir's Orthodox Theological Seminary, 1953) 4-5.

12D.H. Williams, *Retrieving the Tradition & Renewing Evangelicalism: A Primer for Suspicious Protestants* (Grand Rapids: Eerdmans, 1999).

13Thomas Oden, *The Living God: Systematic Theology* (San Francisco: Harper & Row, 1987) xi.

14For example, Bernard Bangley, *Near to the Heart of God: Daily Readings from Spiritual Classics* (Wheaton: Harold Shaw, 1998); Robert Backhouse, *Christian Classics Day by Day: A Year of Daily Readings* (London: Hodder & Stoughton, 1995).

15I am referring to "The Church's Bible" by the Wm. B. Eerdmans Publishing Company, Robert L. Wilken, general editor; and the "Ancient Christian Commentary on Scripture" series by InterVarsity Press, Thomas Oden, general editor.

16James S. Cutsinger, ed., *Reclaiming the Great Tradition: Evangelicals, Catholics & Orthodox in Dialogue* (Downers Grove, IL: InterVarsity, 1997).

17J.I. Packer, "On from Orr: Cultural Crisis, Rational Realism & Incarnational Ontology," in Cutsinger, ed., *Great Tradition*, 155-176, esp. 156.

[18]This is the theological insight providing the stimulus for "Evangelicals and Catholic Together" project. See Charles Colson and Richard John Neuhaus, *Evangelicals and Catholics Together: Working Toward a Common Mission* (Waco: Word, 1995).

[19]Robert E. Webber, *Ancient-Future Faith: Rethinking Evangelicalism for a Postmodern World* (Grand Rapids: Baker, 1999).

[20]Ibid., 153-163. Compare the suggestion by Charry, *Renewing*, 238: "Given the postmodern criticism of Enlightenment rationality, perhaps some of the classical, especially patristic, interpretations of Christian doctrines may be more accessible now than at other times."

[21]David Lyle Jeffrey, *People of the Book* (Grand Rapids: Eerdmans, 1996).

[22]Boniface Ramsey, *Beginning to Read the Fathers* (New York: Paulist, 1985) 22.

[23]Charles Kannengiesser, "The Bible as Read in the Early Church: Patristic Exegesis and its Presuppositions," in *The Bible and Its Readers*, (ed. Wim Beuken, Sean Freyne and Anton Weiler; London: SCM, 1991) 29.

[24]J.N.D. Kelly, *Early Christian Doctrines*, (rev. ed.; San Francisco: Harper & Row, 1978) 61.

[25]Kannengieser, "The Bible as Read", 29.

[26]Douglas Burton-Christie, *The Word in the Desert: Scripture and the Quest for Holiness in Early Christian Monasticism* (New York: Oxford University Press, 1993) 109.

[27]Ibid., 23.

[28]Gregory the Great, *Epistles of Gregory the Great*, Book IV, Epistle XXXI, "To Theodorus, Physician" in *The Nicene & Post-Nicene Fathers of the Christian Church*, Second Series, vol. 12, (ed. Philip Schaff and Henry Wace; Grand Rapids, MI: Wm. B. Eerdmans, 1956) 156-157.

[29]Gregory, "To Theodorus," 929.

[30]Webber, *Ancient-Future*, 189.

[31]Ibid., 134.

[32]M. Robert Mulholland, *Shaped by the Word: The Power of Scripture in Spiritual Formation* (Nashville: Upper Room, 1985) 64.

[33]Ibid., 66.

[34]Kallistos Ware, "The Spirituality of the Icon," in *The Study of Spirituality*, (ed. Chesyln Jones, Geoffrey Wainwright, and Edward Yarnold; New York: Oxford University Press, 1986) 197.

[35]See Helmut Thielicke, *The Evangelical Faith, Volume 1: Prolegomena: The Relation of Theology to Modern Thought Forms*, (trans. Geoffrey W. Bromiley; Edinburgh: T & T Clark, 1974) 129f.

[36]Ibid., 131.

[37]Kathleen Norris, *The Cloister Walk* (New York: Riverhead Books, 1996) 161, 8.

[38]Written by Benedict of Nursia (c. 480-547), *The Rule of Benedict* is, in many ways, the foundational text of Western monasticism. There are many versions available, for example: *The Rule of Benedict in English* (ed. Timothy Fry; Collegeville, MN: Liturgical Press, 1981).

[39]Jean Leclerq, *The Love of Learning and the Desire for God,* (trans. Catharine Misrahi; New York: Mentor Omega, 1962) 76.

[40]Esther de Waal, *A Life-Giving Way: A Commentary on the Rule of St. Benedict* (Collegeville, MN: Liturgical Press, 1995) 108.

[41]Norris, *Cloister Walk,* 217.

[42]Ibid., xx-xxi.

[43]Leclerq, *Love of Learning,* 78.

[44]Norris, *Cloister Walk,* 100.

[45]Leclerq, *Love of Learning,* 25. For more detailed description of this approach, see Mariano Magrassi, *Praying the Bible: An Introduction to Lectio Divina* (Collegeville, MN: Liturgical Press, 1998) or Thelma Hall, *Too Deep for Words: Rediscovering Lectio Divina* (Mahwah, NJ: Paulist, 1988) or Michael Casey, *Sacred Reading: The Ancient Art of Lectio Divina* (Ligouri, MO: Triumph Books, 1995).

[46]Ibid.

[47]Ibid., 26.

[48]Norris, *Cloister Walk,* xx.

[49]Ibid.

[50]Ibid., 218.

[51]Ibid., 92.

[52]Ibid., 94.

[53]Ibid., 95, 103.

[54]I will be using the English translation by Robert Gregg in the "Classics of Western Spirituality" series found in *Athanasius: The Life of Antony and The Letter to Marcellinus,* (ed. Robert C. Gregg; New York: Paulist, 1980) 101-147. Another easily accessible English translation, by Pamela Bright, is found in *Early Christian Spirituality,* (ed. Charles Kannengiesser; Philadelphia: Fortress, 1986) 56-77.

[55]Athanasius, "Letter to Marcellinus," 101.

[56]For a helpful overview of the letter, see Everett Ferguson, "Athanasius' 'Epistola ad Marcellinum in interpretationem Psalmorum'," *Studia Patristica* 16, part 2 (1985) 295-308.

[57]Athanasius, "Letter to Marcellinus", 101.

[58]Ibid., 107.

[59]Ibid., 108.

[60]See Bondi, *To Pray and to Love,* 34-38; Bondi, *To Love As God Loves,* 57-77.

[61]See Rowan Williams, *The Wound of Knowledge* (London: SCM, 1990; 2nd ed.) ch 2.

[62]George Lindbeck, *The Nature of Doctrine: Religion and Theology in the Postliberal Age* (Philadelphia: Westminster, 1984) 117.

[63]Ibid., 35.

[64]Athanasius, "Letter to Marcellinus," 109.

[65]Ibid., 109. Contemporary readers who seek to enter empathetically into the world of the early Christian writers will need to exercise a measure of "interpretive charity" in reading figures such as Athanasius, who was not aware of a need for using gender-inclusive language.

[66]Ibid., 110.

[67]Ibid., 111.

[68]Ibid., 126.

[69]Ibid., 122. Recall that Athanasius uses a numbering system for the Psalter that differs from our contemporary versions. Because he is using the order of the Septuagint, when Athanasius refers to Psalm 138, he is speaking about Psalm 139 in our texts. On the differences between the numbering of the chapters and verses in the Hebrew text, the Septuagint, and the English versions see Peter C. Craigie, *Psalms 1-50* (WBC; Waco: Word, 1983) 42-43.

[70]For a more detailed treatment of the importance of singing, see Pamela Bright, "Singing the Psalms: Augustine and Athanasius on the Integration of the Self," in *The Whole and Divided Self,* (ed. David E. Aune and John McCarthy; New York: Crossroad, 1997) 115-129.

[71]Athanasius, "Letter to Marcellinus," 123.

[72]Ibid., 125.

[73]Ibid., 129.

[74]For a nuanced account of the notion of imitation of the saints in early Christianity, see Wilken, *Christian Past,* chapter 6.

[75]Norris, *Cloister Walk,* 376-377. I am grateful to John Kessler, Robert Wilken and Chris Hall for their encouragement and assistance in preparing this essay.

Chapter 11

Narrative Preaching From the Old Testament:
The Book of Ruth as a Case Study

Roy R. Matheson

Introduction

Don Leggett has had an interest in the Book of Ruth that goes back to his doctoral dissertation. Over the years he has also had a passion for preaching the Old Testament. He has both demonstrated that passion in his church ministry and also passed it on to many of his students. It is with appreciation for 30 years of fellowship in teaching together in the same institution that this paper is offered in an attempt to bring these two interests together.

In recent years there has been an increased interest within biblical studies on narrative criticism. This is due in large part to a growing dissatisfaction with alternative approaches such as source and form criticism. Robert Alter has stated that "No formal aspect of literature has received as much attention in the last 20 years as have the mechanisms of

219

narrative."[1] Form and source criticism tend to trace the history of the text or study discrete units of material rather than focusing on the work as a whole. Dissatisfaction with these emphases has contributed to a search for more rewarding ways to handle the biblical material. Redaction criticism has remedied this to some degree but greater attention to the literary features of the text is required to gain a full appreciation of its meaning.

Evangelicals have tended to applaud these new endeavours since they work with the text as it stands even though they are usually less comfortable with conclusions these studies reach regarding the historical accuracy of the narratives. The impression given by many studies of narrative is that the historical aspect of the text is like the rocket phase of a space shot. Once the flight is in orbit, the rocket (historical) phase is obsolete and can be discarded. Without embracing such conclusions regarding the historical aspects of the text, most conservative interpreters acknowledge that there is much to learn from the study of the literary features of a text.

A second trend that intersects with this emphasis on narrative is a renewed interest in narrative *preaching*. Narrative material has always been a problem for expositors. This is especially true in the Hebrew Bible since so much of the Old Testament is made up of stories. More than one preacher has read an Old Testament narrative only to ask the question, "What am I supposed to do with this?" Narrative preaching has fallen on hard times and usually suffers more at the hands of its friends than its enemies. A survey of the multi-volume collection of Spurgeon's sermons, for example, reveals very little time spent in a book like Ruth. From many decades of preaching at the Metropolitan Tabernacle one of the few messages on Ruth comes from chapter two where Boaz encourages Ruth to glean in the fields at harvest time. This scene of gleaning and reaping quickly becomes a discourse on how preachers are to glean the fruit of their labour. Preachers are often timid (like Ruth) in preaching doctrinal material. They are especially timid when it comes to the doctrine of election, according to Spurgeon![2]

Another example from a more contemporary collection yields yet another sermon on the fields of Boaz in Ruth 2. R. Knox in a sermon entitled *The Gleaner* suggests the fields represent the Eucharist. It is the field Christ cultivated by the merits of his passion; "It was watered by the tears he shed over Jerusalem, by his sweat in Gethsemane, by the blood of his scourging".[3] One can only wonder what the original author of Ruth would think of such observations. Walter Kaiser in a series of lectures on Old Testament preaching accuses many expositors of being closet Marcionites.[4] The above examples would support his contention. For such expositors, if the Old Testament is not ignored, so much New Testament content is poured back into it that it is hardly recognizable. Recent narrative studies remind us that Old Testament narrative deserves better handling.

The term "narrative preaching" is used in two major senses. First, it can mean the scriptural passage is in story form even though the form of the sermon is delivered in a traditionally didactic fashion. Second, it may be used when not only is the text in story form but that the sermon is in story form as well. Adherents of this second definition maintain that since Jesus traditionally told stories to get his ideas across, we are ought to do the same.[5] Two observations are in order here. First, while it is true that Jesus spoke in stories – parables – this was not always the case. For example, there are five major sermons in Mathew around which the evangelist's material is organized. An analysis of the contents shows that the majority of the material is not in parable form but is propositional in nature. Second, Jesus used parables not only because they revealed truth but because they concealed it. The discourses of many modern preachers have the latter result but it is usually not intentional!

Many have championed the idea of having all sermons in story form. Others feel that at the very least, if the text is in narrative form, then the sermon should follow suit. Putting the sermon itself in narrative form has certain advantages. We are part of a culture where people value and identify with stories. If the sermon story is told well it draws the listener in and makes it easier to identify with the biblical character.

Greidanus has pointed out that there are also decided disadvantages to having all, or even the majority of sermons in narrative form. (1) It may isolate the story under consideration from its larger historical context in the Bible. (2) The narrative sermon communicates obliquely and there are occasions where a more direct person to person type of application is needed. (3) The listener may not pick up the truth contained in the incident and go away with a suspenseful story but nothing more. Contrary to popular thinking, one may actually need to listen to a story more carefully than a more assertive approach to the text. (4) An open ended story may fail to make its point. [6]

The remainder of this paper will examine some basic factors that need to be considered in treating Old Testament narrative. These factors will be relevant whether the form of the actual sermon is in a story format or not. Sermons are often weak because they lack imagination in organization and delivery. Many more are weak because the expositor has not spent the requisite time in the text and does not have a firm grasp of either the biblical data or the canonical shape of the narrative. This study will examine the book of Ruth, looking first at selected literary devices, second, at some key theological themes, third at historical and cultural factors, and finally at some canonical issues that bear on preaching.

Literary Aspects of the Story

Plot

Plots are often categorized in a general way as either tragic or comic. The tragic plot describes the downfall of the protagonist while the comic plot describes the ultimate success of the leading character. If this model is followed, Ruth must be described as a comic plot since the story concludes with the well-being of all three of the major characters – Naomi, Boaz and Ruth.[7]

There are a number of features that make for a good plot. Barbara Green suggests features such as continuity, suspense, reliability, distance and closeness.[8] In Ruth one senses all of these qualities. The story demonstrates continuity in that those things which the characters lack at the beginning are supplied at the end. The bitterness voiced by Naomi is replaced by blessing, and her barrenness with fruitfulness. Ruth's widowed state is replaced by marriage. The lack of food is replaced with abundance. This leads Green to identify the leading theme of the book as that of restoration:

> The story's main intent is to relate the restoration of seed, food in the land, food for Naomi and Ruth, a husband for Ruth, a redeemer for Naomi, and an heir (leading to a king) for the whole people. These particular things are all lacking at the outset of the story and they are restored one by one.[9]

An awareness of this motif will enable an expositor to develop the theme that God is in the business of turning barrenness into blessing, whether it be in the fields of Boaz or in more contemporary settings.

Green also identifies suspense as a significant narrative quality. This can be seen in the major sections of Ruth. Each section ends with a comment that indicates the story is far from over, preparing the reader for the next scene. The suspense builds throughout; at the end of chapter three, Naomi tells Ruth, "Wait, my daughter until you find out what happens" (3:18). Ruth's apprehensive waiting is mirrored by that of the reader who now is also anxious to see how the drama will ultimately unfold.

The factors of continuity and suspense present a problem as well as an opportunity for the expositor preaching a series of sermons on the book. The story of the book stands or falls as a unit but it is usually helpful to preach a series of messages on the story. It is usually not helpful in a modern setting to preach a series of sermons as a serial story where one leaves the listener in suspense, having to return the next week to see how things turn out. Each message needs to be self-contained and stand on its own. This is possible if, in each message, one briefly links up what is in the section under consideration (the micro story) to the macro story of the entire book. The expositor needs to relate the part to the whole even if this is briefly done.

The other elements mentioned by Green balance each other out. The reliability factor simply means that the storyteller does not deceive us, but gives whatever is essential for our understanding. The factor of distance may work against this narrative clarity to some degree because what is clear to the first audience is not always obvious to the contemporary reader. Modern readers still puzzle over some of the legal and cultural aspects of the story because we are separated from the events chronologically as well as culturally. This is balanced in another way by what Green calls closeness. In certain stories, notably love stories, one senses that human nature is still the same in many ways and although the distance needs to be reckoned with, it is not as great a barrier as we might initially suppose.

All the above elements make for a good narrative. The development of the plot where issues and problems are presented, and where conflict heightens and is then resolved can be carefully mapped out. Bush, in the introduction to his commentary on Ruth, has carefully and helpfully traced in chart form the various problems and tensions in the story and how each is resolved as the drama unfolds.[10]

Characters and Characterization

Characters refer to the personages that the reader meets in the story, while characterization has to do with all the means the narrator uses to portray them.[11] In Ruth, the characterization is almost completely portrayed through dialogue. With the exception of rare evaluative statements, such as the one found in 2:1 about Boaz, we come to know the characters through their speeches. There is a higher percentage of dialogue in Ruth than any other Old Testament book.

In narrative criticism, characters are often described as either "flat" or "round". "Flat" characters are individuals where only one trait is dominant. Pratt uses the illustration of Isaac in Genesis 22 as he is led to the place of sacrifice. Although in other passages he is portrayed in a variety of ways, his dominant characteristic in Genesis 22 is passivity.[12] A "round" character, on the other hand, is more complex and manifests a group of traits. All three major characters in the drama - Naomi, Ruth and Boaz are round characters. They are not one dimensional, cardboard cutouts. All three are quite complex and thus more interesting.

This complexity of character traits is seen in Naomi. Bush has cogently argued that it is Naomi, even more than Ruth, who is the most important character in the book.[13] It is Naomi's loss that is stressed in the opening scene of the book; it is Naomi for whom a redeemer is provided in 4:14-15 and it is Naomi, even more so than Ruth, to whom a son is given (4:17). All the other characters stand in relation to her. When we meet Naomi in the first chapter, the preacher is immediately faced with a decision. She resists her name Naomi (pleasant) and insists on being called Bitter (Mara). Is this behaviour from which we should distance ourselves? Are these the comments of a caustic old woman who is sour about being dealt a losing hand? Should we not seek to do otherwise and in a more positive vein affirm God's hand in all of life?

Others have seen more in the text. One pastor commenting on some insights in this passage says, "She is not whining or griping. She is with great poignancy articulating her rage. She is not mute and she is not stoic. In classical biblical style, she voices her rage.[14] Campbell points out that her words are couched in language containing strong juridical terms.

> It is a charge of unfaithfulness directed at the God whose relationship with his people is squarely based on the presupposition of his faithfulness and trustworthiness. It is one of *the* characteristic postures of

God's people, who place their trust so completely in
him that they cannot understand when events suggest that God has abandoned them. Such complaints
occur frequently in the Bible, in a way, as it were, of
bringing a lawsuit against God by those who have
been led to trust him. Looked at from this perspective, it is, in a very sense, a profound affirmation of
faith![15]

The more appropriate approach then is not to see Naomi as a
bad example, but rather one who takes her faith seriously and for
whom seeming inconsistencies need to be faced head on. The fact
that the rest of the book is given over to resolving the problem is
confirmation that this is the correct reading of this character. Con-
gregations today are populated with such wounded people who have
difficulty harmonizing what they believe about God with what is hap-
pening to them. The text thus permits them to legitimately voice these
concerns to God and others.

Ruth is also an actor in the drama with many facets to her character. The most natural place to identify is with her affirmation of loyalty in
1:15ff where she affirms her faith in Israel's God. The words are often
used in wedding services (even though they are not addressed to a future
husband but to a mother-in-law!) Another factor in the narrator's description of Ruth is the fact that she is an outsider. The narrator on numerous occasions reminds the reader of her Moabite origins even when
the narrative does not require it (see 2:2,21). "No one with a desire to
shock his or her Israelite readers could have chosen a hero more controversial, even repulsive than a woman from Moab".[16] The story serves as
a 'theological counterpoint' to Nehemiah where Nehemiah calls down
curses on those who have married Moabite wives (Neh 13:23-31). Here
she is not only allowed into the Israelite community but she comes under
the law of Levirate marriage. This law ironically was designed to protect

Israelite families from extinction and their property from dispersion. It was not there to accommodate aliens who may have recently migrated from Moab.

Ruth reminds us that Israel's God is the God of the foreigner as well. His wing span is large enough to embrace not only people of the covenant but those like Ruth who enter from the outside (2:12). In the church today many feel ostracized and marginalized due to social, ethnic or economic factors. Others experience sexual discrimination and harassment. This aspect of Ruth's experience contains a powerful message.

It should not go unnoticed that two of the three leading characters in the drama are women. They are not peripheral to the story, but central. They loom not only large in this story, but in the whole plan of salvation history, as the genealogy at the end makes clear. In the words of one commentator, the women in the Book of Ruth are the foundational elements of society. They are intuitive, and open to creativity, are welcoming, compassionate and sympathetic. The men by contrast appear as hostile and dangerous.[17] It might be debated whether "hostile and dangerous" fits a character like Boaz, but the comments about the female characters accurately describe Naomi and Ruth. In the words of Trible:

> Ruth stands alone; she possesses nothing. No God has called her; no deity has promised her blessing. No human being comes to her aid... Not only has Ruth broken with family, country and faith, but she has also reversed sexual allegiance. A young woman has committed herself to the life of an old woman rather than a search for a husband...One female has chosen another female in a world where life depends on men. There is no more radical decision in all the history of Israel[18]

Elsewhere Trible comments that Ruth outclasses even Abraham as it relates to the matter of faith.[19] In the Genesis narrative Yahweh chooses Abraham, but in this story, it is the opposite and even more significant, in that it is Ruth who chooses Yahweh. These characters speak across the centuries and touch our own culture. Women still are often victimized and vulnerable. In various aspects of our culture, women may yet find it is a "man's world". What is more, in the church women are still denied significant leadership roles. These two characters still encourage and inspire.

One final literary device may be mentioned. In narrative literature each character often has its foil or opposite, and this book is no exception. With Naomi it is the women of Bethlehem; with Ruth it is Orpah, and with Boaz, it is "Mr. So and So", the unnamed kinsman redeemer in chapter 4. There are literary devices in other narratives that are beyond the scope of this study. One may encounter repetition, development of the character from better to worse (or worse to better) and conflict in the life of a character. These also play a significant role in the narrative as a whole. Other features such as the role of the narrator, intended audience, and type scenes are areas that can be profitably explored. An awareness of all of these will make for a stronger treatment of the passage by an expositor.

Theological Factors in the Story

At a first reading, Ruth appears to be an engaging story that has little to do with theology. A careful reading will reveal that this book, like many others in the Bible, is theologically motivated narrative. Each narrative has its own theological message to deliver, and several themes in Ruth function like steel girders in a skyscraper – that is, they are hidden to some degree, but necessary to hold the structure together. Only three will be discussed here – the *hesed* of God, the providence of God, and the restoring and redeeming work of God.

The concept of *hesed* is pervasive in the Old Testament and it is clearly illustrated in Ruth by the relationships of the three major characters to each other, as well as by God himself. Nelson Glueck asserts that the term has to do with God's loyalty to his covenant obligations, a loyalty that God's people Israel should demonstrate as well. Others have modified the concept somewhat since there is more here than merely responding to a contractual agreement. There is also a freedom of decision that is essential. "The help is vital, someone is in a position to help and does so in his own freedom"[20]

In Ruth, the term is used is used in 1:8, 2:20 and 3:10 and its meaning is illustrated in the way the Lord deals with his people and how they in turn deal with each other. Ruth's words of commitment to Naomi in 1:16-17 reflect this *hesed* or kindness.

> Ruth was neither legally required nor customarily expected to remain with her mother-in-law. Thus her speech in 16-17 must be understood as an act of *hesed*, showing her love and loyalty over and beyond what is considered normal and expected... (Naomi) sees no way that Ruth could benefit personally from her continued association with her. Reason alone could not justify Ruth's decision to "cling" to her mother-in-law. Her words and actions are governed by loyalty and love rather than by logic.[21]

Boaz exhibits the same trait in dealing with Ruth, both in the night scene in chapter three and the scene before the court in chapter four. These relationships show, in Hubbard's words, that this behaviour in these chapters in Ruth requires extraordinary commitment, the taking of extraordinary risks and that things be done in the proper way.[22] The word *extraordinary* describes one of the leading traits of this kindness. The difference is seen in the contrasting reaction of Orpah in the scene in chapter one. Orpah returns home to Moab as expected. She does the ordinary thing while Ruth's actions are socially unusual. Her behaviour in relationship to her mother-in-law is extraordinary.

Behind the human acts of kindness is divine kindness. God's treatment of his people is truly extraordinary. He does more than is required and expected. Our human relationships are to be modeled after his. One can see a powerful principle at work here. If business relationships were guided by this trait and if marriages were founded on it, our society and church communities would be revolutionized. If the church members acted this way toward each other, many church splits and fights would be avoided.

The second theological theme is the *providence of God*. Paul Helm in a recent book on providence laments that the concept suffers today from a twofold problem; first the term appears archaic and is seldom used in everyday speech and second, the concept appears as a cold, academic abstraction that is of interest only to theologians and philosophers.[23] The book of Ruth avoids both of these difficulties. The first is avoided in that, although the term is not used in the book, the concept is found in every section. The seemingly cold and impersonal aspect of divine providence is resolved; the theme of providence is illustrated in the events that touch the lives of the books' major characters.

What appears as fate is really providence in disguise. The storyteller works out a correspondence between the actions of God and the actions of people in the story. God's blessings are manifestations of the ways in which God is expected to work and the actors live under God's sovereignty and do work it out.[24] A good illustration of this is the comment in 2:3, "As it turned out, she found herself working in a field belonging to Boaz". The Hebrew expression in other places means "by accident" or "chance". The term does not refer to "blind" or "random" chance. The idea here is that without intending to do so, Ruth ended up where she did. This is repeated throughout the book where things "just happen" to work out as they should. It happens that Boaz' response to Ruth is a positive one and it happens that when Boaz goes to the gate of the city, the unnamed redeemer is there. It also happens that Ruth and Boaz give birth to Obed with all the significance this holds. It just so happens that Ruth thus finds herself in the lineage of Israel's greatest king.

The author does not usually mention divine guidance at these points, but the concept is implicit in the story. God's activity, in the words of Hals, is both continuous and hidden.[25] It is hidden in the sense that the narrator does not have to come out and explain at each point that God is behind all this but it is clear to the original audience. It is continuous because God does not guide by intermittently stepping in to the drama and then retreating from the story for long periods of time. It is God's story from beginning to end. Such a theme has a multitude of parallels for us. God often directs from the shadows and does not always have to be centre stage to be in control of the everyday details of our lives as well.

A third emphasis is that of *redemption*. Fisch calls it the *Leitmotif* of the book.[26] In a book of 85 verses the Hebrew root *g'al* (to redeem) is used over 20 times. Although Hals in his work on the theology of Ruth basically ignores this theme, it is a key to the story.[27] At a basic level the vocabulary of redemption has to do with Boaz' purchase and recovery of a piece of property. However Boaz acts as a redeemer for Ruth as well. The fundamental idea is that of fulfilling one's obligation as a kinsman,[28] a duty which often involves financial obligation, as here.

A factor that must not be overlooked is that Yahweh is the ultimate *go'el* or redeemer and moves on behalf of his people in that role. In Proverbs 23:10, the Israelites are told not to move ancient boundary markers because their defender (*go'el*) is strong and will take up a case against an unscrupulous individual. In Isaiah 54:4-5 Yahweh is the redeemer who rescues Israel from widowhood, a picture that is especially appropriate for the story of Ruth. God is in the business of redeeming and rescuing people, particularly in situations where the individuals cannot rescue themselves and need outside help.

Boaz, in his actions in chapters 3-4, is simply following the model of God himself. Just as God's *hesed* is the model for human relationships, so it is with redemption. The applications for preaching then are twofold. Firstly, like Boaz, we are called to the aid of people who need outside help. Secondly, Boaz illustrates and typifies for us, the redemptive work of God on our behalf.

The question for the preacher is to what extent one ought to introduce the New Testament teaching of redemption into this text. On the one hand, we need to exercise care and not pour all the Pauline teaching on redemption into this chapter and minimize the historical context of Ruth itself. On the other hand, we recognize that Ruth is part of the canon and as such contributes to a rich theme of biblical theology that is found in all of Scripture. Perhaps Leggett provides a balanced perspective when after a lengthy historical and exegetical study on redemption in Ruth, he concludes by saying:

> When Boaz shows covenant loyalty, he is acting as an agent of Yahweh and can as such be mentioned as a type of the great Agent of Yahweh, the Lord Jesus Christ. In the actions of Boaz as *goel*, we see foreshadowed the saving work of Jesus Christ, his later descendant. As Boaz has the right of redemption and yet was clearly under no obligation to intervene on Ruth's behalf, so it is with Christ.[29]

Cultural and Historical Factors in the Story

A number of items in the story need to be explained if an expositor is to make any sense of the activities. At the heart of the story are the actions of Boaz in response to the initiative of Naomi and Ruth. Leggett's monograph analyzes in detail how Boaz functions as a *go'el* and how his responsibilities relate to the laws of Levirate marriage in such places as Leviticus 25 and Deuteronomy 25. Another custom requiring explanation is the removal of the sandal in Ruth 4 and what that implies. Explaining such practices is not as easy as one might suppose because there are differences of opinion among Old Testament scholars on these complex issues. However, a tentative decision must be made and explained as briefly and clearly as possible.

One cultural issue in the narrative is the action of Ruth in going to the threshing floor of Boaz in the middle of the night. From a modern perspective, this looks like a case of sexual entrapment. Ruth, at Naomi's suggestion, waits until the middle of the night, comes and uncovers the legs of Boaz and leaves early in the morning so she will not be seen. In addition some of the vocabulary used to describe the story is sexually suggestive. The repetition of the verb "to know" may remind the reader that the term is a euphemism for sexual relations (Gen 4:1). The word "lie" is repeated a number of times in the scene on the threshing floor (3:4,7,8,13,14) and might reinforce this notion. The word "uncover" in 3:7 is used of a number of illicit sexual acts (Gen 9:21, Lev 20:18, Isa 57:8).

Bernstein is undoubtedly correct when he suggests that the vocabulary used is by design and is intended to highlight the sexual tension in the scene.[30] There is sexual attraction but not the sexual act. One reason the reader knows this is that we already have been given a series of character references, not the least of which is the statement of Boaz in the middle of the scene, "The Lord bless you my daughter... this kindness is greater than which you showed earlier: you have not run after the young men, whether rich or poor." (3:10) Ruth is acting in kindness (*hesed*) and will not act out of character by compromising herself sexually. She is "a woman of noble character" (3:11). She is going to act in such a way that will be in everyone's best interest – that of Naomi, Boaz and Ruth herself.

Canonical Factors

Another avenue that would be profitable to pursue would be to study the role of Ruth in the canon. The Book of Ruth is like a snapshot that has merit and beauty in itself. Once a snapshot is placed in a collage it takes on deeper meaning by virtue of its relationship to the surrounding material in the work. The first verse of Ruth places it in the historical context of the Judges and it is for this reason the Septuagint places it immediately after that work. The story of Ruth

and the concern for acting in the prescribed legal way is a contrast to the
lawless acquisition of women in Judges 21. Ruth also parallels the book
that follows. First Samuel traces the history from the time of the Judges
to the reign of David. Ruth with its genealogy at the end does the same
and so both books take the same journey. [31] The story of Tamar in
Genesis 38 is another canonical parallel to Ruth. Both are outsiders who
lose their husbands and end up childless. Both need a near kinsman to
come to their aid and raise up seed. Both conceive but the manner in
which this comes about is totally different. A study here in intertexuality
will reap some significant insights since the stories contain some interesting parallels as well as contrasts, and since both these women eventually
make their way into the genealogy of Israel's Messiah in Matthew 1.

Conclusion

Sensitivity to all the features discussed above presents a formida-
ble task for a pastor whose time is at a premium. Rather than pursue all
these items it is more tempting to find an alliterated outline to impose on
the story. While it may not be possible to explore every area suggested, it
is still better to pursue the goal of preaching the text as theological narrative. The canonical shape of the passage will determine to a large degree
which of these literary, theological, historical-cultural and canonical factors will be most productive in a given book or passage.

A narrative analysis such as has been suggested for the Book of
Ruth will yield significant dividends. It may entertain the congregation, but more significantly, it will edify them. It will honour rather
than violate the form in which the author has chosen to present the
material. It will enable the listeners to hear the voice of God clearly
and naturally from the text rather than in a form distorted by a homiletical grid that is imposed on the material.

Narrative material is like high octane fuel – very powerful if
used properly but very dangerous if handled carelessly. This is especially true of narrative material of the Old Testament. If the text is han-

dled with care and if the form as well as the content of the story is dealt with sensitively, the pulpit ministry will flourish and the people of God will prosper.

Notes

1 Cited by David Gunn and Danna Fewell in *Narrative in the Hebrew Bible* (Oxford: Oxford University Press, 1993. Although he is talking about narrative in general, Alter's other work, *The Art of Biblical Narrative* (New York: Basic Books, 1981) demonstrates that his comment applies equally to biblical narrative.

2 C.H. Spurgeon, *The Metropolitan Tabernacle Pulpit* (Pasadena, Tx: Pilgrim Publications, 1969) 7. 445-50.

3 Ronald Knox in *Twenty Centuries of Great Preaching* (ed. Clyde Fant and William Pinson; Waco: Word, 1971) 10. 147-48.

4 Walter Kaiser, *The Old Testament in Contemporary Preaching* (Grand Rapids: Baker, 1973) 14-15.

5 For a discussion of how to use narrative as the form for the sermon see Eugene Lowry, *The Homiletical Plot: The Sermon As Narrative Art Form* (Atlanta: John Knox, 1980).

6 Sidney Greidanus, *The Modern Preacher and the Ancient Text* (Grand Rapids: Eerdmans, 1988) 152-53.

7 For an author who tries to do this with the plot of the parables see Don Via, *The Parables: Their Literary and Existential Dimension* (Philadelphia: Fortress, 1980). Classifying all parables as comic or tragic is difficult especially when the plot is not highly developed.

8 Barbara Green, "The Plot of the Book of Ruth", *JSOT*, 23 (1982) 55-56.

9 Ibid., 56.

10 Frederick Bush, *Ruth and Esther* (WBC; Dallas: Word, 1998) 39-40.

11 Peter Miscall, "Introduction to Narrative Literature," *NIB* (Nashville: Abingdon, 1998) 2. 548.

12 Richard Pratt, *He Gave Us Stories* (Philipsburg, NJ: Presbyterian and Reformed, 1993) 142.

13 Bush, *Ruth*, 49.

14 James Howell, "Between Text and Sermon, Ruth 1:1-18," *Interpretation, 23* (1982) 281-84.

15 Edward F. Campbell, *Ruth* (AB ; Garden City: Doubleday, 1975) 31-32.

16 Andre LaCocque, *The Feminine Unconventional: Four Subversive Figures in Israel's Tradition,* (Minneapolis: Fortress, 1990) 85.

[17]Ibid., 106.

[18]Phyllis Trible, *God and the Rhetoric of Sexuality* (OBT; Philadelphia: Fortress, 1978) 173.

[19]Ibid.

[20]R. Laird Harris, "Hesed" in *Theological Wordbook of the Old Testament* (ed. R. L. Harris, G. L. Archer and B. K. Waltke; Chicago: Moody, 1980) 1. 305.

[21]Kathleen Farmer, "Ruth" in *New Interpreter's Bible* (Nashville: Abingdon, 1998) 2. 908. It should be noted that the 'over and beyond' aspect of *hesed* is more prominent in some passages than in others. In other contexts, the emphasis falls more on a choice based on a relationship. The way in which *hesed* is shown will depend on the nature of the relationship. For a significant treatment of all these aspects see Katharine Sakenfeld, "Love (OT)" in *ABD* ed. 4. 375-81.

[22]Robert L. Hubbard, *The Book of Ruth* (NICOT; Grand Rapids: Eerdmans, 1988) 72-74.

[23]Paul Helm, *The Providence of God* (Downers Grove, IL: InterVarsity, 1994) 17.

[24]Campbell, *Ruth*, 29.

[25]Ronald Hals, *The Theology of the Book of Ruth* (Philadelphia: Fortress, 1969) 15-19.

[26]Harold Fisch, "Ruth and the Structure of Covenant History", *VT* 32 (1982) 435-36.

[27]Hals, *Ruth*, 15-19.

[28]Leon Morris, *Judges, Ruth* (TOTC; New York: InterVarsity, 1968) 282-83.

[29]Donald Leggett, *The Levirate and Goel Institutions in the Old Testament with Special Attention to the Book of Ruth.* (Cherry Hill, NJ: Mack, 1974) 298. A work that is more allegorical in nature and finds spiritual parallels in minor details of the story is J. Vernon McGee, *Ruth: The Romance of Redemption* (Wheaton: Van Kampen, 1954).

[30]Moshe Bernstein, "Two Multivalent Readings in Ruth," *JSOT* 50 (1991) 19.

[31]David Jobling, "Ruth Finds a Home: Canon, Politics, Method" in *The New Literary Criticism and the Hebrew Bible* (ed. J. Cheryl Exum and David Clines, Sheffield: JSOT 1993).

9 781894 667050